ROUTLEDGE LIBRARY EDITIONS:
THE RENAISSANCE

Volume 6

THE WOMEN OF THE MEDICI

THE WOMEN OF THE MEDICI

YVONNE MAGUIRE

Routledge
Taylor & Francis Group

LONDON AND NEW YORK

First published in 1927 by George Routledge & Sons Ltd

This edition first published in 2020
by Routledge
2 Park Square, Milton Park, Abingdon, Oxon OX14 4RN

and by Routledge
52 Vanderbilt Avenue, New York, NY 10017

Routledge is an imprint of the Taylor & Francis Group, an informa business

British Library Cataloguing in Publication Data
A catalogue record for this book is available from the British Library

ISBN: 978-0-367-25398-1 (Set)
ISBN: 978-0-429-29609-3 (Set) (ebk)
ISBN: 978-0-367-27248-7 (Volume 6) (hbk)
ISBN: 978-0-367-27143-5 (Volume 6) (pbk)
ISBN: 978-0-429-29245-3 (Volume 6) (ebk)

Publisher's Note
The publisher has gone to great lengths to ensure the quality of this reprint but points out that some imperfections in the original copies may be apparent.

Disclaimer
The publisher has made every effort to trace copyright holders and would welcome correspondence from those they have been unable to trace.

PLATE I

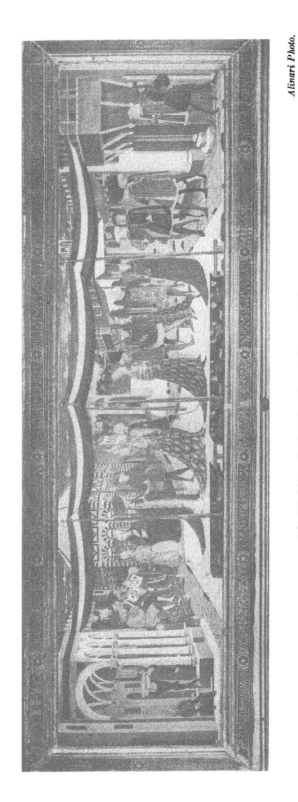

The Wedding of Lisa Ricasoli and Boccaccio Adimari

[*front.*

THE WOMEN
OF THE MEDICI

BY

YVONNE MAGUIRE, M.A.

LONDON
GEORGE ROUTLEDGE & SONS, LTD.
BROADWAY HOUSE: 68–74, CARTER LANE, E.C.
1927

Made and Printed in Great Britain at
The Mayflower Press, Plymouth.   William Brendon & Son, Ltd.

TO

C. E. M.

PREFACE

THIS book is based on the essay which was awarded the Gamble Prize by Girton College in 1923. It has been written under considerable difficulties, in many places, and since it has been completed in the interior of China, far from documents and libraries, I can only ask pardon for any small inaccuracies that may have crept in.

I was drawn to the subject of the Medici Women by a general interest in the women of Renaissance Italy, coupled with the fact that practically nothing about these leading women of Florence exists in English. My first real source of information was Mrs. Ross's book, *The Lives of the Early Medici as told in their Letters*, which give a number of letters written by these ladies. I have collected many more letters and documents than are contained in that book, but I must thank Mrs. Ross for her kindness in allowing me to quote from her book, and also for her encouragement to a follower along her own lines.

Unfortunately, for geographical reasons, I have not been able to consult the original documents myself, but all the letters listed from the Medici Archives in Florence have been copied for me by Dr. Ferdinando Sartini, of the Archivio di Stato, to whose helpful kindness and courtesy I am deeply indebted. All the translations, either from these manuscripts or from Italian printed sources, are my own work, and my own responsibility.

Although the work is based on the correspondence of the women of the Medici family, it does not pretend to be a complete collection of their letters, but I have tried to include as many as possible, especially those of any importance. In the text I have omitted such portions as are obscure or confined to the complications of contemporary politics, but in almost every case the complete document will be found in the notes. The exceptions are due to their excessive length, or to the omission of such items as long Biblical quotations in Latin, etc. etc.

It is impossible to mention by name all who have so kindly helped me in the preparation of this book, but I would like to make special mention of Dr. Sartini for his work in copying the originals, of Mrs. Ross for allowing me to quote from her book, as well as first rousing my interest in the subject ; of Signor Roberto Ridolfi for communicating valuable information ; of Commendatore Ulrico Hoepli of Milan for finding many Italian books for me ; of my sister, Miss Veronica Ruffer, for verifying references, etc., and of Dr. Eileen Power for much kindly help and encouragement.

To Mr. R. W. Carden, who has been kind enough to see the work through the press for me, I owe more than I can say, but I wish to absolve him from all responsibility for any statements of fact or opinions contained herein.

My thanks are due to Mr. John Murray and Colonel Young for permission to reproduce from *The Medici* the illustrations of The Medici Palace in the Via Larga, and Lucrezia Tornabuoni, by Botticelli, in Kaiser Friedrich Museum, Berlin ; also the portrait of Maddalena Cibo, and the Villa of Careggi. Also to Messrs. Chatto and Windus for the illustrations of the Contessina de' Bardi bust in Museo Nazionale, Florence, from *Pieraccini*, and the facsimile of her writing reproduced in Ross, *The Lives of the Early Medici* ; also the portrait of Clarice Orsini, formerly ascribed to Botticelli, called La Bella Simonetta, in Palazzo Pitti, Florence, reproduced in I. del Lungo, *Women of Florence.*

YVONNE MAGUIRE

PEIPIAO, NORTH CHINA,
   May 24, 1926.

CONTENTS

LIST OF ILLUSTRATIONS

WOMEN OF THE MEDICI

CHAPTER I

INTRODUCTION

IF we stand on the hill of San Miniato at sunset it is easy to understand why Florence is called " The City of Flowers." Flowers are everywhere, in the city, and on the slopes of Fiesole ; the emblem of the commune is a red lily, and the cathedral is dedicated to Our Lady of the Flowers. But, above all, the city, with its towers and cupolas nestling in the valley, is like a flower in its beauty, with its bright marbles glistening in the clear Tuscan air.

Other Tuscan cities may be more beautiful, but the most picturesque are cities of the dead, mere museums for tourists, whilst Florence is modern and progressive, although she has preserved her beauty almost intact. The modern Florentine lives and works among the beautiful buildings of his forefathers.

During the Renaissance Florence became the Athens of Italy, and her sons were leaders in every branch of the revival. Such men as Dante, Petrarch, Lorenzo de' Medici, Giotto, Botticelli, Leonardo, and Michelangelo, have conferred undying fame upon their native city.

In the days of Imperial Rome, Italy was merely a province, and after the fall of the Empire she sank into the gloom of the Dark Ages, no less than did other parts of Europe. But her gloom was never as deep as that of the North, and her political history was very different. Northern Europe was feudalised, and though the various Teutonic invaders of Italy tried to transplant the system, they never really succeeded, but were themselves absorbed by the race they had conquered. After the fall of the Western Empire, Italy was without any central authority, and this, together with the growth of the power of the Church, helped the rise of the independent communes. By 1100 the cities had nearly all achieved their independence, and, though they owed nominal allegiance to the Pope or the Emperor, the history of Italy henceforward consists almost entirely of the quarrels, both internal and external, of these small city-states.

They had struggled successfully to emancipate themselves from their overlords, but they had not learnt to tolerate one another, still less had they any conception of the federal idea. The Lombard League is the only example of an extensive alliance between them, and even that rapidly collapsed. The stronger cities were always trying to subdue their weaker neighbours, and the records are filled with confusing and complicated accounts of wars that lasted for years. Their causes were often absurd, such as the theft of a pail which caused a lengthy conflict between Modena and Bologna. Confusion is worse confounded by the fact that, in many cases, both sides claimed the victory, always adding " with great slaughter," until, as Mrs. Ross says, " the bewildered reader wonders how anyone was left alive to note down the incessant fighting."[1]

Gradually the larger cities conquered the smaller until at the beginning of the fifteenth century Lombardy, with Genoa and Venice, controlled the North ; Tuscany and Rome, with a fringe of Papal states, occupied the Centre ; and Naples held the South. Florence was virtually mistress of Tuscany, except for Siena and Lucca, but her subject cities often revolted, and were the cause of many troubles.

In spite of all this warfare, the Italian cities were not blessed with internal peace. There were everlasting quarrels between nobles and burghers, burghers and plebeians, Guelphs and Ghibellines, Blacks and Whites, and these quarrels led to bloody battles within the cities themselves. The streets were narrow, and the leading families built high towers from which they could hurl missiles at their opponents below. It is a suggestive fact that in every Italian palace the *Piano Nobile*, inhabited by the master and his household, was on the first floor, whilst the ground floor was given up to offices and store-rooms, with windows that could be barricaded for defence when required.

Gradually the cities' warlike spirit waned, and from sheer exhaustion they yielded to the sway of a tyrant. This brought them a certain measure of internal tranquillity, and wars were henceforth carried on by mercenaries, so that the burgher could pursue his business in peace. But the demand for mercenaries brought into being a new force to disturb the sorely harassed land, and with the rise of *condottiere* families like the Sforza, the Este, and the Gonzaga, there was less and less hope for peace.

Florence had been torn by factions as fierce as those of any other city, but she did not fall under the sway of a tyrant in the same way as did the rest. The tyrannies of Milan or Ferrara were founded on force and maintained by arms, but the rule of the Medici in Florence was based on wealth and personal prestige. Cosimo, Piero and Lorenzo were never more than *primi inter pares*, and as soon as Piero the younger forgot this his family was driven out of Florence.

Probably more books have been written about Renaissance Italy than about any other period of history except the French Revolution, and a large proportion of the books about Italy deal with Florence and the Medici. But the history of the family was so closely interwoven with that of the city that historians have dwelt chiefly on matters of national importance, and have neglected the homely details of daily life. This is particularly so with regard to the women of the family. Cosimo and Lorenzo, and even Piero, were such dominating personalities that we tend to think that their wives and daughters were mere nonentities. They did not play as great a part in politics as women like Isabella and Beatrice d'Este, but they were persons of importance, nevertheless.

The Medici archives in Florence contain a number of family letters which give us glimpses of domestic life during the years of the Medici supremacy. Unfortunately there is no such wonderful series as the contemporary correspondence of Alessandra Macinghi degli Strozzi with her exiled sons, but industrious search has revealed quite a number of illuminating documents that give us an idea of the helpmeets and companions of the first citizens of Florence.

CHAPTER II

THE IDEAL WOMAN

FROM the beginning of the Renaissance we have several descriptions of the ideal wife, and Contessina de' Bardi, the wife of Cosimo, Pater Patriae, almost came up to this ideal in fact. The growing deviation from this type in succeeding generation keeps pace with the change in the position of women, which we can see by comparing Contessina de' Bardi with Alfonsina Orsini, or Alberti's Ideal Wife with Castiglione's Court Lady.

Leo Battista Alberti (d. 1472) wrote a dialogue entitled *Della Famiglia*,[1] in which a certain Giannozzo Alberti discusses the best way of conducting the family affairs.

Speaking of his wife, he says that soon after marriage he took her all over the house and showed her everything, and then

> " Locking the door I showed her all the things of value, the silver, the tapestries, the fine clothes, the gems, and the places in which they were all kept. For I did not wish any of my precious things to be hidden from my wife. . . . Only my books and papers, and those of my forbears I kept hidden and locked, both then and thereafter, so that she should neither read, nor even see them. . . . I always kept my papers, not loose in my sleeves* but locked up in my study . . .

* The long flowing sleeves of mediæval gowns were often used as pockets, as is done by the Chinese to this day.

5

into which I never allowed my wife to enter, either alone or with me."

He went on to tell her that she was never to meddle with his affairs in any way, and, in order to discourage her, he added that women who knew too much of masculine affairs got the reputation of being too fond of men. Her duty consisted in being faithful to him, looking after the family and seeing that the household was well ordered. He also exhorted her to be modest in her dress, and not to use cosmetics, for " the ancients forbade their women to paint their faces." He went on :—

" When I had shown her everything we shut ourselves into our room, and kneeling down we prayed to God that we might make good use of our wealth . . . and live long together in happiness and concord, with many male children, and that He would grant to me riches, friends and honour, and to her faithfulness, modesty and the gifts of a good housekeeper."[2]

The need for good housekeeping is much dwelt on by Alberti, for he forbids his wife to gossip with the maids, but begs her to " take the pleasant exercise of going every day from the top to the bottom of the house to see if everything is in its place."

All through the fifteenth century we get praises of the good housekeeper, but possibly she was not found so frequently as of yore, since her virtues are so much dwelt on, as an example to the modern generation.

The Florentine bookseller, Vespasiano da Bisticci (1421-1478), wrote a collection of the *Lives of Illustrious Men*, among which he included a number of women. His ideal wife was " a mirror of virtue," with a modest manner, kind and helpful to the sick and to the poor, but not over-generous with her husband's goods, and

not too religious, but sufficiently so to be a good wife
and mother.

Writing of Alessandra de' Bardi he says :—

"I have known Florentine women, even those of
the highest birth, to be the first to rise in the house,
and go through it from cellar to granary, putting a
hand to all that was doing."[3]

At about the same time Matteo Palmieri wrote :—

"The duty proper to a wife is heedfully to govern
the house well, provide for its wants, know all that is
going on there, be watchful as to all that affects it,
confer with her husband, ascertain his will, and follow
it in such wise that his command, opinion, and
custom shall serve as her law."[3]

Girls were married at an early age, and although their
whole upbringing had been intended to fit them for
this, and for nothing else, anxious mothers must often
have felt that their little daughters were hardly strong
and wise enough to fulfil the duties and bear the burdens
that awaited them. One such mother gave her daughter a set of rules of conduct on her marriage which
show what a Florentine husband expected of his wife :—

The whole document reads[4] :—

"My dearest daughter,—I beg and command you
that you will not grieve because I have given you
in marriage, and sent you away from me, so that you
may not anger your new husband, to whom I have
married you. My sweet daughter, if it were right
that you should stay with me until the end of my
life, you should never leave me, for so great is the
love I bear you. But reason requires, and our honour
demands, and it is seemly for your age and condition
that you should be wedded, so that your father and I
and all our family may rejoice in you and the children

7

that by the grace of God will come to you. Now I tear you from my bosom ; now you pass from the power of your father into that of your husband and lord, to whom you must not only be a companion, but an obedient servant. Above all, in order that you may know how to serve him obediently, listen to my instructions, and obey them as commands, for if you follow them you will keep the love and grace of your husband, and of all others.

The First Commandment is to take care not to do any of those things which might anger your husband, or justly provoke him to wrath. And take care not to be merry when you see that he is wrathful, nor to be angry when he is merry ; and when he is worried or burdened with trouble, or many thoughts, do not try to attract his attention, but stand aside until he is more serene.

The Second Commandment is to take care to know what dishes please him at dinner and at supper and to see that they are prepared for him. And if you do not like some of these dishes, I want you to pretend that you do like them, for it is right and proper for a woman to share the pleasure of her husband.

The Third Commandment is that when your husband is sleeping, either from weakness or weariness, or some other reason, you must take care not to wake him without good reason, but if you must do so, do not do it suddenly, or in haste, but quietly and gently, so that he may not be wrath, for in this matter men are easily angered.

The Fourth Commandment is that you must guard faithfully both his honour and your own, and never touch the box or purse or other place in which he keeps his money, so that he may not suspect you ;

and if it so happens that for any reason you do touch it, do not take anything, but put it back carefully. Do not give anyone anything of his without permission, nor lend it, for he is so much your lord that even for the love of God you must not give to the poor without asking him. Therefore take every care of his property, for, as a man is praised for generosity, so a woman is praised for her care of her husband's goods.

The Fifth Commandment is that you must not be too anxious to know your husband's secrets and his affairs, and if he tells you anything, take care not to repeat it to anyone. And take heed also not to repeat outside the house the words that have been said privately within, even if they are of little importance, for it is an evil thing that others should know the affairs of your household, especially from your own mouth, and the woman who acts thus is foolish and silly, and will be hated by her husband.

The Sixth Commandment is that you must love and trust in a proper manner your servants and your household, especially those who are beloved by your husband. Take care not to scold them nor dismiss them for any light cause, for you will be hated for this and may be so abhorred by the household for so doing that you will never get rid of the blame, and may easily come to be hated by your husband and other people.

The Seventh Commandment is not to do any great thing of your own accord, without the consent of your husband, however good it may seem to you. And take care not to say to him ' My counsel was better than yours ' even if it was so, for that would make him very angry and cause him to hate you.

9

The Eighth Commandment is not to require of your husband anything unseemly, or that he would not wish to do, or a thing that you think might displease him, or be dishonourable, even if it is not the cause of evil, harm or destruction.

The Ninth Commandment is to take care to keep young, fresh and beautiful and clean, in a modest manner, without anything immodest or any ugly ornament. For if your husband finds you adorning yourself immodestly, he might easily suspect you, but if you dress modestly he will love you and cherish you the more.

The Tenth Commandment is not to be too familiar with your household nor too humble, especially with those who have to serve you, whether varlets or damsels, men or maids ; for too much intercourse leads to trouble, and familiarity breeds contempt. Therefore it is better to be a little proud and haughty towards them, for it is not a good sign to see the servant disdainful in the presence of her mistress, and in vulgar speech the people say ' Where the maid rules, the mistress is a fool.'

The Eleventh Commandment is not to be too much of a gad-about, nor to go forth too much from your own house, for you must know that the woman who stays at home and goes about little, is the joy of her husband, as saith Solomon, who knew well. It behoves the man to see to matters outside the house, in order to obtain what is necessary for within. Similarly it behoves the woman to look after the affairs of the family and the household, which you could never do well, my daughter, if you were a gad-about. Also I desire and command you not to talk too much, for speaking little suits a woman well, and shows modesty. For even if a woman is very foolish, if she speaks little, she is thought wise. Also I command you to be discreet, and not to desire to know too much, nor to give heed to soothsayers, nor to their witchcraft and incantations, for it is most unseemly for women to know as much as men about masculine affairs.

The Twelfth Commandment, and the most important, which I want to impress upon you above all, is that you should not do anything by word or deed or act that might make your husband in any way jealous. For this will destroy his love more than anything else, and he will always suspect you, and be always burning like a flame, and you will be hated, not only by him, but also by all his family and friends, and you will be covered with such infamy that you will never get rid of it, for such misdeeds make a stain that can never be washed out. And let this be the greatest commandment of all, for I assure you that a wife cannot please her husband better than by being chaste, and the opposite is equally true. Take care to honour and reverence him in every way that is seemly, and when he returns home, always greet him cheerfully, and joyfully do honour to his relatives even more than to your own, for he will do the same to your family. If perchance, on the arrival of some honourable person, you are busy with some menial housekeeping duty, quickly put away your distaff and spindle, and hide your menial work, whatever it may be, so that you will not look as if you had been brought up on a farm. In matters of love do not depart from modesty, as I told you when we spake together, so that too great a show of affection may not lessen his love for you too soon, but take care that love and not anger shall move him, and let him always use a little loving force, for this loving constraint is due to your modesty."

Such documents show us the ideal of womanhood, but for the other side of the picture we must go to the novelists. They often exaggerate greatly, but they give us many amusing little side-lights on women and their ways.

Alberti had objected to the use of cosmetics, and we find repeated complaints of the use of paint and false hair in contemporary writers, and many sumptuary laws were passed to check these and other abuses in feminine dress. Franco Sacchetti tells a tale about these laws and the difficulty of enforcing them. This duty was entrusted to the Podestà, a foreign lawyer who only held office for a year at a time, and a certain Messer Amerigo of Pesaro found that the ordinances relating to women's dress were beyond his power to carry out. He therefore came to the Priors and complained that the women were so full of arguments that he could do nothing. He said that if he met

"a woman with a fringed peak to her hood, and my notary says to her 'Tell me your name, for you have a decorated peak,' the good woman takes this peak, which is attached to the hood by a pin and taking it in her hand she says 'It is a garland.' I go on and I find one with many buttons in front. I say to her 'You must not wear these buttons,' and she replies, 'Nay, Messere, but I may, for these are not buttons, but studs, and if you do not believe me, look and see, and they have no shanks, and besides, there are no button-holes.' The notary goes to another who is wearing ermine and says 'How is this, you are wearing ermine,' and wishes to inscribe her. The woman says 'Do not inscribe me, for these are not ermine, they are sucklings.' The notary says 'And what is a suckling?' and the woman replies 'It is an animal.'" [5]

By the beginning of the fifteenth century these sumptuary laws were falling into disuse, although magnificence in dress was increasing, and scattered among the Medici papers we find several descriptions of splendid costumes, which contrasted with the plain serge gowns still in everyday wear.

One sumptuary ordinance that persisted longer than others was the regulation of the number of dishes that might be served at feasts and weddings, and in the accounts of some of the Medici festivities we read that they had only " such dishes as were customary."

Though the Medici were the richest citizens of Florence, they were not given to ostentation, but spent their money on fine buildings and wonderful works of art, rather than on food and clothing, and their women lived soberly and without undue luxury to the end.

CHAPTER III

THE FORERUNNERS

ALL through their history the Medici were representative of the bourgeoisie against the nobility,
and of the lower classes against the rich traders. They
are occasionally mentioned in early documents, but the
first prominent member of the family was a certain
Salvestro, who headed the rising of the Ciompi, or
wool-carders, against the wealthy merchants who at
that time held all political power. The result of this
insurrection was that the franchise was extended to
include what were known as the Minor Arts, and the
name of Medici became associated with the opposition
to the oligarchy of wealth.

The important branch of the Medici family was not
descended from this Salvestro, but from a certain Averardo, the son of their common ancestor, Chiarissimo.

Averardo lived about 1280, and his wife, Benricevuta,
bore him a son, another Averardo, who married
Mandina di Filippo Arrigucci of Fiesole. Their son,
Salvestro Chiarissimo, married Lisa di Sinibaldo
Donati,[1] and although we know nothing more of her
than her name, she belonged to a family which was
well known in Florentine history.

The Donati palaces stood between the Corso and
the church of San Piero Maggiore, and some of the
family were important in almost every generation.
Dante's wife was Gemma di Manetto Donati, a near
relative of the famous Guelph leader, Corso Donati,

14

whose name has been handed down to posterity in Dante's poem.[2]

Corso was a very prominent personage in the strife between Black and White Guelphs in Florence, and in 1308 he plotted to obtain the lordship of the city. The plot was, however, discovered and he was condemned to death. He fled through the Porta Santa Croce, but was overtaken by some Catalan mercenaries, and, after being dragged by his horse for some distance, he was slain.

He had been married three times, first to one of the Guelph family of the Cerchi, but, when his politics changed, he poisoned her, and married one of Ghibelline Ubertini. Late in life he married the daughter of the *condottiere*, Uguccione della Faggiuola, hoping to be able to count on the support of his father-in-law in his attempt on the lordship of Florence. But Uguccione was one of the leaders of the conspiracy that brought about Corso's death.

Corso based his policy extensively on political marriages, and in 1288 he desired to ally himself with the powerful and turbulent Black family of Della Tosa. Therefore, since no other member of his family was available, he abducted his sister, Piccarda, from the convent of the Poor Clares, and married her to Rossellino della Tosa. She died soon afterwards, and is numbered among the Blessed in the Florentine calendar, under the name of Sister Costanza. Dante has immortalised her by placing her among the inhabitants of the Moon, who, after taking religious vows, had for some reason been forced to abandon them.[3]

Though so closely related to the turbulent Messer Corso, Salvestro de' Medici took care to keep out of his affairs, so that he did not suffer proscription and exile, but laid the foundations of his family on a firm and stable commercial basis.

Salvestro and Lisa had a son, named Averardo Bicci, who was twice married. His first wife was Giovanna di Lotto Cavallini de' Bonagiunsi, whose name does not convey anything to the historian. After her death he wedded Giacoma, the daughter of Francesco Spini, and though we know nothing further about her, we do know something about her family. The Spini palace stood on the Piazza S. Trinità, which was a favourite spot for dances and other festive gatherings. On May 1, 1300, a number of girls were dancing there when they were interrupted by a brawl in which the young men of the Donati, Pazzi and Spini families attacked those of the Cerchi. This street fight had very serious consequences, for it brought to a head the feud between the Black and White Guelphs, which not only led to Dante's exile, but largely changed the history of Florence. The head of the family at this time was Geri Spini, who was the Papal banker and aimed at achieving the position afterwards held by the Medici. He rebuilt the ancestral palace and lived there in great magnificence, as Boccaccio tells us in the *Decameron*. In 1321 he entertained some of the barons who accompanied Charles of Valois, and in every way he was one of the leading citizens of Florence. The Medici were increasing in importance when they were able to ally themselves with such a family.

The first historically important member of the Medici family was Giovanni Bicci, the son of Averardo. He established the family fortune on a firm basis, and played an influential, though unobtrusive part in the affairs of state.

In 1386 he married Piccarda, the daughter of Edoardo Bueri. She was born in Verona in 1368, of a Florentine family, and was one of the most beautiful women of her time. She was an excellent housewife, and good to the poor, but she had also been well educated and was fully able to look after affairs during Giovanni's absences from Florence. In 1429, when he lay dying, Giovanni told his sons that he owed his great wealth to fortune, but its preservation was due to his wife's help. He also commended her to the special care of his sons, saying :—

"I leave you in possession of the great wealth which my good fortune has bestowed upon me, and which your good mother and my own hard work has enabled me to preserve. . . . I commend to you Nannina, my wife and your mother, see that after my death ye change not the habits and customs of her life." [4]

Giovanni and Piccarda had five children, Cosimo and Lorenzo, who played so large a part in the history of Florence ; Damiano, who died in 1390 ; Antonio, who died in 1398,[5] and a daughter who died on the eve of her marriage.

Piccarda died unexpectedly on April 19, 1433, and Carlo Marsuppini, the Chancellor of the Republic, composed an oration in her praise, which is still to be found among the manuscripts of the Laurenziana. She was buried in the same grave as her husband in S. Lorenzo, in the Old Sacristy. Their sarcophagus, which is decorated with *putti*, stands in the middle of the sacristy, and is now covered by a table, which makes it practically invisible. Traditionally this work has always been ascribed to Donatello, but modern criticism assigns it rather to Buggiano, Brunelleschi's foster son. We know from the *Denunzia de' Beni*, or tax register, for the year 1433, that Cosimo had commissioned Buggiano to execute a tomb, and it is probable that this is the one in question.[6]

CHAPTER IV

CONTESSINA DE' BARDI

GIOVANNI BICCI DE' MEDICI was a wealthy and important citizen of Florence, but not a power in the state. His wife, Piccarda, is known to us only from Marsuppini's oration and one or two scanty allusions in contemporary chroniclers. In the next generation we have Cosimo, Pater Patriae, and his wife Contessina, many of whose letters have survived.

Giovanni was a trader rather than a politician, and he amassed an immense fortune, which he used to obtain a personal following among the citizens, and thus prepared the way for his son. He held office on several occasions, but did nothing notable. He was always a member of the peace party, which did not wish to squander the resources of Florence on foreign wars, but desired prosperity at home, and low taxation. The only measure with which his name was associated was the Catasto, which was intended to be a more equitable method of assessing taxation. He was certainly a member of the Council which originated it, and tradition has always ascribed its introduction to him, although, as a matter of fact, his own taxes were enormously increased.

Giovanni died in 1429, having never been more than a business man who dabbled in politics, but his son Cosimo made himself the chief power in the state, and when we come to his descendants, the commercial origin of the family fortunes recedes more and more into the background.

Cosimo created his own position in Florence and while, for the last thirty years of his life, he held the city in the hollow of his hand, he was careful not to assert himself, but worked through his chosen instruments. He was shrewd and witty, a good business man, a lover of the new learning, and a clever politician.

In Italy, as in the rest of Europe, methods and manners were still often primitive, and an inconvenient opponent frequently perished by the assassin's dagger. But this was not Cosimo's way. Instead of killing his enemy he ruined him, a more subtle and often more effective form of revenge. By Florentine law, a citizen who was in arrears with his taxes could not hold office, so Cosimo paid the debts of his adherents, but caused his enemies to be assessed very highly until, by falling behind with their payments, they lost their political rights. The introduction of the Catasto was an effort to equalise the incidence of taxation, but it soon became as unfair and as open to manipulation as previous methods, so that Guicciardini, writing in the following century, could say :—

> " The Medici never allowed a fixed method and legal distribution of the taxes, but always reserved to · themselves the power of bearing heavily on individuals according to their pleasure . . . they made use of the taxes to win the people over, while they set themselves up as lords of all." [1]

Cosimo was born on September 27, 1389, and some time after 1413 he married Contessina, the daughter of Giovanni de' Bardi, Count of Vernio, and Emilia Rainieri Pannicchieschi, of the family of the Counts of Elci.

The Bardi were from the earliest times leading

members of the Arte di Calimala, and were originally enormously wealthy. They lent large sums of money to Edward III of England, and his refusal to pay brought about a financial crisis in Europe. As a slight recompense for not paying his debts, Edward made two members of the Bardi family Canons of Lincoln in 1343, and conferred the Deanery of Glasgow on another in the same year. Another interesting member of the family was Messer Simone di Geri de' Bardi, the husband of Beatrice Portinari.

Contessina, called The Little Countess, in memory of the great Countess Matilda, was not particularly clever or cultured, but she was shrewd, like all the Tuscans, and in her letters we see her as a fond mother and a good housewife, much concerned over domestic details.

Her eldest son, Piero, was born in 1416, and Giovanni in 1421, but there is no record of any other children.

Among the many hundreds of letters in the Medici archives, the earliest one from Contessina seems to be the following, dated 1430. Cosimo was often away on business in his earlier years, but he did not write to his wife over much, and we have many complaints on this score. In 1430 the plague was raging in Florence, so Cosimo took his two sons with him to Verona and Ferrara, whilst Contessina retired to the family villa of Castelluccio. Giovanni did not like Ferrara, and on June 6 his mother sent him a letter full of good advice. Her letters were generally to the point, but her style was bad, for she jumped from one subject to another, and then back again, without any warning. On this occasion she said :—

" I wrote to you a few days ago and shall have little to say now. By a letter from Ser Alexo I hear that you are all well, thanks be to God. I

PLATE II

Contessina de' Bardi.   Bust ascribed to Donatello (?) in the
Museo Nazionale, Florence

[*face p. 20*

hear that you both want to return here, and do not like staying there. You ought to be glad to be there for business reasons, and so as to learn something, besides here it is not healthy anywhere. Wherefore I beg you, my son, that you will not try to return before the sickness departs, and please say the same to Piero. Tell me how many suits he has had made, for I do not know what he is wearing, for he has not written to ask for his cloth-lined garments. It has been very hot here for some days, and I expect it is the same with you, so take care to keep cool. I do not know if Cosimo has yet sent for his summer clothes, but I expect he is thinking of returning any day. Take care to caress him and see that he is comfortable, but everybody tells me that he is so fat, which is excellent. Commend me to Monna Dina, and salute Monna Ginevra, and thank them from me, for Ser Alexo tells me that they treat you like brothers. I should like to know whether you are doing anything at the Bank, either you or Piero, and whether Cosimo makes any use of Piero. Write and tell me. I will say no more. Christ guard you.

At Castelluccio, June 6, 1430.

LA CONTESSINA." [2]

When Cosimo first entered political life, the government was practically in the hands of the Albizzi faction, who represented the aristocratic and old-fashioned oligarchy of wealth. Cosimo put himself at the head of the poorer and less important citizens, who were opposed to this plutocracy. A disastrous war with Lucca increased the unpopularity of the government faction, and after the fighting had dragged on for four years, Cosimo and Palla Strozzi went to Ferrara in 1432 to negotiate for peace, which was finally concluded in April, 1433. Cosimo's success in this affair increased the enmity of Rinaldo degli Albizzi, who said :—

> " Little is wanting to Cosimo but the actual sceptre of government, or rather, he has the sceptre, but hides it under his cloak. . . . The people have chosen him as their advocate, and look upon him as a God. . . . The people are all Mediceans." [3]

The Albizzi therefore decided to rid themselves of Cosimo at the first opportunity, but he retired to his villa in the Mugello, in May, and gave them no chance to attack him. In September, the new Signory was entirely favourable to the Albizzi, and Cosimo was invited into the city to confer on an important matter. As soon as he reached the Council Chamber, he was seized and imprisoned in a small room in the tower of the palace of the Signory, called the Alberghettino. At first he was afraid of being poisoned, but his gaoler, Federigo Malavolti, reassured him by sharing his meals, and after a few days he was allowed to receive food from his own house.

The Albizzi meanwhile hesitated. Some of the party wished to put Cosimo to death at once, but the majority were afraid to do this, and eventually he was banished to Padua for ten years. He was four weeks in prison and all that time his friends were working on his behalf, and considerable sums of money passed before he was set at liberty. The Gonfalonier received a thousand crowns, but in his *Ricordi*, Cosimo remarked

> " They had but little spirit, for if they had wanted money they should have had ten thousand or more to deliver me from that peril." [4]

Cosimo's place of banishment was very soon changed to Venice, where he was received more like an ambassador than an exile, and was able to carry on his business as usual. He was accompanied by his brother Lorenzo and his cousin Averardo, and his two sons, Piero and Giovanni. Contessina does not seem to have been with them, but probably retired to one of the Medici villas outside Florence. Women were seldom included in the political proscriptions of Florentine history, but remained behind to look after the family affairs and work for the return of the exiles. Two prominent examples are Gemma Donati, Dante's wife, and Alessandra Macinghi degli Strozzi, neither of whom were banished with their families.

After exactly a year of absence Cosimo was recalled, and Rinaldo degli Albizzi and his chief partisans were exiled in their turn. Very little blood was shed in this revolution, but all the prominent anti-Mediceans were banished and were kept away from Florence till they died. Cosimo would not run the risk of a counter-revolution, and was strong enough to keep his enemies abroad.

When Cosimo and Lorenzo returned in 1434 they left Piero and Giovanni in Venice, until they saw how things turned out in Florence. When it was clear that he was going to remain at home, Cosimo sent for his possessions from Venice, but decided to leave Piero there for a time, to go on learning the business. He wrote him a letter which is interesting as a medley of domestic details and paternal advice, and also shows that he was already collecting and lending books :—

" Send by the women who are returning the things mentioned in the letter given to Ser G., and look closely thyself, as is but right, after what is sent here and what remains there.

Put the books that are in my desk into a small strong-box so that they should not be opened, and see that the others which we lent should be sent back in such a manner as not to be spoiled.

It seems to me that thou shouldst remain at Venice this winter, for there is nothing doing here, and thus thou canst devote thyself to learning something of the affairs of the bank and of book-keeping. I have ordered a book which thou art to keep according to instructions which Antonio Martelli will send thee. In this way thou wilt learn book-keeping properly, and canst return here at Lent.

Be careful to conduct thyself well at home and abroad, so as not to put either me or thyself to shame. Consort with our friends according to usage ; make thyself acquainted with what is doing in the company and learn what is going on.

Try to get back that book on ethics from the son of Messer P. Corro [Cornaro ?] and the Sallust and Suetonius I lent to G. Lignacci, in one volume. If they have done with them, get them back before S. Lucia [December 13]. Also get back a small volume of Chrysostom which they say they want to translate. Keep the books from Nicola de' Servi as is said in the minute given to Ser G. and send back twenty or twenty-five volumes of our books on each subject. Thou canst put them with the quilts, or in other bales, so that they should not be spoiled, and take care that those which remain are not gnawed or spoiled.

As I said before, for many reasons I think it would be better for thee to remain at Venice, for nothing of any good is doing here. But if thou wishest to return here, do as thou wilt. Naught else to say." [5]

After his return from exile Cosimo played an increasingly important part in public affairs. At first he was necessarily an opportunist, but he was gradually able to mould circumstances more and more to his own will.

In 1436 war broke out between Florence and Milan, and dragged on for some time with varying success, until in 1437 Cosimo went to Venice, his nominal ally, to try to get more effectual help. He was not very successful and went on to Ferrara to persuade the Pope to transfer the Church Council from that city to Florence.

Although Cosimo was a banker and a politician, he took an interest in the minutest details concerning the administration of his various country villas. While he was in Ferrara Contessina wrote him a long letter full of the affairs of Careggi :—

" This evening I received a letter from you, and I understand what you say about sending the barrels to Careggi. When they arrive I will do as you say. I have had a letter from Antonio Martelli * in which he says he is sending you nine bales of our linen which were in Venice. I expect they will have arrived, so please see that they put them in a dry place, so that the linen cloth is not spoiled. At Careggi all are well, as usual, and may God grant that things may be well there in future. It is true that we were somewhat frightened by one of our labourers, who lives where Starnone used to be. He is well again, and I do not think he had the disease. By Giovannino I wrote to you asking you not to be too sparing with paper and ink, if it does not trouble you. Ginevra † and Pierfrancesco ‡ are in Val d' Arno and Amerigo Cavalcanti is staying with them, and they

---

* The Martelli were devoted servants of the Medici, continually mentioned in the letters.
† Ginevra Cavalcanti, wife of Cosimo's brother, Lorenzo.
‡ Pierfrancesco, son of Lorenzo de' Medici and Ginevra Cavalcanti.

are all well, as you will have heard from Giovannino. Lorenzo § and I are here, and we are well enough. If you need anything, let me know. Take care to keep well above all things and take care of yourself in every way. No more now, except may Christ guard you.

In Florence, March 4, 1437.

La Contessina commends herself.

I had the little keys from Matteo. If you want them, let me know. He tells me he put that Santelena in the little bag with the other medals which you brought from Venice, and he is very surprised that you did not find it. He certainly remembers putting it into the bag with the others, and it was one of the first things he did after you left. He wrote to you to-day and answered about this. The men who owed the rent have paid Piero d' Orlando, as they were ordered by Lorenzo.

To Chosimo de Medici in Ferrara." [6]

A *santelena* was really a medal brought back from the Holy Land by a crusader or pilgrim, but all religious medals were often so-called. Such medals were very popular in the Middle Ages, and were regarded as mascots, able to ward off evil. Louis XI of France [*d.* 1483] was so credulous that he had little images of saints fixed on the brim of his hat, and even enlightened patrons of the new learning, like the Medici, could not free themselves from these superstitions.

Cosimo had again taken Piero and Giovanni with him to Ferrara, and we have two letters from Contessina to her younger and favourite son. Professor Pieraccini has made an exhaustive study of the Medici from the medical point of view, and he says that we have copious

§ Lorenzo de' Medici, Cosimo's brother.

evidence that Giovanni was addicted to excessive eating and drinking. At this time, when he was only twenty-one, we find his mother already exhorting him to moderation :—

> " In the name of God on the 15th of March, 1437.
>
> I have received a letter from you and I see where you want me to put your things. Do not worry, for I will look after everything. I should be glad to know how you are finding the doublet you had made there, and also whether you received the trunk full of clothes. Also I would like to know how your eczema is, and to remind you to take some of the quassia I gave you, and put in the phial in your saddlebags. Take care what you eat, especially this Lent, or the eczema will get hold of you again. I should be glad to know what you are doing, and the same about Piero, and whether you have yet been able to do any business. Giorgio tells me you had very bad weather going there, but even if it was bad, you arrived safely, by the grace of God. May it please Him to send you back here safe and sound. I would like to know who waits on you and looks after your things, and where you sleep.
>
> Please take the trouble to write me a few lines sometimes, so that I may have frequent news of you. I will say no more. Christ guard you.
>
> MONNA CONTESINA DI COSIMO IN FLORENCE.

To Giovanni di Cosimo de Medici in Ferrara." [7]

In reply to these many questions, Giovanni duly wrote and gave an account of himself, but he had to confess that he had not been taking care of his health. On April 20 his mother replied :—

> " A few days ago I had a letter from you. I see you are all well, but cannot tell me when Cosimo is

coming back. I hear you have again had a little eczema, which displeases me and if I had been able to take care of you as I had begun to do, I believe you would have been well by now. Please tell Piero that Tanccia and Franciescha want to have those Indulgences. It is getting warm and I think you will need your summer clothes. Please send back one of your trunks, so that if you write for your clothes I shall have something to send them in, and send it to the house in Florence. Do not forget this or I shall not be able to send you anything. Piero Francesco says he would like you to write him a letter, and Piero also. Remind Piero that he must buy a straw hat this summer, and see that he has it well and cleanly made. I will say no more. May God preserve you to me for a long time.

At Castellaccio, April 20, 1438.

MONNA CONTESSINA.

To Giovanni di Cosimo de Medici, Ferrara.'' [8]

Contessina's sons were by this time grown men, but she still looked after their wardrobes, and we have continual references to their clothes, but, unfortunately, very few to her own. We often hear of fur-lined cloaks and capes, for Italy can be bitterly cold in winter, and when travelling had to be done on horseback or in litters warm clothing was very necessary. She also often speaks of stockings, but these were rather leggings, made of cloth, than knitted or woven hose as we know them, which were not introduced until the following century. Queen Mary is said to have been the first Englishwoman to possess a pair of silk stockings.

Piero and Giovanni went to stay with their uncle Lorenzo at Prato in the autumn of 1438, and on October 14 Contessina wrote to Piero :—

" You write to ask me to send you your grey lynx cape, because you say you have felt cold. I do not know why this was, for if you had sent to ask me I should have sent it as I did the other. It seems to be decided that you should all return to Careggi on Monday, where all is well, thanks be to God. It will be a lucky hour, for it seems to me a thousand years until everyone is back at home. I am sure you will all be very busy, especially Ginevra,* so help her all you can and know, and arrange all your own things, and do not leave one here and the other there, and tell the other boy the same. It would be well if you each had a pair of slippers made. You have some stockings to go with the slippers, but he has not, so I am sending the sorriest pair he has, which will be quite suitable with the slippers. Tell him this, and tell him also to send back those new boots which are not right, and to tell the bearer of this to show them to Francesco Martelli, who had them made. And if you want to send anything in the bag of Antonio Martelli's servant, do so, provided there is no duty to be paid. I was going to send some patterns of woollen cloth, but as you are returning I will not trouble. Tell me what you are sending, and write by this servant. I am sending you your porter. No more. Christ guard you.

From Florence, October 14, 1438.

La Contessina.

To Piero di Cosimo de Medici in Prato." [9]

Contessina's dowry had included the old Bardi palace on the other side of the Arno, and here she and Cosimo lived in the time of Giovanni Bicci, and here Piero, and probably also Giovanni, was born.

* Ginevra Cavalcanti, wife of Cosimo's brother, Lorenzo.

The Medici had originally had a house in the Via Larga, and then later one in the Piazza del Duomo, but two years after his father's death, Cosimo decided to build himself a great palace, worthy of housing the art treasures he had already begun to collect. He chose a site at the corner of the Via Larga and the Via de' Gori, quite close to the family church of S. Lorenzo, and at first he intended to employ Brunelleschi as his architect. His plan was so grandiose, however, that Cosimo gave the commission to Michelozzo instead, and the outcome is one of the finest and most imposing palaces of the early Renaissance.

As soon as the building was begun, Cosimo commissioned the sculptor, Donatello, to execute various statues for the adornment of the cortile. These included the famous David, now in the Bargello, the Judith, which was formerly in the Loggia dei Lanzi and is now in front of the Palazzo Vecchio, and the medallions copied from antique gems which are still in their original places.

The palace was begun in 1430 and took over ten years to build, but in 1440 Cosimo and his family took up their abode there. It is built in three orders of architecture, Rustic on the ground floor, Doric above, and Corinthian above again, the whole being crowned with a massive cornice which adds greatly to the fine effect. From the great entrance door one passed through an archway into the beautiful cortile, adorned with priceless statues, whence a fine marble staircase led up to the main apartments, the ground floor being used chiefly for store-rooms and offices. Beyond the palace, along the Via Larga, were extensive grounds, containing many works of art, both ancient and modern.

Nearly all the Medici were of an infirm habit of body, and Contessina's two sons were perhaps the most delicate of the family. She was always worrying about

PLATE III

The Medici Palace in the Via Larga (now Riccardi Palace)
Via Cavour, Florence

[*face p. 30*

them and sending them good advice, whilst they very often visited the various Tuscan baths.

The habit of patronising medicinal springs is a legacy from the Romans which has persisted all through the Middle Ages and the Renaissance in Italy, up to our own day; and the Medici were great frequenters of baths. They chiefly went to Petriolo and Bagno a Morba, though in later years Lorenzo also tried Filetta, Speda-letto and Bagno S. Filippo. The chief diseases we hear mentioned, besides the plague, are gout and rheumatism, eczema and boils, all of which point to errors in diet, and in some cases to uncleanly personal habits. Medical science was very rudimentary, and some of the medicines given to patients are terrible, but the patronage of mineral baths was a step in the right direction.

Contessina herself seems to have enjoyed excellent health, for we hardly ever hear of her going to the baths, but Cosimo and his son were frequent visitors. In 1443 Giovanni was at Petriolo, and Contessina was very anxious to join him, and wrote on September 13 :—

" The reason for this letter is that at table this morning Cosimo told me that Maestro Mariotto had gone to stay with you for eight days, but that when the said Maestro Mariotto returns he would be glad if I would go and be with you. But please ask him to stay with you as long as you think you need him, and Cosimo also would be glad if he stayed with you, and he wishes you to provide for him in such a way that he may be content. But if he returns I will put aside everything in order to be with you, for on no account do I want you to be there without him and without me. So let me know his intentions, for if I had known about it before he went, there would have been no need for him to take this

trouble, for I should have gone. Tell me if you got wet the day you left, and if you need anything, write to me. No more. May Christ guard you.
In Florence, September 13, 1443.

MA CONTESSINI DI COSIMO.

To Giovanni di Chosimo de' Medici at Siena or Bagno a Petriolo." [10]

In the following spring Piero and Giovanni went together to Petriolo for their health, at a time when Cosimo and Contessina were also both unwell. On March 16, 1444, a certain Giovanni Cafferecci wrote to Giovanni from Florence :—

" Madonna Contessina has such eczema that she can hardly bear it. I expect that as soon as Cosimo is better she will come and join you." [11]

At the same time Contessina herself wrote to her son :—

" I have not written to you since you left because every day I have had news of you in Matteo's letter. Cosimo has been much better and was thinking of joining you. But I have again got a boil on my side and have not been able to get up for several days, but it is beginning to get better. I would like to come and stay with you, if only to see if I can get rid of this return of my eczema, for to be in this condition cannot be good for me or for anybody else. Cosimo, thanks be to God, gets better every day, and I could quite well leave him. Although Matteo writes that you are well, I should like to have a letter from you yourself to say how you think the baths are suiting you, and whether they are doing you more good than at other times. I expect you have been having bad weather, for it has been very cold here. Be careful not to get yourself too wet. If you want anything from here, let me know, and you shall have it, and also tell me how the cook serves you. Salute Maestro Paolo and everybody else from us, and may God send you back in good health. There is no more to say. Christ guard you.

Florence, March 15.

Gianesse is studying the Politics well, and has got to the fifth book.

MA CONTESSINA.

To Giovanni di Cosimo at Bagno a Petriolo." [12]

The following week Contessina was much better, for on March 20 she was well enough to think of starting for Petriolo, and wrote :—

" I note what you say about my coming to the baths. I should have come several days ago if I had not had a boil which gave me considerable pain. Now, by the grace of God, I seem to be so much better that I intend to leave here on Monday morning, but there is no need for you to send anyone for me, as I shall come in good company from here." [13]

Although, after the Council of Constance in 1415, the Popes had nominally returned to Rome, the turbulence of the populace often made it impossible for them to maintain themselves there. For this reason Eugenius IV lived for a number of years in the monastery of S. Maria Novella in Florence. But in 1443 he decided to return to Rome and put himself under the protection of Alfonso of Naples. This was very unpopular in Florence, which was then at war with Naples, and it was even suggested that the Pope should be forcibly prevented from leaving Florence. Wiser councils prevailed and Eugenius was allowed to get to Rome, but Cosimo realised the necessity of keeping in close touch with the

D

Pope, and therefore sent as his ambassador, first a certain Averardo de' Alberti and, later, his own son Giovanni. Averardo was not favourably impressed with Rome, and wrote to Giovanni on March 22, 1444 :—

" The condition of this city thou must have heard from others, so I shall be brief. There are many splendid palaces, houses, tombs and temples, and other edifices in infinite number, but all are in ruins and much porphyry and marble from ancient buildings, and every day these marbles are destroyed by being burnt for lime in scandalous fashion. What is modern is poor stuff, that is to say the buildings ; the beauty of Rome lies in what is in ruin. The men of the present day who call themselves Romans are very different in bearing and in conduct from the ancient inhabitants. *Breviter loquendo,* they all look like cowherds. Their women are generally handsome in face ; all the rest is uncommonly dirty ; the reason, they tell me, is that they all cook. They seem agreeable, but one seldom sees them. Amusements there are none, save to go to these pardons (indulgences) which are perpetual, and in these days of Lent the women frequent them, as well as those who, like me, have nothing else to do.

Ex Urbe delacerata (From the ruined city) 22 March, 1443/4." [14]

Giovanni's visit to Rome filled Contessina with concern. He was never strong, and Rome was notoriously unhealthy. Plague and malaria were very prevalent, and the ruined condition of the city made it most insanitary. Contessina was also troubled because Giovanni was very careless about his health, and was very remiss at writing letters, so that she had considerable difficulty in getting detailed news of him. Almost as soon as he had left Florence she wrote :—

" Since you left I have had no news of you except from Vicho, who said that you were well when you left Siena. I do not know how you have been getting on as the weather has been so bad. Now, however, I think you must be near Rome. May God keep you safely, for this week has seemed to me like a year. I beg of you to let me know how you are, and whether you had a troublesome journey. Remember to take care of yourself above all things, and if you need anything let me know. We are all well, thanks be to God. I will say no more. Christ guard you. February 21st, 1444.

MONA CONTESSINA.

To Giovanni di Cosimo de Medici. Rome." [15]

In spite of his mother's exhortations, Giovanni did not write to her, and three weeks after his departure she sent him a stern reproof :—

" Since you left you have not written me a line or a word, and I have neither had letters from you, nor anything written with your own hand, which worries me. For although I get news of you from others, if I do not hear from you personally I fear you may be ill. . . . Take care of yourself, and write with your own hand, and also put a little money in the Bank." [16]

Hereupon Giovanni did at last write and give some account of himself, but Contessina was still very worried about the unhealthy climate of Rome, for on March 20, she wrote :—

" I have to-day received one of your letters, and I see you are well. May it please God to keep you so. I have been told that there is fever there, as there was last summer ; I beg of you that if you are not comfortable you will come away, for those are bad fevers.

35

You saw how Bartolommeo di Nanni di Nettolo had enough of them ; do not wait to do as did Piero at Ferrara. I have a small jar of very good raisins ; I will send it to you during the next few days ; when it arrives, give it to Monsignor di Capua.

Lucrezia is well and is getting fat, and her whole person has improved. She asks me to remind you of her paint. If you want anything I can do for you, let me know. Commend yourself to the Holy Relics and pardons there, and especially to the Holy Face, so that you may become Holy.

Tell Riccio that all his people are well, and that I have had capons given to the women, and spices, and saffron, and sweetmeats for the confinement ; and Matteo, who comes from the Mugello, says that he has had the stakes taken to his vineyard. No more. May Christ guard you. Salute Roberto on my behalf.

In Florence on March 20, 1444.

MONA CONTESSINA.

To Giovanni di Cosimo de Medici in Rome." [17]

It was usual to send presents to the mother of a new-born child, and, in spite of much legislation on the subject, these tended to become more and more sumptuous as time went on. In this particular case Contessina seems to have sent the customary gifts and no more.

Giovanni remained longer in Rome than he had originally expected to do, for he wrote home for some clothes and his mother replied on April 11 :—

" I have just received your letter asking for your rose-coloured *lucco*, lined with fur, a cloak and some boots. The hat I am sending you by Benedetto Altoviti, and all the other things I will send during next week. I have received your tunics, the hams and the bundles you sent. . . ." [18]

The *lucco* was a long loose gown, generally tied round the waist, worn by all Florentine citizens, and may be seen in portraits of Dante.

During the years 1445–1450 we have no letters from Contessina. For some unknown reason, all those belonging to that period have been lost or destroyed.

In 1450, shortly after the birth of his eldest son Lorenzo, Piero went to Trebbio with his family, and Contessina wrote to him on February 6th :—

" I am sending you a quarter of a goat, a hare and a kid, so I will not send you any veal. I have received your letter and trust that God will one day grant us this grace, and I send you the capers. Giovanni was very anxious to try to go up there to-day to see Lucrezia and the children, and said that it seemed such a long time since he had seen you. With great difficulty I prevented him and did not let him come, so that he should not overtire himself. Tell Lucrezia that I will have the baby's petticoat relined, and that she shall have it on Monday, finished. Tell her also to make him suck well, and take care of all the children. Cosimo is well ; this morning his knee pained him a little and he had a touch of the gout. But I think he will soon be well, for it is nothing much. If you or Lucrezia need anything, let me know. I will say no more. Christ guard you.

In Florence on 6 February, 1449–50.

MA CONTESSINA IN FLORENCE.

To Piero di Cosimo de Medici at Trebbio." [19]

At this time Florence, in alliance with Venice, was at war with Naples, and in every way it was most important to keep on good terms with the Pope, so Giovanni went to Rome once more.

Contessina was exceedingly concerned about this, for

the plague was raging there, and, apart from her natural anxiety about her son, she felt that, as Cosimo was growing old, and Piero was such an invalid, it was necessary for Giovanni to take especial care to keep out of danger. She therefore wrote to him on February 24, 1450 :—

"I have not written to you since you left, for there has been no need, but now I must write, for we hear that the plague is raging there, even among better-class people. I beg of you, for the love of God, and the love I bear you, to return as soon as possible, for you know how we suffer, Cosimo and I, when you are there. Your brother also is worried, and if Cosimo had known that there was plague he would never have allowed you to go. Cosimo has perpetual fever, as he had when you left, and the doctors say it is not gout fever, and you know he is getting on in years, so that one cannot know what may happen from day to day. Therefore do please return as quickly as possible, for you know how much he has to do. I will not write more to-day. Piero and his family have come to Careggi, for he also has had fever. Tell me how that trouble of yours is . . ." [20]

At the end of 1450 Giovanni went to Volterra, presumably in some official capacity, and just before Christmas Contessina wrote him a letter full of domestic details. She was busy preparing for the festival of the Epiphany, and required some provisions. She also apparently proposed to make the tunic which had been presented to Cosimo into a garment for herself. While Giovanni was at Volterra, his brother Piero and his cousin Pierfrancesco had gone on an embassy to Rome, so she looked forward to the visit of Messer Rosello, a poet and a canon of Florence, who was coming to spend the holidays with her :—

" In the name of God on December 18th, 1450. I had your letter yesterday. All the things you ask for you shall have by the first messenger going to you. Cosimo continues to improve, and now he is only slightly ill, though he is not quite free of fever, but it is slight. Your slippers were finished, but he had made them black, so they must be remade, and I will send them by the first messenger. We have not yet had news of the arrival of our party, but those who met them on the road said that they were well. When we hear, I will let you know.

Although I wrote to you that we paid too much money for the pigs I should be glad if you would send a pig or a goat, so that we might have it for Christmas, that is if they are given you. If we have to buy them, we do not want them. Messer Rosello says he wishes to spend Christmas with me. He has brought Cosimo a fine tunic of marten and sable made in the Polish fashion, a pair of gloves, and the tooth of a fish a foot long. As we have to prepare for the feast of the Magi, these things will make a change from my cloth of gold.

There is little or no plague here. Only three or four cases in eight days, and no one speaks of it as they are not people one knows. I should be glad to know how you are, and whether you think you are better or worse. I shall be very glad of your return when you do come back.

Antonio degli Strozzi has been here, and has worried me greatly. He is going to see you during the holidays. Tell him whatever you think best, but if he says I promised him anything, do not believe him, for he got nothing definite from me. Take care how you deal with him.

Tell the women that I do not write to them, for there is a dearth of writers until Matteo returns from

Rome, which should be to-morrow. Salute them and greet them from me, and caress the children, and kiss them with my love, and if the women need anything I can do, send to tell me.

No more by this. God guard you.

MA CONTESSINA IN FLORENCE.

To Giovanni di Cosimo de Medici, personally, in Volterra." [21]

Among the citizens exiled in 1434, when Cosimo returned to Florence, were several members of the Strozzi family, including the famous Messer Palla, and Matteo, the husband of Alessandra Macinghi. Those who were allowed to remain were excluded from public life for many years, but at last, in September 1450, Antonio degli Strozzi became one of the Priors. The hearts of his kinsfolk were greatly rejoiced, and Mona Alessandra hoped he might effect the recall of her beloved sons. He was unable to do this, but he approached Contessina and hoped to persuade her to influence Cosimo, though without effect. Later on we find that Filippo endeavoured to achieve the same result through Piero's wife, Lucrezia.

Although she was a fairly copious letter writer, Contessina very seldom wrote with her own hand, but depended on scribes and secretaries. Very few of the ladies of the period wrote their letters themselves, but if they did they made especial mention of the fact, by adding to their signatures the words " Manu propria."

Giovanni remained in Volterra, but he was still a bad correspondent, and on January 3 his mother wrote :—

" In the name of God, on the 3rd day of January, 1450 (s.f.). I am only writing this because it is now several days since we had a letter from you. I expected Antonio degli Strozzi to return and give us news of you by word of mouth. But I will say that

Michele came and gave me news of you, and said you expected the party from Rome on Friday. But I must tell you that it would not be possible for them to be there, for they were expected at Siena that evening. But all the same they may have arrived there, and if they have, do not fail to let me know how they are. According to what Ruberto wrote to C. they were to leave on Monday. If they arrived here we will let you know. No more by this. Christ guard you. Written in haste.

MONA CONTESSINA IN FLORENCE.

To Giovanni di Cosimo de Medici in Volterra." [22]

Piero's wife and children were staying at Volterra with Giovanni, and on his return from his Roman embassy he joined them there for a few days. Cosimo and Contessina had been there previously and had left some of their things behind, as appears from the following letter :—

" In the name of God, on the 5th day of January, 1450 (s.f.). The other day I wrote to you in haste. I have heard of the return of Piero and Pierfrancesco. May God be praised, for we are very glad that they have returned in good health, but I hear that his foot has worried Piero a little. I do not know what you will decide about staying or returning. If you return here, put all your things together in one place, so that if you need anything, you can send and ask the women for it without driving them mad. I think Cosimo has written to you about the strong safe he wants. Here the plague has lessened, and I shall be glad of your return, but perhaps it would be better to wait a little, but do not fail to come back if it is necessary. Tell me what you are going to do. I wrote to you the other day, asking you to look in the linen-cupboard in my room for a pair of scissors that belong to Cosimo, and if you find them, send them in that strong-box. No more by this. Salute Pierfrancesco from me, and say he is welcome back, and that I am very anxious to see him. May Christ guard you

MA CONTESSINA IN FLORENCE.

To the worthy gentleman Giovanni di Cosimo de Medici in Volterra, personally." [23]

Piero soon returned to Florence, but intended to go back to Volterra to fetch his family about January 15, though he was delayed by bad weather. Giovanni wrote to ask his mother what his brother's plans were, and she replied :—

" It is some days since I wrote to you, and now I have a letter from you asking when Piero is coming. . . . Piero intended to start to-day, for yesterday was the vigil and to-day is the feast. But until the weather mends a little he will not go, although he says he wants to be there for S. Antonio, unless it rains so much that he cannot start. Cosimo is getting better, but very slowly, and Piero is well, so please tell Lucrezia. Here all are well at present, and Maestro Mariotto says there is nothing in the neighbourhood, so I think Piero wants to bring back his family, as soon as there is good weather and the roads are good, but he is coming and will tell you what he thinks. I have not sent Pierfrancesco's things, because I hear that he and Ginevra want to return here. . . . I will say no more now, except to ask you to kiss the babies from me. . . ." [24]

As he gained increased power in Florence, Cosimo gave up going on foreign embassies, because he wished to remain at home to manage affairs. But in the case of certain important missions, he took care that one of his sons should be sent as one of the ambassadors, so that

Giovanni went to Rome on several occasions, and after the peace of Lodi in 1454, Piero went to Venice. He fell ill there, and on July 21st, Contessina wrote to him :—

" I have just received a letter from you saying that you were feeling better, and improving every day, which pleases me. I expect you wish for news of Cosimo. During the last few days he has improved greatly, so that he has escaped this time, and has little fever. You say you have bought the quilts and bed-ticking, which is well. If you want to send them to Careggi before your return, do as you think best. Your family are all well. It seems a thousand years till you come back, and I hear no mention of it. I do not know how long this business of yours will be, for it is now regretted. I will say no more now. Christ guard you.
In Florence, June 21st, 1454.

MA CONTESSINA.

To the noble gentleman Petro de Medici, Florentine Ambassador in Venice." [25]

Piero was married as early as 1443, but Giovanni waited ten years longer before he took a wife. He married Ginevra degli Alessandri on January 20, 1453, but she is a very shadowy figure and very few of her letters remain. She was devoted to her husband, but he seems to have repaid her affection with neglect, and would not write to her for weeks when he was away from her. In 1454 she bore her husband a son, called Cosimo after his grandfather.

In April 1455 Ginevra and her husband went to the Baths of Petriolo. Soon after their arrival she received a letter from an old family friend, Pippa di Bartolo Tedaldi, who addressed her letter on the outside to " The wise and discreet young Monna Ginevra, wife of Giovanni di Cosimo, at Bagno a Petriolo." She said :—

43

"IHS   April 2, 1455.

Dearest as a daughter.   On the 29th of last month
I had a letter from you, together with two excellent
almond tarts, one of which went to Nicholaio, while
I kept the other myself.   This was very dear to me,
not so much because of the tarts, but because I see
that everywhere you remember me, and also your
father, which rejoices me.   I have heard that you
reached the Baths safely, praise be to God.   Now I
should be glad, and it would console me greatly,
to hear how you are and how the baths are affecting
you, for I hear that you have already bathed several
times without doing yourselves any harm, so I beg
that, without troubling yourself unduly, you will write
me a couple of lines and tell me how things are, for
this would please me greatly.   The family in your
house is well, and your Cosimo sucks well enough, and
is in good health.   Monna Contessina must be telling
you all the time how things are.   Commend me to
Giovanni, and if there is anything I can do here for
you, let me know, and it will be a great pleasure
to do things which will be a pleasure to you.   No
more . May Christ guard you.

Your Pippa di Bartolo Tedaldi in Florence.
To the Wise and Discreet young Monna Ginevra, wife
of Giovanni di Cosimo, at Bagno a Petriolo." [26]

The Medici had a house at Petriolo, for when Giovanni and Ginevra were expecting to return, Contessina
wrote to her daughter-in-law :—

"I see that you are hastening back. . . . Piero
will go there on the 20th of this month, so leave the
things that he will need, and leave Riccio and Gian-
netello, and consign everything to them if you should
leave before Piero's arrival.   He will stay at Bagno

a Macereto for about six days to bathe his eczema. Bring back the women you took with you, for Monna Lucrezia is taking Monna Meo and some of these slaves, so she will need no other women. Your baby is well and has cut two teeth, and I think he will become so accustomed to these nurses that he will give up the breast, both by day and night, and he will do it of his own accord. I think that having cut his teeth like this, he will do very well." [27]

Much of the housework at this time was done by slave-girls, chiefly Circassians and Tartars, who were bought in the open market, especially in Venice. Sometimes they were valuable and faithful, but more often they were a great source of trouble to their mistresses. The Commune of Florence levied a tax on every slave that entered the city, and insisted on baptism. If a slave bore a child to a free man, the child was also free, and the father was responsible for its upbringing. We do not hear much about the slaves belonging to the Medici, but Cosimo had a son by a Circassian slave-girl he bought in Venice in 1427. This boy, who was named Carlo, was brought up in the Medici palace with the other children, and afterwards entered the Church. He held numerous benefices, and became Papal collector and nuncio in Tuscany, and a protonotary apostolic. In 1460 he became archpriest of Prato, where he died on March 29, 1479. He shared the family taste for art, and was a great collector of manuscripts and antiquities.

Before Giovanni left Petriolo in 1455 his mother wrote to him :—

" I expect you will have received a letter written by Tita, that is to say, my Tita, saying that Milla wants to go to the Baths and take with her the said

Madonna Tita and a servant. Therefore she would like a little accommodation in the house, for they have no man with them, and they would feel safer, especially as Piero is going there. So let me know if you can find room for them. I expect they will arrive before Piero, as he is staying at Macereto for six days. As they have no man with them they will be better and safer in the house. I do not think they can do with less than two beds and somewhere to cook. . . ." [28]

After his visit to Petriolo in the spring, Giovanni's health was considerably improved, and in the summer he went to Milan. On July 8, his devoted wife wrote to him :—

" By the hand of Francesco I have heard that you had arrived safely as far as Bologna, praise be to God, for it seems to me a thousand years till you return, and I can hardly await the day and hour, my desire is so great. I must tell you that we went to Fiesole with Piero and Lucrezia and Agnolo della Stufa and the choir boys of S. Giovanni, where they enjoyed themselves very much, and the daughters of Ser Antonio performed miracles and things of the other world, which mystified everybody present, and we stayed so long to watch them that it was the second hour of the night before we returned to Florence. There is any amount of water, and the wall has given way. Piero thinks it well that it was so gentle. Perhaps it was best that it happened thus, otherwise it might have hurt someone. I hear from Cosimo that you are not going further than Milan, which pleases me greatly. Please tell Ser Francesco not to forget the veils I told him about. Cosimino had such a cold that he seemed to be stifled, but he is a little better now, and the Maestro tells me it is nothing to worry about. No more now. I commend myself to you, and commend me to the Duke, and tell him that I beg him to do that which he wrote to Cosimo about you. Cosimo is well, and all the others, and I beg you to reply to me with your own hand. No more. Christ guard you as much as my heart desires.

July 8, 1455.

Your loving Ginevra commends herself to you.

To Giovanni di Chosimo de Medici in Milan." [29]

Giovanni was habitually a bad correspondent. When he was a young man in Rome his mother complained that she did not hear from him, and now, when he was in Milan, he did not write to his wife. When he had been away for over a month she wrote :—

" Oh, if I could have written that I had seen a line from your hand." [30]

The rest of the letter deals with the wall at Fiesole that had collapsed, and was giving a great deal of trouble. Giovanni was building himself a villa on the slopes of Fiesole, and the incline was so steep that the work was often very difficult.

Cosimo did not approve of the site chosen by his son, for he considered the property stony and sterile, and the cost of building in such a position excessive. But Giovanni said he had chosen the place because it gave him such a magnificent view. Cosimo replied that he thought the finest view could be obtained from Cafaggiuolo. But Cafaggiuolo lies low, and Giovanni could not understand, until his father explained " From there everything I can see is ours, which is not the case at Fiesole."

Cosimo was the old-fashioned burgher who preferred

the sight of his own property to any natural prospect however fine, but Giovanni was a man of the Renaissance, attracted by natural beauty.

When Ginevra was at the Baths she made friends with a Genoese lady, a certain Ginevra di Campofregoso, who lived at Sarzanella, and we have a letter from her when she wanted Cosimo's goodwill for one of her men. She wrote on August 31, 1456 :—

" Since I left the Baths I have not had any letters from you to tell me how you were, and what good results you had from the Baths. I have not written to you either until now, because nothing has happened worth telling you about. But since the bearer of this has occasion to go to my compeer Cosimo, I have decided to write to you and at the same time send you two little shirts for your son, not as a present, for they are unworthy of Your Magnificence, but in order to remind you of me. Please let him wear them for my sake. And if in future there is anything I can do for you, I beg you to let me know, for I will not cease to do that which is pleasing to you. I beg you to commend me to my Magnificent compeer, to your husband, and to all your family, for I offer myself to them with all I have and all I am. I beg you to be willing to let me know often how you are, for it will always give me the greatest pleasure to know that you are well. The bearer of this has been in our household for a long time, and we are all very fond of him. Since he has got to transact some business with the Magnificent Cosimo, I beg you to commend him to him, and to show that my intercessions carry weight with you, whom may God keep in happiness. Clarice, Maria, and the others who were at the Baths with me when you were there, beg you to bear in mind that business about which you will hear in due course.

From the Castle of Serzanella, August 31, 1456.

GENEBRA DE CAMPOFREGOSO.

To the Magnificent and beloved as a sister, Donna Genevre de Medicis." [31]

(The word *compare*, here translated compeer, is frequently used, but its meaning is vague. Strictly it means godfather, and was used by persons who had together been sponsors of a child. By so doing they were regarded by the Church as related and within the forbidden degrees of marriage, and so the term compare came to be used for distant relationships.)

Housekeeping was no easy thing in those days, especially with so many houses and villas to look after. In Florence the whole family lived together in the palace in the Via Larga, but during the summer they scattered among the various villas they owned in the neighbouring country. Each of these properties produced a certain quantity of necessary things, some of which were sold, but the majority kept for family use.

But they all moved about a great deal, and it was often necessary to send things from one villa to another, as they were required, and we get many letters full of such matters, which throw light on the conditions of the day.

In the spring of 1457 Lucrezia was at Cafaggiuolo, recovering from an illness, and Contessina was with her, though she was most anxious to join Giovanni and Ginevra at Careggi, and on May 13 she wrote a letter full of household affairs to her daughter-in-law :—

" I have not written to you for several days, because Filippo has not been down there. Lucrezia is much better and is getting stronger every day, so that I am thinking of coming on Saturday or Sunday without fail, for it seems to me a thousand years, for love of Cosimo, until I can be there. I am sending you a mattress and a feather bed for the children's little bed, and I am also sending you a carpet, the cover from your room, and the flax which you need for the linen up there ; a pair of my sheets, a table-cloth, a doll's cover, and two pairs of my slippers. I send two curds to my Cosimino, and to you three pairs of capons, and two bolsters with the feather bed. I have a letter from Giovanni to say he cannot come and see about his things, but they can be left until the middle of June, unless I find that Piero's men need them. I am not writing to Cosimo because I know you will give him news of us. I will say no more. May Christ guard you.

In Cafaggiuolo, May 13, 1457.

CONTESSINA DI COSIMO.

To Monna Ginevra di Giovanni di Cosimo at Careggi." [32]

Contessina returned to Cafaggiuolo and spent most of the summer there, for on October 25 she wrote thence to Giovanni, who was still at Careggi :—

" A boy came to-day with a letter for Francesco Fracasini, who was not at home, as he had gone to Gagliano, so I opened and read it, and saw what you were asking for. I send you three couple of goats' cheeses, for we have no more in the house, but I think we shall soon have more, and if you want them I will send some.

I am sending up fifty-three pounds of formed cheese, so that the factor may sell it to those pot-makers, and anyone else who may be suitable, but if you need any in the house, take it and let him sell the remainder.

Facsimile of Contessina's writing

[face p. 50

Tell Ginevra to send Marco's son to the bleacher of Monte Domini for me, to get our towels, whether they are done or not, and tell her to look into matters there and see whether they have sold the dry meat, and whether they are doing so to the best advantage.

Cosimino is very well, but Cosimo has got pains again. I will say no more. May Christ guard you. In Cafaggiuolo, October 25, 1457.

CONTESSINA.

Tell Ginevra to send me a barrel of vinegar, from that on the terrace, by the first messenger, and tell Antonello that he can pick the oranges on Averardo's house, and send me some here and also use them there.

I have now decided to send you thirty couple of cheese, and a sack of moulds of cheese and some bad cheeses. Tell Felice to sell the cheese as best he can, and the moulds he had better sell to a carpenter who may find them useful. The sack with the pieces are ours, take care of them."

On a separate sheet.

" Send back our sack, and the little sack in which the cheeses and the moulds come.
To Giovanni di Cosimo de Medici at Chareggi." [33]

Ginevra was still at Careggi at the end of November, for Contessina, who did not think the younger woman such a good housewife as herself, wrote to her from Cafaggiuolo about the making of oil, which had not been done well that year.

" I received the oil this evening, and you can tell Felice he is a fool who does not know whether oil is good or bad. That barrel you sent is not very successful, but the half-barrel you have sent now is better. He must take the dregs of that oil which, as you know, was so good, and then he must boil it, as he has done with the dregs every year. Then when it has settled he must clean the jars well, so that the new oil can be put in them, but take care he does not mix the bad and the good.

I will see that you receive the things you commissioned Matteo to get, but take care not to do anything that might harm you. Cosimino is well and is a good boy. Do not forget to have his pills made. You were wise to have his coat lined. . . . I am sending you back the sack which contained Madonna Lucrezia's flax." [34]

In the following summer the positions were reversed, and Contessina was at Careggi and Giovanni at Cafaggiuolo. The family butler had been giving trouble, and Contessina was trying to replace him. She wrote to her son on June 7, 1458 :—

" I would like you to have a little talk with that man who is building a house for his wife and children at San Piero a Sieve, and find out if he would care to come to us as butler, for on no account will I have our man back in the house. But if he cannot be got, you must go and see Giovanni Guicciardini when you come back, and we can try the man he has spoken about several times. Please send me some of those salted cheeks and some tongues and some lard. No more. Cosimino is well." [35]

The little Cosimino, the son of Giovanni and Ginevra, spent a large part of his time with his grandmother, and she mentions him in many of her letters. In September, 1459, he was with her at Careggi, while his parents were at Petriolo, taking the baths, and on September 24, Contessina wrote to them :—

" I have not written to you since you left, but I expect you are anxious to have news of us, especially of Cosimino. We are all well, thanks be to God. But Monna Lucrezia has not quite recovered, though she is better. Cosimino is looking very well, so do not worry, and if he gets no worse, you will think he has been remade on your return. Please let me know how the woman serves you, and how you all are, and if the baths are doing good to Giovanni's hand and foot. I expect you have heard from Cosimo that Guglielmo will b with you to-morrow, for to-day he lunched Cafaggiuolo. . . ." [36]

Giovanni's health became more and more precarious, and in August, 1460, when he and his wife were at Bagno a Morba, Contessina was very annoyed to hear that he had been told of the illness of Cosimo and Piero. It was considered most important to keep cheerful and avoid depression in times of illness, and great ladies, like Isabella d' Este, even sent their pet dwarfs and buffoons to cheer their friends on their sick-beds. On this occasion Contessina wrote :—

" Dearest Children. We have just received your letters, which have given us much joy and pleasure, since you are so much better. May it please God that the improvement continues, so that we may have this pleasure and consolation in our old age. It annoys me that you were told that Cosimo and Piero had been ill, for I did not want you to have any sad news, so that the Baths might have their full effect. They have only been slightly ill. Cosimo had a little flux, but he soon recovered, and is now well, and Piero had slight pains and is not yet quite well, but you know how it was at other times. So take care to keep well. Cosimo has given up the trouble of being one of the Eight, and has put Pierfrancesco in his place ; the same might be done for you. I should be glad, Ginevra, if you would tell me how the Baths are, and how Mona Nanna serves you. If I can do anything for you here, let me know. Mona Pippa has that trouble you know about. The rest of the family are well.

At Careggi, August 28, 1460.

Your CONTESSINA.

To Giovanni di Cosimo de Medici and Ginevra his wife at Bagno a Morba, Volterra." [37]

During the next few years much grief came to Cosimo and Contessina. On November 18, 1459, Cosimino, the son of Giovanni and Ginevra, died, and in 1463 Giovanni himself, until Cosimo felt that his work was likely to die with him, since Piero was too great an invalid to take much part in politics. But Cosimo had builded better than he knew, for the power of the family was upheld by Piero and bequeathed to Lorenzo, who raised it to an unprecedented height.

In September, 1461, Piero and Lucrezia were at the Baths of Corsena together, and Contessina wrote them a letter full of family and domestic news :—

" Since the boys who accompanied you returned we have had no news, which surprises us somewhat. You wrote that Guglielmo was coming there for the Fair, but I expect he stayed in order to be there for the Feast [of Lucca ?]   Monna Cosa also says that she has had no news. I should be glad to know how the Baths suit you, and how you manage about the discomforts that I expect you have. I heard that your hand had been troubling you a little, and I should like to hear whether you have had any more pain. We are here at Careggi, and Bianca is with us. She is very well, as are all your other children. Cosimo and Giovanni are well, by the grace of God. Lorenzo is a good boy and they are all pleased to be with me. And Lorenzo is looking well. Tell Matteo not to forget his promise to Cosimo to write often. If you want anything from here, let me know and I will do it gladly. Lucrezia's linen will be finished on Tuesday, and I will send it to be bleached.

At Careggi, September 10, 1461.

To Piero di Cosimo de Medici et Ma Lucretia at Bagno a Corsena." [38]

In 1462 Ginevra tried yet another of the Tuscan springs to cure her ills, for on August 18, we find her writing to her husband from Bagno ad Aqua :—

" This is only to tell you that I am well and am taking baths desperately while the weather is good, for I shall be lucky if it does not rain. But the greatest piece of luck would be to hear that you yourself were coming for me, but I do not expect this, for I never have any luck. However I am thankful that you are alive. I am so covered with a heat rash that I feel as if razors were cutting me, and I cannot sleep, but I think soft treatment will send it away. . . . " [39]

Contessina was an excellent housekeeper, and a devoted wife and mother, but she was not Cosimo's intellectual equal, and, though full of superstitious piety, she could not understand his interest in the problems of the Soul and the Life Eternal.

In July, 1464, Cosimo was at Careggi, where he spent much of his time in study and in Platonic discussions with Marsilio Ficino. He also spent many hours in silent meditation, and when Contessina asked him the reason for this, he replied :—

" When we are going to our country-house, you are busy for a fortnight preparing for the move, but since I have to go from this life to another, does it not seem to you that I ought to have something to think about ? " [40]

When Cosimo was dying on August 1, 1464, he would have no one in his room except Contessina and his son Piero. By his own wish he was buried as a private citizen, but in Piero's *Ricordi*, we find a list of the funeral expenses. A large number of masses were said for the repose of his soul, and mourning was purchased for several members of the family and household.

" Madonna Contessina, wife of Cosimo, had of cloth 30 *braccia*, and also eight veils and two kerchiefs." [41]

The other members of the family received 20 *braccia* of cloth, with two veils and one kerchief, except " Maria Nannina, daughter of Piero di Cosimo," who received only cloth, probably because she was still unmarried. The five maids and the four slaves received a small quantity of cloth only. Another recipient of cloth was " Maestro Mariotto di Niccolo, our doctor," who is so often mentioned in Contessina's letters.

Contessina now faded into the background, though she survived not only her husband but both her sons. Giovanni had died in 1463, and Piero only lived till 1469, when he was succeeded by his son Lorenzo, the greatest of the family.

In 1463 the old lady was ill, but she soon recovered, and in the summer of 1467 she was at Cafaggiuolo with Piero's children, for the factor, Francesco Fronsini, wrote to Piero on August 26 :—

" Madonna Contessina and the boys are well, and may God preserve them so. . . . Lorenzo wants to level the land here, in front of Cafaggiuolo. We need candles here, both of wax and of tallow. I spoke to Madonna Contessina about it, and she told me to take some of those white ones from Venice, but they seem too good for Cafaggiuolo. If you agree, please ask Madonna Lucrezia to send some others, and especially tallow ones for the use of the household." [42]

Later in the year Contessina wrote the last letter which has come down to us. It was addressed to Lucrezia :—

" My dearest Daughter. I received a letter from you this morning, from which I see with joy that you are better. We must be grateful to God and give thanks to Him, and pray to Him continually that He may free you entirely from your ills. I hear continually from Piero of your progress, so do not tire yourself by writing to me. I am sending you the spices you wanted by the bearer. I have received the knives and will have them attended to as you wish. Do not worry about Ginevra, for I have provided everything needful for her household, and will continue to do so. Visits to Laudomina* have been paid on your behalf, and everything necessary has been done. She is very discontented, although it was a boy. We are all happy and well here, thanks be to God. May you be the same there. No more at present.
October 25, 1467." [43]

Although Contessina was getting on in years she was still full of energy, for in the summer of 1468,

* Daughter of Agnolo Acciaiuoli and wife of Pierfrancesco de' Medici.

when she was again at Cafaggiuolo, Fronsini wrote to Piero :—

> " Yesterday morning Madonna Contessina, Lorenzo and Giuliano, with the entire household, went on horseback to the house of the Frati del Bosco. There they heard High Mass said before the picture of S. Giuliano, sent by you, which the friars had decorated handsomely. . . . Madonna Contessina rode Lorenzo's mule and was astonished at managing better than she expected. . . . She rides always with two boys at the stirrups, and we will do our best to relieve her of the fatigues and troubles of housekeeping." [44]

Contessina abstained almost entirely from affairs in general, though Antonio degli Strozzi tried to make her influence Cosimo on behalf of his kinsmen, and in 1471 a certain Alessandro Bardi di Vernio wrote to her to ask her to persuade Lorenzo to take one of his sons with him on his forthcoming journey to Rome.[45] This is the last trace of her in the correspondence.

Contessina was very pious, and spent her dowry on rebuilding the convent of S. Lucia in Via S. Gallo, where Catherine de' Medici afterwards spent part of her girlhood. It was probably for this convent that Filippo Lippi painted the picture of the Virgin adoring the Child who is sleeping in a flowery meadow, with the little S. John in the background.

Contessina died in October, 1473. On September 25 we hear that she is well, but on October 26 Luigi Pulci says he found her dead on his return to Florence a few days earlier. We have no account of her burial and do not even know whether she was buried with Cosimo in S. Lorenzo.

Vasari says that he saw a bust of Contessina by

Donatello in the Medici Guardaroba, but unfortunately this cannot now be traced. Personally I should think the bronze bust of an old woman in the Bargello might thus be identified. This has been ascribed to both Vecchietta and Donatello, and is apparently worked from a death mask. As Donatello died in 1466, he cannot have worked from Contessina's death mask, but since there is no definite proof of his authorship, it is pleasant to think that this peaceful old woman was Cosimo's wife.

Contessina was an old-fashioned Florentine woman, a good housekeeper and a loving wife and mother. Her importance depended not on her personality but on that of her husband, so, after his death, she was rapidly overshadowed by her son's brilliant wife, and faded from life without ostentation, as she had lived.

Cosimo's wife was not clever, nor did she play a great part in the history of Florence, but she is typical of the women of the earlier days of the Renaissance. She tried to live up to the precepts of Alberti, looked after her house and her husband, and did not meddle in politics. She had more affinity with the days of Dante than with the High Renaissance, but she is fascinating because she is the first real woman of Florence to emerge as more than the mere shadow of a name.

CHAPTER V

LUCREZIA TORNABUONI

CONTESSINA'S daughter-in-law, like herself, was a member of an old Florentine family, and she too was careful of her household affairs. But she was also a highly cultivated, intellectual woman, who wrote poetry and took part in politics, and was on friendly terms with the most eminent authors and scholars of the age. She marks a definite stage in the transition from the old-fashioned burgher's wife to the Grande Dame of the Renaissance.

As commerce increased the wealthy citizen found it more and more necessary to go on long business journeys, and he soon fell into the habit, whenever possible, of leaving his affairs in the hands of his wife. He therefore desired her to be able to read, and write, and cast accounts, so that she might guard his interests at home, manage his country estate, and even keep watch on his business in town during his absence. Thus the education of women gradually improved, until, in the full tide of humanism, they shared their brothers' studies, and became excellent Greek and Latin scholars.

With increased mental cultivation women began to take a growing interest in public affairs, but in Florence their influence always remained indirect, and women rulers such as Isabella d' Este and Caterina Sforza were unknown. Although actually ruled by a veiled despotism, Florence always chose to consider herself a Republic, in which women had no part. The Medici were themselves very able politicians, but they did not let their women share activities to any great extent. The two exceptions to this rule were Lucrezia Tornabuoni and Alfonsina Orsini. Alfonsina was the evil genius of her generation, but Lucrezia was the finest and most interesting woman of the family.

Lucrezia Tornabuoni belonged to an ancient Florentine family, descended from the noble Tornaquinci, whose ancestor Giovanni, at the age of seventy, commanded the guard of the Carroccio at the battle of Montaperti in 1260. In 1393, under a certain Simone, they abandoned their nobility, changed their name to Tornabuoni, and became prosperous traders.

Simone's son, Francesco, married Selvaggia di Maso degli Alessandri, and had at least ten children, of whom the best known were Giovanni and Lucrezia.

Giovanni, who was the younger, was for many years the head of the Medici Bank in Rome, where he amassed an immense fortune. He was a great patron of art, and towards the end of his life he commissioned Ghirlandaio to adorn the choir of S. Maria Novella with a great series of frescoes. On the occasion of his son's marriage with Giovanna degli Albizzi he employed Botticelli to paint the two frescoes discovered in the Villa Lemmi and now in the Louvre.

Lucrezia Maria was born in 1425, for in the Catasto of 1427 her father states that she is one and a half years old. This does not quite tally with the ages given on later occasions, but it is probably accurate, as her father would be less likely to be mistaken than either her husband or her son. We know nothing about her education, but we may suppose that she shared lessons with her brothers, for in after years

61

she was a well-educated and well-read woman, though we do not know if she was a Greek or Latin scholar.

She was married to Piero, Cosimo's elder son, on June 3, 1444, when her name appears in the " Libro delle Gabelle dei Contratti," but there is not any contemporary record of the festivities. Cosimo had not yet attained his commanding position in the state, so that the wedding was a purely private affair, though probably on a sumptuous scale. Three years later, in 1447, a much less wealthy citizen, Marco Parenti, spent 372 lire 18 soldi 1 denaro on his wedding breakfast, as well as 94 lire 4 soldi and 1 denaro to the apothecary for almond paste and various other spices, sweets and condiments. The entertainment was provided by pipers and trumpeters, a fluteplayer and a harpist, who together received 6 lire 6 soldi.[1]

A marriage had previously been arranged between Piero and Gualdrada di Francesco Guidi, Count of Poppi, and although the betrothal had already taken place, Cosimo decided against it for political reasons, and found a wife for his son among the good Republican citizens of Florence.

Lucrezia bore Piero seven children, four sons and three daughters. Lorenzo was born in 1450 and Giuliano in 1453, but the other two boys died in infancy, as well as one of the girls. The daughters were named Bianca and Nannina, and married respectively Guglielmo de' Pazzi and Bernardo Rucellai. Piero also had a natural daughter, Maria, who was brought up with the rest of the family, married Leonetto de' Rossi, and became the mother of Cardinal de' Rossi.

Lucrezia was always delicate, and was continually being sent to the Baths, first to Petriolo and then to Bagno a Morba. The first letter remaining to us was addressed to Piero from Petriolo on May 17, 1446 :

PLATE V

Lucrezia Tornabuoni, by Botticelli.   In the Kaiser Friedrich Museum, Berlin

[*face p. 62*

"In the Name of God on the 17th day of May, 1446.

My Lord and Master. Yesterday I had a letter from you telling me what to do about the baths. I had intended to do all the things you advise in your letter, and everything that Maestro Giovanni orders, for nothing will seem wearisome or unpleasant which will help me to regain my health. I think, by the grace of God, it will be restored in a way that will please you all.

I see you have purged yourself, and are going to the villa. I am glad to hear it. Take care of yourself and do not worry about me, for I shall return cured. We will do honour to Maestro Giovanni, and give him good cheer, for he deserves it.

If it were convenient to you, and pleased you to come here, I should be very glad, but if it is inconvenient or troublesome, I shall be content if you let it be.

I am glad Bianca Maria is well again, and I pray to God that all will go on so as to please you and me and her husband. I will speak of you to Maria Nanna and to Filippo. I have saluted them and they commend themselves to you and to all the rest. Commend me to Cosimo, and to Mona Contessina, and to Mona Ginevra and Giovanni, and salute Piero.* No more at present. Christ guard you. In Petriolo.

If you can conveniently and suitably leave Franceschino with me for the rest of time, I shall be very glad, for he is very useful to me here, but do whatever pleases you best.

From your LUCREZIA who commends herself.

To the Worthy Gentleman Piero di Chosimo de Medici, my honoured husband, in Florence." [2]

* Probably Pierfrancesco, son of Lorenzo de' Medici.

Lucrezia's two daughters, Bianca and Nannina, were older than Lorenzo, who was born on January 1, 1450. In February of that year the little family were at Trebbio, and the following Christmas Lucrezia took her children to stay with her brother-in-law, Giovanni, at Volterra. She was too much taken up with her small children and the many festivities to answer letters, and on January 15, her brother Marabotto wrote to her very reproachfully on this score.[3]

Whilst Lucrezia was at Volterra Piero went to Rome on an embassy, but stopped to see his family on his way back at the beginning of January. He then returned to Florence, but on January 16 or 17, he fetched his family from Volterra back to the city.

In April, 1455, Piero and Lucrezia again went to Petriolo, and in July of the same year we get a glimpse of them in a letter from Ginevra to Giovanni. Ginevra and Piero and Lucrezia took the choir boys of S. Giovanni up to Fiesole, where they were greatly entertained by a conjuring exhibition performed by the daughters of Ser Antonio, which pleased them so much that they did not get home until late that night.

In 1456 Piero drew up an inventory of his possessions for the purpose of the Catasto, and under the heading of " Clothing of Piero and Mona Lucrezia " we find the following garments which must have belonged to Lucrezia, as well as some others the ownership of which is not so clear.

A petticoat of black brocaded velvet, faced with sable.

A dress of crimson and gold brocade damask, faced with ermine.

A skirt of light and dark purple, faced with green brocade.

A dress of light and dark crimson faced with fur.

A dress of black damask faced with red taffeta.

A cloak of blue taffeta brocaded in silver, with silver sleeves.

A coat of light and dark crimson with gold brocade sleeves.

A coat of figured material with gold brocade sleeves.

A skirt of fine red Milanese serge faced with gold brocade.

A rose coloured petticoat faced with marten and embroidered.

A skirt of black cloth faced with black velvet.

A rose-coloured house dress with sleeves of black taffeta.

A lining made of the backs of grey miniver.[4]

Special mention is made always of the sleeves because these were separate articles of clothing presumably attached to an under-bodice.

In February, 1457, Lucrezia was at Cafaggiuolo with her children, for on the 28th, she wrote to Piero, who had gone to Florence on business :—

" I have to-day received a letter from you, which was very dear to me, since it told me how you were. I see that by the grace of God, the ride did not trouble you much, which pleases me. Mona Contessina had already told me this, and also that you were greeted with great rejoicings, and truly, as you say, we have much to thank God for. So make up your mind to suffer a little discomfort gladly, for these things cannot be done without weariness. . . . I see that all the family are well, and it has been a great consolation to me to know that they are all in good health, and I thank you, and I beg you, if we are. not to return, to come back here as soon as possible, for it seems a thousand years since we saw you, especially to Giuliano.

Lorenzo is learning the verses the master left here, and teaches them to Giuliano. No more now. Commend me to Cosimo and to Mona Contessina. We are all well. May Christ guard you.

February 28, 1457." [5]

Piero decided that his family were not to return to Florence, but to go to Careggi from Cafaggiuolo, and Lucrezia found that a great many domestic matters required attention before she could make the move. She wrote to Piero on March 3, 1457 :—

" This evening I received your letter saying you have decided that we are to go to Careggi. I must see how we can clean and scour and to do all the needful things, and get in the necessary provisions, as you write. When I had received your letter this evening, I decided to send the things on the enclosed list. There is also a list of the things that are to be left at Careggi, so that if you want anything there before I come, you will be advised.

Please let me know what there is in the way of wine and corn, and also anything else you want, for none of the flasks you left with Averardo have been touched.

I wanted one of the sheets without hem-stitching from the antechamber, but you have sent me one from the bed in our room. I am sending you this back, together with Cosimo's squirrel-lined tunic which you asked for. Please send by Filippo the sheet without hem-stitching that belongs to the antechamber there, for I want it for the same room here, and in exchange I sent one of three and a half breadths with you when you left here.

Please ask Madonna Contessina what we are to do about Madonna Giuliana when we leave here.

All Madonna Contessina's pieces of cloth are

here, except one linen one which will be finished very soon. Does she want them sent to Careggi? Bleaching-time approaches, but here there is no one to do it, so please let me know what to arrange.

We still have about twenty brace of pigeon here. It would be a good thing if Madonna Contessina would have them there, for here they will only be a useless expense. . . .

The sheet you are sending should be put in the bag in which I am sending you various things."[6]

In 1459 Galeazzo Maria Sforza, the son of the Duke of Milan, visited Florence in order to cement the alliance recently made by Cosimo with the old *condottiere*. He was entertained in a most sumptuous manner, and gave an account of the festivities in a letter to his father.

He described the beauties of Careggi, where he lunched with the whole family, except Giovanni, who acted as a kind of steward and saw that everyone was served, and that there was nothing lacking. After the meal was over, the company went into another room, where they were entertained by a certain Maestro Antonio, who accompanied his song on the zither. He sang a song describing all the great deeds of the Sforza family, which greatly pleased the young prince, who was also greatly struck by the fact that " he mingled so many old stories, names of ancient Romans, fables, poets, and the names of all the Muses, that it was a great work." [7] To our modern taste it sounds as if it must have been a terrible hotch-potch.

This performance was followed by a dance in which Lucrezia, Ginevra, Bianca, Laudomina, and Marietta Strozzi took part, who all danced together in the Florentine fashion, which seems to have involved a good deal of jumping and leaping.

The educational principles of the famous Vittorino da Feltre were widely diffused in Italy, and Piero's two sons were brought up on his system. Their tutors included some of the greatest scholars of the day, such as Christoforo Landino, Marsilio Ficino and Giovanni Argyropoulos. Their chief teacher was, however, Gentile Becchi of Urbino, afterwards Bishop of Arezzo and Lorenzo's lifelong friend.

In 1461 Piero and Lucrezia were at Corsena, and Gentile wrote them a letter which shows the studies that were considered suitable for a boy of eleven.

"Lorenzo is well, but your absence is always in his mind. So far we are well on with Ovid, and have read four books of Justin, both history and fable."[8]

In 1463 Giuliano was at Pisa, where he was taken seriously ill. His mother hastened to his side, and wrote to her husband in Florence :—

"I write you several letters on the same day so that, in case one goes astray, you will have another giving you news of Giuliano, as we agreed to send by anyone going to you. I wrote to you yesterday that, as Giuliano was better, I did not think it necessary to make the change Maestro Mariotto suggested, but in the evening I wrote that the fever had returned as usual. This last letter was written at the seventh hour. Later he did not rest as quietly as on other nights, and he seemed more restless than he should be with the decrease of the fever. I want you to know every little change, so that you may understand better what Maestro Mariotto writes, and that you may decide, not according to my opinion, but according to what you yourself think best, judging from our news. Pulse, appetite, and natural functions are all good in Giuliano. The fever is almost the same as on the fourteenth day, and has decreased but little since. He is not as cheerful in the day time as I should like, because he is exhausted by the fever. The Maestro says this is the nature of the phlegm that remains in him. I want you to know this.

Do not get depressed, however, for Giuliano is strong ; he walks about the room, and, though pale, his complexion is good ; therefore I give you these details for your information, but not because Giuliano seems to me seriously ill, or because I do not think the improvement is going to last. We commend ourselves to you.

November 24, 1463.

Thy LUCREZIA at Pisa.

Giuliano has just woken up, and the Maestro says he has never found him as free of fever as now, and that convalescence always brings weariness. Please note." [9]

Medical science was still in a very rudimentary condition at this time, and diagnosis was usually extremely vague. An enormous variety of ailments were classed as " fever " and supposed to be due to some pernicious phlegm in the patient. The chief remedies were purging and keeping the patient cheerful.

In 1450 Antonio degli Strozzi had tried to persuade Contessina to influence Cosimo on behalf of his exiled kinsfolk, but without success. In 1464 Filippo himself sought to enlist the sympathies of Lucrezia, and sent her a Christmas present of fine linen, which pleased her greatly. On April 19, 1465, she wrote to him :—

" I have your letter in reply to mine thanking you for sending me the linen. This pleased me as much as your present, for I see that you trust me as I would wish. I spoke to Piero as you asked me to do. . . . He heard everything most willingly, and I think he will do it, for he speaks of you with so much affection and wants to do something to please you. . . ." [10]

Mona Alessandra's comment on the affair was somewhat sarcastic. She wrote to her son :—

" I see Mona Lucrezia di Piero has written you a nice letter about the linen. It would be well to repay you by a thing which would cost her no more than words, for she could recommend you to Piero, so that you might return home." [11]

Mona Alessandra was no friend of Lucrezia's, but the latter did speak to Piero on behalf of the Strozzi family, and their sentence of banishment was revoked in 1465, after which they were free to return home if they wished.

In June, 1466, Lucrezia's daughter Giovanna, generally called Nannina, was married to Bernardo, the son of Giovanni Rucellai. This was a political alliance arranged by Piero in order to strengthen his position, for the Rucellai had been among Cosimo's opponents in the early days of his supremacy. This marriage was the sign of a complete reconciliation between the two families, whose interests were henceforth identical.

Old Giovanni Rucellai was immensely proud of this alliance, and gives a long account of the wedding in his Reminiscences.

The dowry was not very large, for, including the value of the trousseau, it only amounted to 2500 florins, which

Biagi computes to be worth about 60,000 lire or £2400 in modern (pre-war) currency. The Rucellai were, however, more anxious to ally themselves with the Medici than to obtain a large sum of money, for they were wealthy enough themselves.

The trousseau was very wonderful, and will bear comparison with the outfits of Royal princesses. There were at least fourteen dresses, one of white velvet embroidered with pearls, silk and gold, with open sleeves lined with white fur ; one of zetani, a special kind of thick silk, trimmed with pearls and with ermine-lined sleeves ; one of white and gold brocaded damask with pearl-trimmed sleeves ; one of silk with crimson brocade sleeves, and ten more of various materials embroidered with gold and pearls. A chemise of Rheims linen was also included, for this material was considered a great luxury, but we hear of no other underwear.

But, since a burgher's wife in the same year had " eight new hem-stitched chemises," [12] it must have been merely omitted from the list. Head-gear was well represented, for the bride received a head-dress of crimson stuff worked with pearls, two caps trimmed with silver, pearls and diamonds, and a Milanese hat with a fringe. She had eight pairs of stockings and four pairs of gloves, and many pieces of stuff, embroidered pillow-cases, scarves and purses, an embroidered fan, needles and needle-cases, ivory combs, three mirrors, a jug and basin of silver enamel and endless other things. For her devotions there was a Mass Book decorated with minatures and silver clasps, and a wax figure of the Bambino Gesù dressed in damask embroidered with pearls. There is also mention of a richly adorned box, presumably the usual bridal *cassone* or chest in which the bride kept her possessions. These wedding-chests were usually either beautifully carved or painted by the most eminent artists, and at least one *cassone* decorated by Botticelli has come down to us, so that we may well suppose that Nannina's " richly adorned box," had been executed by one of the great artists patronised by her father.

The dowry of 2500 florins can hardly have included the bride's jewelry, for there was a necklace of diamonds, rubies and pearls which alone was worth 1200 florins. She also had a jewelled hairpin, a pearl necklace with a large diamond pendant, a snood embroidered with pearls, and a hair-net of coarse pearls. Her rings numbered twenty, six of which were presented by her husband, two when he came to fetch her, two at the wedding, and two on the first morning of wedded life. This last gift was a relic of the old Lombard custom of " Morgengabio," when the bride was purchased by a present given on the day after the wedding. Bernardo also gave his bride a hundred florins, as well as some other money, which she probably distributed in almsgiving.

The wedding celebrations began on Sunday, June 8, 1466, when the bride was escorted to her new home by four of the leading citizens, namely Manno Temperani, Carlo Pandolfini, Giovanozzo Pitti and Tommaso Soderini.

The Rucellai palace had been built for Giovanni by Bernardo Rossellino from the designs of Leo Battista Alberti, and was a real gem of early Renaissance architecture. It had only been completed a few years before, and on this occasion it was hung with brocades and garlands of flowers. Although the rooms were spacious they were insufficient for such a concourse of guests, wherefore a red awning had been erected on the little Piazza Rucellai. In the centre of this pavilion was a table adorned with the most beautiful silver ware in

Florence, for on such an occasion the Rucellai did not content themselves with their own lovely possessions, but also borrowed from all their friends. In the street next to the palace there was a temporary kitchen, where fifty cooks were kept busy throughout the three days that the festivities lasted.

The sound of music accompanied the bride and her four attendant cavaliers from the Via Larga, and a large concourse of people followed the procession, for such occasions were a festival for the whole city, not merely a private entertainment for the families concerned.

On the bride's arrival dinner was served, and this was followed by dancing until supper-time. Fifty Florentine ladies, together with fifty young men, allmost richly and sumptuously attired, had been especially invited to dance, but a great number of other guests were also present. About a hundred and seventy persons were served at the first table, and countless others at the lower ones, so that on one occasion about five hundred guests were entertained.

There were two banquets a day for three days, but Giovanni says the dishes were the customary ones, wonderfully cooked and prepared. The victuals mentioned do not sound unusual, and it is notable that poultry was very prominent, but that sweets, which were a very great luxury, were much more sparingly used.

On Sunday the first meal consisted of boiled capon and tongue, large joints of meat, and roast pullets with sugar and rose-water. In the evening jelly, roast meat and pullets with fritters were served. On Monday there was boiled turkey and sausages, and roast pullets, and the same in the evening, together with a cake called " tartara," made of bread, almonds and sugar. On Tuesday morning dinner consisted of meat with quails, and in the evening the same with the addition of jelly.

Besides all this food, at each meal twenty boxes of sugared pineseeds and other sweets were distributed among the guests.

The whole feast was reckoned to have cost more than 6000 florins (or 150,000 lire to-day). The purchases included seventy bushels of bread, two thousand eight hundred white rolls, four thousand wafers, fifty barrels of trebbiano wine, three thousand fowls, fifteen hundred eggs, four calves, and twenty bowls of gelatine, whilst twenty piles of wood were burnt in the kitchen. Besides this enormous quantity of food, there were probably many things brought in from the Rucellai estates, which are not included in the list of purchases.

The proceedings closed on Tuesday with the customary jousting, which began in front of the Palazzo Rucellai, and went past the Canto dei Tornaquinci to the Via Larga, where the festivities ended in front of the Medici palace.

Thereupon Nannina settled down to married life in the famous palace. She bore her husband five sons, Cosimo, Palla, Piero, Giovanni and Tommaso, and one daughter, Lucrezia, and we have one or two letters written by her to her mother in succeeding years. Bernardo was a clever man, but he had rather an uncertain temper, which occasionally put his wife in an awkward position. He was a writer of some repute in the vulgar tongue, which he was so anxious to cultivate as a literary medium that he refused to speak or write Latin under any circumstances whatever. On one occasion he was sent to Venice on an embassy and there made the acquaintance of Erasmus. The Dutch scholar knew no Italian, and always conversed in Latin, but this Bernardo refused to do, so that they were not able to have much intercourse. Erasmus says " I told him he might as well attempt to speak to a deaf person, as to talk to me in Italian, of which I knew no more than Chinese, but still I could not get a word from him." [13]

Shortly after these wonderful wedding festivities a plot was hatched to assassinate Piero on his return to Florence from Careggi, which was only frustrated by the presence of mind of the young Lorenzo. He was riding ahead of his father's litter, when he overheard some talk by the roadside which made him suspect that something was wrong. He managed to send a message to Piero to take another road whilst he himself went on to Florence to take the necessary precautions there. As a result a number of the leading citizens were banished, but the Medici power was more firmly established than before. The nominal head of the conspiracy was Luca Pitti, but Piero felt that, alone, he was too weak a man to be formidable, so he was not exiled, but allowed to remain in Florence. But he suffered an even more humiliating punishment. Whereas before he had been courted and fawned upon by all the citizens, he was now neglected and ignored, and his power and prestige utterly destroyed.

At the beginning of 1467 Lucrezia went to Rome to open negotiations for the marriage of her eldest son with a daughter of the house of Orsini. She left Florence in the middle of March, and announced her arrival in Rome in a letter to Piero dated March 28. On April 5 she wrote to say that she was only waiting for the weather to clear before she started for home, but a few days after she was taken ill, and wrote on April 13 :—

" On Saturday I wrote and told you the course of my illness, and then yesterday morning I took some medicine, which has done me so much good that it is a long time since I felt so well, or better purged. I am following the doctor's orders and letting myself be cherished, so as to get well, and all these people are

75

looking after me so well that, unless the trouble is within me, I shall return better than I went. When you receive this we shall have started, and every day seems to me a thousand years until we do so, but we must thank God for everything and have patience. Messer Giovanni Canigiani has visited me several times, and has been as kind to me as if I had been his daughter. I am greatly indebted to them, and they have begged me to stay until I am quite well again. All our friends among the Cardinals have sent and offered me all their possessions, and even the Holy Father sent some of his treacle more willingly than I can say. I cannot tell you everything, but if it pleases God I shall soon be able to tell you all our doings by word of mouth, and it will take more than a day. No more now, except that I commend myself to Mona Contessina, and salute the whole family. May God guard you.

In Rome, April 13, 1467.

To Piero di Cosimo de Medici in Florence.'' [14]

Lorenzo at this time was seventeen years old, and was the leader of a band of young men who met together for recreation, and also for religious observances. They wished to have special privileges from the Pope, so Filippo Martelli was commissioned to obtain the desired indulgences from Rome. He therefore wrote to Lorenzo giving an account of Lucrezia's health, and also reporting on the success of his mission :—

" A few days ago I had a letter from you, which pleased me greatly. I did not answer so as not to have to tell you of Madonna Lucrezia's illness, for I knew that our Giovanni was writing every day to the Magnificent Piero. Now that God has utterly restored her to health, I am writing to tell you that she is very well, and better than when she first came, and we went to-day with great joy to Santo Nofri in Trastevere, where we thought of you a hundred times. Her visit has been most valuable, for she has not only fulfilled her vow, but she has acquired high favour with all this Court, and especially with these gentlemen, in such a way that even if she had no more than her presence, her conversation and her appearance, it would show that she was greater than her reputation. I know that the Cardinals have talked about her, and have decided that no finer lady ever came to Rome. God leave you the desired comfort that you have in her and she in you and yours. I think they will leave in four or five days, and you will hear everything by word of mouth.

We have sent off an indulgence for your company on the lines suggested by Messer Gentile, who will bring the Bull. The right of choosing your confessor *in articulo mortis* is omitted. If you want this for yourself and all your companions, of whom I understand there are about 700, it will cost you 150 denari, and possibly more. Messer Gentile and I did not think we should go to this expense without consulting you, and awaiting your answer. It shall be done as you command. The other right, that of communicating in the company itself, will be granted to you by His Holiness, except at Easter, for this has been a difficulty with the enclosed Religious. On that day he requires them to go to the Parish Church, and he will not change for anything. If you want it for other days, let me know, and the Bull will be sent. The above indulgence we received for nothing.

I am surprised that Bartolommeo Buonconti has not answered the three letters I wrote him. As soon as I hear that the horse is all right, I will send for him, and we will keep him here as long as you wish. For this it would be well to send me a letter addressed to His Majesty the King, so that he may give me a licence to take him away.

I have no more to say except to beg you to commend me to the Magnificent Piero and to yourself, and may the Lord keep you in happiness.

Your servant FILIPPO MARTELLI in Rome.

To the Magnificent Gentleman Lorenzo de Medici in Florence." [15]

Lorenzo was always passionately fond of horses, and on several occasions he exchanged animals with the King of Naples, whose stud was famous.

Lucrezia duly set out on her journey, but at Fuligno she was taken ill with inflammation of the lungs, and had to remain there a considerable time. Probably she had been weakened by her previous illness, and caught cold in the bad weather she encountered.

On April 30, Gentile Becchi reported to Lorenzo :—

" I expect you have seen all the reports of Madonna Lucrezia's illness which have been sent to Piero, but you will be glad of more news, for the piety of a good son hangs on the health of such a mother. If you had seen her under these circumstances and the pain of the present illness, you would have thought she was at the end of her resources. We wrote to Piero at the 13th hour of yesterday, Wednesday, the 29th of this month, that she had a double laxative, followed by brandy, in order to destroy the mucus, and this had an admirable effect, and the doctors think she is out of danger and cured. She has been improving ever since, resting all day and not crying out as she did, and she passed the night with much less discomfort than previous nights, though it is true that after resting all day she did not

78

sleep all the time. They have now repeated the dose, which did excellent work. She has the three best doctors in these parts, and she lacks nothing, so you can be at rest. I wrote to you from Rome that if you wished me to return before the others you should let me know, for although I am useful here, I would as soon serve in my usual place. Giovanni is expected from Rome to-day, and Madonna Lucrezia will only wait to make sure of herself for a few days. If you want to reply here what you did not reply to Rome, I will come at once, for there are so many people that I can leave. To tell you the truth I am anxious to see you again. I commend myself to you.

April 30, 1467 at the 10th hour.

Thy GENTILE in Fuligno.

To the Magnificent Laurentio Petri Cosme de Medicis, Florence.[16]

By May 4, Lucrezia was well on the way to recovery, although she had not yet left Fuligno. But she wrote to her husband :—

" I do not know if it is these doctors, or your letter received this evening, but I feel so well to-day that I hope to start on my way in three days if the improvement continues. Maestro Girolamo will tell you in greater detail how I am, but I think you will approve. I am sorry for all the trouble I have given you on this journey. But, believe me, I should have been ill wherever I was, for I have brought up so much phlegm and nastiness that must have been there a long time.

Commend me to Mona Contessina, and tell her that as soon as these doctors allow it, I will return to her, so that she can take greater care of me. But here, thanks be to God, I lack nothing, and I do not know if I should have had so much care at home, certainly not in Rome. . . . If you want me to send back Messer Gentile for Giuliano, let me know if it is necessary before we leave. I will take care of myself as you say, so as to get well. Meanwhile and always I commend myself to you, and pray you to have patience with me." [17]

She was not able to travel quite as soon as she expected, but had to wait until the second week in May. Even then she had to travel very slowly, and on May 15 her brother, Niccolo Tornabuoni, wrote to Piero :—

" We are at Castiglione Aretino, and as it is about the eighteenth hour we are just leaving for Arezzo, which we shall reach without fail to-night. Mona Lucrezia has been much better for the last two days . . . and she looks as if she was getting on well. She rests better when asleep, and has less pain than usual and less fever. We are travelling very slowly in order that she may have as little discomfort as possible." [18]

Even after her return to Florence Lucrezia did not regain her strength for a long time, for still in July Piero speaks of her as an invalid, and in September she went to Bagno a Morba, accompanied by Lorenzo, who had eczema. Lucrezia herself was said by the doctors to be suffering from depression and indigestion.

There was a rumour that some of the Florentine exiles were going to attack Bagno a Morba with the intention of seizing both mother and son and holding them as hostages. Lucrezia therefore sent Lorenzo back to Florence and Piero thought it wiser to keep him there. He was very disappointed and wrote to his mother on September 19 :—

" I had expected to be with you several days ago, but as it is now cooler Maestro Mariotto did not think it would be good for my eczema to go there, so I have not come. Piero has promised . . . that he will go and see you, either with Messer Benedetto or soon after. Take care that we find you better. . . . We are all well at present, and Piero is very well and lacks nothing except more frequent news of you, for, owing to carelessness on the part of either the scribe or the messenger, news of you has so far been very scarce. So . . . please let us hear from you more often, and take care of yourself, so that you may get the full benefit of your stay. . . .

Please send me back my purple tunic, as I have nothing to wear. The other things do not matter at present." [19]

A large number of letters remain from this visit. Not only had Lucrezia been seriously ill, but the political situation was very troubled. Piero was not the strong man Cosimo had been, and although he had successfully weathered the storm of the previous year, matters were still very unsettled, and the exiles were making great efforts to return to Florence.

On September 30 Lucrezia's brother, Leonardo, wrote to her :—

" At this moment . . . I have your letter of the 28th, and I cannot tell you how consoled and over-joyed we all are to hear that the improvement continues. . . . From Piero, who has letters from the doctors every day, we have had all the news. . . .

Bartolommea, as you know, is about to be brought to bed, and it might happen at any time now. I should be glad to know what name you think I should give the child, whether boy or girl. She has written to tell me to discuss it with you, and I will do as you say. May God bring the matter to a good conclusion, with safety to them both." [20]

Lucrezia does not seem to have been a very good patient, for her correspondents are always begging her to obey the doctors' orders. She was a woman of lively intellect who probably found the life at the Baths very dull, and tried to relieve the monotony of the treatment by continuing her interest in affairs. But the doctors wanted her to rest and to concentrate on her cure, and two of the physicians attending her at Bagno a Morba wrote to Piero soon after her arrival :—

"We have received your letter in reply to our first one. Now we must inform you that we arrived here safely at the hour of lunch. Last night Madonna Lucrezia had a little more fever than the night before. She said she thought it was due to drinking rather more than usual, because she was so thirsty from an argument. I gave her a soft drink, and she supped well, but it is necessary to curb her, for her stomach cannot digest all that her appetite desires. This morning the fever had lessened, and she began her baths in the name of God, and stayed in the bath for a third of an hour without feeling any discomfort. We will take great care and do all we can. It would be well to keep on exhorting her to obedience in your letters, but in such a way that she will not think it was our suggestion, for that would displease her. On our part we will omit nothing that can be done for her cure. . . .

Your servants AUGUSTINUS et CANTES phisici." [21]

After receiving this Piero wrote to his wife on October 1 :—

"Have faith and obey the doctors, and do not budge one jot from their orders, and bear and suffer everything, if not for yourself and for us, for the love of God who is helping you. Do not do anything besides what you are there for. Do not worry about us, for we are well and lack nothing. . . . " [22]

He went on to tell her that prayers were being offered up for her recovery in all the churches in Florence, not only by her family and friends, but also " by those who do not know you, and whom you have never known."

Pieraccini considers, judging from the following letter, that Lucrezia suffered from rheumatic gout. Presumably Benedictus was another doctor sent by Piero to attend Lucrezia, as appears from Lorenzo's letter. Benedictus wrote on October 3, to Piero :—

" JESUS.

Magnificent and honoured sir, salutation. I have just received a letter from you which shows your most worthy and pious nature towards your parents. Although the doctors' letters to your Magnificent father were more cheerful and consoling, nevertheless, I promised you when I left that I would write punctually and tell him every variation as if he was present to know it like the doctors themselves. So I will write the symptoms and progress as they occur from day to day.

The doctors' letters during the first few days will have told you how much benefit and relief she has experienced from the waters of the baths for all three kinds of pains from which she suffered. The first were in the breast, on the left-hand side, and sometimes as far as the shoulder. When these had been relieved came the usual ones in the stomach and the spleen on the left side of the body. These usually last for several days, but this time, after the remedies had been applied, they only lasted for an hour and a half. Then followed the third pains, in the right thigh, in the form of a very painful sciatica, but by the grace of God, they lessened so much yesterday morning that she rested very well last night, without any pain. Now since these attacks have been conquered so rapidly, we have a manifest sign that nature is stronger than the cause of the pains. We are not omitting to do anything which might be fitting for a great queen.

Commend me to the Magnificent lady Contessina and to the Magnificent Piero and all your family.

From the Baths in the County of Volterra, October 3, 1467, at the 16th hour.

BENEDICTUS REGUARDATI, knight and physician.

To my Most Honourable and Magnificent Gentleman Laurentium de Medicis." [23]

Lorenzo was exceedingly disappointed at not being allowed to join his mother, and wrote to her again on October 4 :—

" I am very sorry that since I wrote to you the pains have returned, but I am glad to hear from your letters that they did not last long, so that perhaps this time they will have left you altogether. . . . I have remained here for the reason I gave you, and I may have to stay so long that I shall not be able to return to see you there, as I would like to do. . . . We are all well, especially Piero, and we are longing to see you, and we hope to see you soon in good health. . . ." [24]

Lucrezia's sojourn cost more than had been expected, and she had to write to Piero for more money, whereupon he replied :—

" I wrote to you at length last night by Giovanni da Monte Castelli. The bearer of this will be Antonio di Pace, and it is only to say that I am sending you forty florins, half in gold and half in small money. Note this, and ask for anything else you require, and pray to God that He may cure you." [25]

Lucrezia was always anxious to help her various protégées, and tried to obtain posts and preferment for them, and a great many of her letters deal with such matters. Even when she had been so ill, she interested herself in a certain Ser Paolo da Monte Castelli, and wrote to ask Lorenzo to use his influence to have the wardenship of a little hospital conferred on him. This preferment was in the gift of the Consuls of the Arte degli Speziali (the Druggists' Guild), and Lucrezia thought that a certain Filippo would be able to arrange matters for her. She said :—

" You know what the men of Monte Castelli have done for me, and we are duly grateful to them. . . . At Pogibonati it appears there is a certain little hospital which is in the gift of the Consuls of the Arte degli Speziali. The bearer of this is Ser Pavolo di Monte Castello, the chaplain of Pogibonati, and an old friend of the family, who would like to have that hospital. So please speak to Filippo, and tell him I am writing to him also, and do everything in the proper quarters, so that Ser Pavolo may get the hospital, which would give me great pleasure. I am getting better all the time, as you will have heard from Maestro Augustino and Maestro Cante. . . ." [26]

Lucrezia made a long stay at the Baths on this occasion, but on November 4 Benedictus was able to write to Piero :—

" The Magnificent Mona Lucrezia continues to improve, and is willing to do the veriest tittle of what is recommended for her health. She does whatever is necessary, and prays to God for good weather, so that all may go as you wish. . . ." [27]

She remained another ten days, but at last, on November 13, Piero wrote :—

" I shall not write at length, especially as you are just returning, which I desire greatly. . . ." [28]

Among Lucrezia's correspondents at the Baths was a certain Suor Bartolommea, who described herself as " the unworthy Prioress of Santo Domenico." She wrote from Pisa and, after asking after Lucrezia's health, begged her to ask Piero for help, since the soldiers were taking possession of the houses of the convent's tenants. She concludes " Only Piero the father, and you can help."

Lucrezia's health had benefited so much from her stay at Bagno a Morba that she went there again in 1468. There does not seem to have been any very definite season for visiting the Baths, for we find Lucrezia and the rest of the family going there at all times of the year, except perhaps the depth of winter.

All Lucrezia's many brothers were very devoted to her, but their number is apt to be somewhat confusing. Niccolo very often acted as her escort when she travelled, and in 1468 he accompanied her to Bagno a Morba. They arrived on May 22, and Niccolo at once wrote to Piero :—

" I wrote to you in Lucrezia's name from Poggibonsi, and told you how by the grace of God she had arrived safely and was well, and hoped to arrive here at the Baths the next day. But this was not the case, for we had gone too far on the previous day, and either because of the strange bed, or because of the things that were in it, she did not sleep at all the night at Poggibonsi, so we left late. We therefore went to see some relations of Messer Bartolommeo and Giuliano and others at Colle, with Antonio da Pela. We did this in order not to do worse. Giuliano will tell you everything by word of mouth. This was on Saturday. On Sunday we were on the road soon after dawn, and arrived at Colanaca, where we heard Mass, and then we went on and lunched beneath Radighondoli. After a short rest we went on, we on horseback, and Lucrezia in the litter, and reached Bagno safely at the hour of vespers, all well content, and without any harm to Lucrezia, who is well.

On Monday she rested, and has begun the clysters as ordered by Messer B. This morning, in the name of God, we shall begin the bath on the plain, and then we shall proceed gradually according to the orders and instructions of Messer B. without omitting anything. Lucrezia is very well and very cheerful." [29]

She did not cease to attend to business nor relax her efforts on behalf of her friends and servants when she was at the Baths. On May 31 she wrote to Lorenzo asking him to get the brother of one of her servants, a certain Bartolommeo di San Miniato, appointed to the parish of Brozi, which was vacant owing to the death of the priest in the previous winter. She does not say in whose hands the appointment lay, but only " I beg and pray you that you will do your best with whoever it may concern." [30]

She remained at Bagno a Morba about six weeks, and again found the waters very beneficial, for already, on June 14, there are encouraging reports of her progress.

On July 1, shortly before her return to Florence, she wrote to Piero :—

" I have been getting better and better and am now well. Now the time of return approaches, but as I lost three days by my journey to Volterra, it seems best to me, an it please you, to postpone my return. I had thought of leaving on the 7th, but now I think of leaving on the 10th or 11th without fail. I have quite given up the idea of returning by Volterra, owing to the plague which has been doing damage there for the last four days, so I shall come by Colle. This we have decided among ourselves, and if I hear nothing more from you before the time of our departure approaches I will send the boy to tell you about the horses and mules." [31]

Owing to Piero's many infirmities he was obliged to entrust a great deal of public business to Lorenzo while he was yet a mere boy. But he feared that this might make him think himself too great a man, and that by his arrogance he would undermine the family prestige in Florence. He therefore looked to his wife to moderate these ideas. In 1469, shortly after his marriage, Lorenzo went to Milan to stand proxy for Piero as godfather to the Duke's infant son. He made his arrangements on a magnificent scale, which displeased his father, who wrote from Careggi to Lucrezia who had gone to Florence :—

" You know that I did not want to allow Lorenzo to go, for various reasons, but especially so as not to seem to attach importance to this mission. Since we decided upon it yesterday I have not heard what has happened. But I understand that the thing has become known, which displeases me. Therefore I insist on their being here to-night and starting to-morrow morning without fail. If they do not do this, I will arrange something else.

88

Tell this to Spanio, and tell Lorenzo that he is not to go beyond his orders in any way, and not to make such a fuss. He is not an ambassador, and I will not have the gosling teach the gander to drink. Make haste and return here this evening for certain." [32]

Piero had been almost a lifelong invalid, suffering terribly from rheumatic gout, and he died at Careggi on December 2, 1469, and was buried in San Lorenzo. His position in the city passed to his nineteen-year-old son Lorenzo, who was greatly helped by his mother in the difficult task of ruling Florence.

In 1471 Galeazzo Sforza, now Duke of Milan, paid another visit to Florence, accompanied by his wife, Bona of Savoy, and his two daughters. They came with an immense retinue, all sumptuously equipped, and were entertained on a most lavish scale. They shocked the good citizens of Florence by eating flesh in Lent, and were the unwitting cause of a great disaster, when the church of S. Spirito was burnt down. A mystery play of the Descent of the Holy Ghost was being given when the church caught fire and was almost entirely destroyed.

Although Galeazzo was the richest prince in Italy, he confessed that his magnificence and ostentation were as naught besides the wonderful art treasures collected by the Medici.

The diarist Luca Landucci, who was living and writing in Florence at this time, gives no account of the Milanese visit, but he tells us that on May 26, 1471, he bought some of the first cargo of sugar that ever came to Florence from Madeira. His diary is full of little items of this kind, but utterly ignores important events.

In 1472 Lucrezia was asked to intervene in an un-

usual case. A young German (or more probably Dutch-
man), named Piero, had set up a workshop in Poggibonsi
with seven looms. He was aged thirty-six and was
described as " a perfect master of linen-weaving . . .
not only an upright man, but holy in his life and
conversation, as he shows in his life and in his speech
to all who know him." [33] This virtuous man was
arrested and condemned to death for bigamy, and
Lucrezia was asked to intervene to save his life. His
story was sufficiently romantic. Sixteen years before,
when he was living at Antwerp, he had married a
wife, but before a year had passed " one morning in
anger, she ran away on to a ship and went to Libya."
Piero sought her for some time, but was unable to
find her, so he came to Italy, where he worked in
Florence, San Casciano and Poggibonsi. His wife
meanwhile took two husbands in succession, both of
whom died, and then Piero's mother heard of the
woman's death and wrote and told her son. Therefore, in 1464, he had married a girl of Poggibonsi,
who bore him two beautiful boys, and a little girl,
now aged six months. This wife had died two months
previously.

In December, 1470, the first wife arrived in Poggibonsi. She was not dead, but said she was on her
way to Rome with a company of German pilgrims.
She made her quondam husband give her a document
in the presence of Germans, in which he acknow-
ledged her as his wife, and promised to go back
to her in the following September. Having got her
evidence the jealous woman went at once and denounced the man to the ecclesiastical authorities as
a bigamist, so that he was now in danger of death.
The whole community was much perturbed, for not
only was the man popular with everybody, but it
was felt that he had been grossly misled and injured

by the woman. Not only had she left him, and taken two husbands herself, and let him believe that she was dead, but she had also been a prostitute, so that the feeling was entirely on the side of the man, who was felt to be the injured party. But legally he was guilty, though it was thought that a strong letter from Lucrezia would probably save his life.

We do not know how the matter ended, but we must hope that the poor man was reprieved.

Lucrezia's correspondent on this occasion was a certain Ser Francesco d' Antonio, a notary of Bibbiena, who was extensively employed by her both on public and private business. He must have been quite a good man of affairs, but he was always very anxious to get Lucrezia to use her influence so that he might be appointed to some small post in the government service. However, it is quite probable that Lucrezia did not pay him a fixed fee for his services, but rewarded him by obtaining these positions for him. Under the Florentine constitution offices were only held for very short periods, so Ser Francesco had always to be looking for another post.

In June, 1472, he wrote to his patroness to thank her for paying twenty-five florins for the dowry of a poor girl from Bibbiena, and also thanking her for " arranging matters with Pierantonio Cennini, the Captain in the mountains." [34]

In August there is another letter from the same man, which seems to show that accountancy was somewhat complicated in those days. He begins, as usual, with a long paragraph invoking heavenly blessings on Lucrezia, and then goes on :—

> " I left with Madonna Bice the record, which I sent you, of those thirteen florins due to me, and Arigo was to collect them and send them, as I told

you at Careggi. When you have received them, please ask Arigo how much he wants for the work he did for you. . . ." [35]

In 1472 Catherine, the exiled Queen of Bosnia, appealed to Lucrezia for help. She was the widow of the last King of Bosnia, who had been defeated by the Turks and had been living in Rome since 1466 as a pensioner on the Pope's bounty. She died in 1478 and was buried in Araceli. The Medici were the Papal bankers, but their Roman branch had been paying the Royal pension in cloth instead of in cash, and the poor lady was in money difficulties. She wrote to Lucrezia in Latin :—

" Please ask your sons to order their Bank to pay us the pension assigned to us by the Holy Church in money and not in cloth, for neither I nor those who are with me, are accustomed to this kind of trade." [36]

A certain Papinus de Macthei de Sartis de Artiminio became, in later years, Lucrezia's chief correspondent in Rome, but in 1473, when we first hear of him, he was a notary in the Val d' Elsa, and sent her some figs from Certaldo :—

" Although this year my figs are not so good nor so fine flavoured as they have been in other years, nevertheless, I am sending you some by my brother Antonio, the bearer of this. I beg you to blame the figs rather than me. . . ." [37]

Lucrezia was always anxious to obtain ecclesiastical preferment for her friends and dependents, and in August, 1473, she had expected to present a small living to one of her household, when she heard that Lorenzo had promised it to someone else. She therefore asked him to resign it in favour of her candidate.[38]

In all accounts of Lucrezia her charity is much dwelt upon, especially the fact that she dowered poor girls and rescued prisoners. These latter suffered incredible hardships, and it was always regarded as a meritorious act to obtain their release. In August, 1473, the leading citizens of Galatea applied to her for help for one of their countrymen, who was accused of false coining. In their own words :—

"Several months ago, one Ser Michele, a priest, was taken by the lords of the Mint for coining money and after torturing him they put him in the Stinche.* Thus you will understand that he has already atoned for his sins and is purged of them. . . ."[39]

They go on to say that some of his family who reside in Galatea are anxious to obtain his release, and beg Lucrezia to use her influence to this end.

Another of Lucrezia's correspondents was a priest, Christofano d' Antonio di Maso, who may have been the domestic chaplain of the Tornabuoni family, and was employed by them and by Lucrezia on confidential business. On September 25, 1473, when Lucrezia was visiting Pisa, she received a letter from him, giving her news of the whole family :—

"First, Mona Contessina is very well, and Giuliano the same. I have been to see Mona Bianca † many times. She is well, and her children are coming to spend three days with Mona Contessina to her great joy. Lucrezia ‡ has a little eczema, but otherwise she is well, and is well cared for by Mona Nanna, whom she obeys like the

---

* The Florentine prison.
† Lucrezia's daughter, married to Guglielmo de' Pazzi.
‡ Lorenzo's eldest child, born 1470.

clever little thing she is. Piero's * complexion is good, and he is joyful and happy, by the grace of God, and often comes to the door leading to Terzola and calls everybody, saying, ' Granny, Father, Mother,' in a way that would make you laugh if you saw it. Maddalena † is well also, and every day when I come back from Casa Tornabuoni I go and stay with her a little. Then I say to the wet-nurse, ' Go for a little walk,' for this pleases her, and she gets some exercise and keeps well, so that her milk comes better. She is very pleased and says, ' I will pray to God for you.' In truth she is most diligent. Cosimino, the son of Mona Nannina ‡ is well, but he does not want to read, and says ' I did not come into the country to read,' and Mona Contessina is not pleased. After All Saints it will be better. . . . I know you have many petitioners, but when something of small value comes to you, please remember me. . . . All your relations are well. Mona Bartolommea § and Mona Francesca ‖ go often to see Mona Contessina and the children. . . ." [40]

After her subjugation by Florence, Pisa's prosperity decayed, and her University, which had flourished in the Middle Ages, sank into obscurity. Lorenzo was anxious to conciliate the Pisans, and spent many months at his house in the city. He also restored the University and incorporated it with that of Florence. Both were governed by the same statutes, but Pisa was intended to concentrate on the study of law, theology and medicine, and Florence on philosophy and philology.

* Lorenzo's second child, born 1471.
† Lorenzo's third child, born 1473.
‡ Lucrezia's daughter, wife of B. Rucellai.
§ Wife of Leonardo Tornabuoni.
‖ Wife of Giovanni Tornabuoni.

The University was reopened in the autumn of 1473 in the presence of Lorenzo, who had spent part of the previous summer in the neighbourhood, together with Lucrezia and Clarice, and his sister Nannina. The rest of the family returned to Florence in October, but Lorenzo remained for the formal opening at the beginning of November. His mother therefore wrote to him on October 29 :—

> " We were much looking forward to your spending All Saints' Day with us. Now we hear you want to reopen the University before leaving, so, as we cannot celebrate the festival together, we are sending you your share of good things by Maso del Ciave, and we hope you will enjoy them with your friends for our sakes. We are sending you geese, chestnuts, and macaroni stuffed with meat.
> There is no other news. We hope for your return." [41]

In that same year we get one of the few letters we have addressed by Luigi Pulci to his patroness. He asked her to help a friend of his, one Andrea Ughi, who was unable to pay his debts and had been mulcted of his vineyard by his chief creditor, Urbano Cattani, who refused to wait for his money. This letter is of no importance except that it gives us the approximate date of Contessina's death. It was written on October 26, 1473, and begins :—

> " On my return I did not find our Madonna Contessina, which grieved me sorely. I would like at least to have seen her. . . ." [42]

Luigi Pulci is remembered for his long burlesque poem of " Morgante Maggiore," but in his own time he was more notable as one of Lorenzo's men of affairs. His poem grew up piece-meal, and was not a definite piece of composition. Pulci was a member of the intimate family circle of the Medici, and, in order to enliven their repasts, he was wont to improvise long and often absurd poems. Many of these were based on the Carolingian legend which, in its prolixity and endless ramifications, was known to every Tuscan. Lucrezia saw that there was something better than the average storyteller's improvisations in Pulci's verses, and she persuaded him to write them down and polish them into a literary form, and the result was the *Morgante Maggiore* as we know it. It is based on the story of Orlando and Rinaldo, but Pulci dwells more on the absurdities of the giant Morgante and the lesser giant Margutte, who accompanies him, than on the deeds of the paladins. He also invented a new character, Astarotte, the devil of dogma, who introduces all sorts of modern arguments into the old tale.

Pulci was probably himself a sceptic, though he recanted on at least one occasion. Nannina Rucellai strove very hard to reform him, but he was too much of a jester to remain devout for long.

At the beginning of 1474 Giuliano went to Pisa to study. He took part in various festivities, and in a letter to his mother, written on May 16, we get news of these, but none of his studies :—

" . . . We have arrived safely and are all well. Here we are among a thousand grandeurs, as you shall hear at greater length by word of mouth on our return. Yesterday we lunched with our Rector, which was magnificent, and he wore his hood. To-day we dance, and to-morrow we joust, which, as is the custom of this country, should be very fine. . . ." [43]

In May, 1474, Ser Francesco d' Antonio again tried to obtain a government post with Lucrezia's help.

Such appointments were nominally drawn by lot, but actually Lorenzo's nominee stood an excellent chance of being chosen. Ser Francesco was at S. Marcello at the time, but hoped for the governorship of Vico Pisano, and wrote to Lucrezia on May 25 :—

" Some days ago I wrote to ask you to beg the Magnificent Lorenzo to appoint me as the new Vicar of Vico Pisano, whose name is to be drawn on the 27th of this month. Since I cannot come myself to the drawing, I am sending Ser Giovanni di Ser Goro da Poppi, who will act for me when necessary. Wherefore I beg of you as much as possible to take my part as you have always done. This place is much sought after by our equals, and it is necessary to be prompt and careful. If my name is drawn I will show my gratitude to you and to Lorenzo in any way you may wish. I know it is presumptuous to give you as much trouble as I do, but I have faith in the great love I bear you, which makes me apply to you in all my needs, so I hope you will pardon me.

I had ordered some trout to be caught, but the weather was not suitable. However, I send you these, which are but few. Another time I will send more, so pray pardon me. I wrote and asked you to tell me if you desired anything that this mountain country produces. You have not answered, so I suppose you want nothing. I can have no greater grace from God than that you should command me. No more. I commend myself to you always, and may the Lord keep you happy. I am always at your service.

In San Marcello, May 25, 1474.

FRANCISCHUS SER ANTONII notaris.

To the Magnificent Lady Lucrezia de Medici, who is most singularly great. Florence.[44]

Lucrezia was regarded as wielding great influence over various appointments, for we have any number of letters asking her for help in that way. In November, 1474, she was asked to recommend an applicant for the new Chancellorship of Pisa. A certain Ser Niccolo da Volterra, who was then at Pisa, wrote :—

" I only write this because I cannot come in person. The reason is that my wife is dying, and I cannot leave her as I have no one to look after her.

Here it has been decided by the Priors and Council of Pisa that Lorenzo shall be authorised to appoint a Chancellor of the Priors, who is not a native of Pisa or the surrounding territory. Therefore, since, as you know, I am suitable for such a post, I beg you to do me the favour to recommend me . . . I also recommend to you the daughters that I have." [45]

Ser Francesco d' Antonio apparently did not obtain the Vicariate of Vico Pisano that he asked for, as in May, 1475, we find him at his native Bibbiena, anxious to obtain another appointment. Lucrezia had recently acquired some property in the neighbourhood, and had asked him to report upon it, whereupon he wrote :—

" This is to tell you about the formation of the river where it could be made into a lake. I got my information from a trustworthy person who goes there every year to fish. He says that the river passes through your land for six miles, and that there it is all flat and suitable for riding. It is a beautiful river, full of trout and crabs, and a lake could well be made. It is very flat, and the wall would be twenty-five *braccia*, making the lake a third of a mile each way, and it would be very beautiful. It is three miles from the hermitage of the Camaldolesi, and the place is called Campo Romano, because the Roman army once camped there. The thing could be done at small cost. . . . Felindazzo tells me that Niccolo has presented it to you. I am very glad, and the Vicar of Poppi has forbidden fishing there.

As I told you, this summer I must stay at home, and I should be very pleased if you would give me something to do. If I were appointed Captain of Bagnio I could look after this matter for you very conveniently, for I have men here . . .

Checha gave a piece of your cloth to the apothecary to see, and as she had no one to bring it back to her, he sold it without saying anything. You can find out the length from Ugo, and she will make him pay well for it, which he says he is willing to do.

Please do not forget your promise to come. We are now full of flowers, and there are the most beautiful little kids you ever saw at five soldi each. Frate Zacheo is expecting you. . . ." [46]

A fortnight later Ser Francesco wrote again. He was very worried because he had had no reply to his last communication, and the time for the appointment of the Captain of Bagnio was drawing near. In the event of not obtaining this, he begged Lucrezia to obtain for him the Vicariate of Certaldo. He was a persistent man. [47]

In 1475 Lucrezia's daughter, Bianca de' Pazzi, wrote and asked her to buy some land on her behalf, without mentioning her name. The vendors were the mother and the widow of a certain Giovenco, a member of a collateral branch of the Medici, and Bianca did not wish to appear in the transaction personally, possibly because her husband's family had not been on good terms with Giovenco. [48]

Ginevra degli Alessandri, Lucrezia's sister-in-law, was also interested in the matter, and wrote to Lucrezia :—

" I am writing to you because I hear that Francesca, the widow of Giovenco, wants to sell the farm of Magugnago, and that your Madonna Lucrezia is going to buy it. If you do not want it, please arrange that the rents may provide doweries for poor girls, or be otherwise used for charitable purposes, as you may think best. . . ." [49]

The whole transaction is very obscure, and it is very tantalizing to find, as we are always doing, phrases like " I desire it for many reasons, which I will tell you when I see you," or " the bearer will tell you more." Through the mists of ages we get glimpses of things, but it is seldom we have enough documents to piece together the whole affair.

In 1476 Lucrezia was asked to obtain the pardon of an exile. Her petitioner was a certain Galasso di Savoia, whom Levantini-Pieroni describes as the Duke of Savoy. He wrote :—

" Martino da Cataccione, my great friend . . . is banished from Florence owing to a difference he had with his brother. . . . I beg you to do him this favour, so that he may be with his wife and children, instead of going to the bad by wandering about the world." [50]

In the same year Lorenzo's little son Piero wrote to his grandmother from Trebbio. He was five years old and a thoroughly spoilt child, and he dictated the following letter :—

" Please send me some figs, for I like them. I I mean those red ones, and some peaches with stones, and other things you know I like, sweets and cakes and other little things, as you think best. **We** are at Trebbio with Madonna Ginevra, who spoils us. . . ." [51]

There is no record of Lucrezia's visits to the Baths between 1468 and 1477, so possibly she enjoyed such good health during those years that the treatment was not necessary.

In 1477 she decided to buy the Baths at Bagno a Morba and improve and equip them in the most up-to-date manner. The accommodation was of the most primitive description " with bugs as big as capers," but she built a house for herself and her family, and an inn for visitors, and she rebuilt the Baths entirely.

Bagno a Morba lies ten miles south of Volterra, but passed into the hands of Florence in 1388, when Doctor Ugholino da Montecatini accompanied Coluccio Salutati, then Chancellor of the Republic, in order to report on the value of these medicinal springs. His verdict was highly favourable, and the township, which was largely ruinous, was rebuilt and walled in, and became known as a place for the cure of gout and rheumatism. But Lucrezia's account of the rooms there, before she acquired the property, is not attractive. She wrote to Lorenzo :—

" We have arrived safely at the Baths. . . . We are keeping the ambling cob and the sorrel, for they are most suited to the place. Therefore have patience if we did not send back the cob as you said, for none of the others stood the journey so well. It seemed to be best to keep enough so that, if anything happened, we should not have to go on foot, to which the others agreed. If, however, you really need it, let me know and send me a better one, and I will let you have it. Here they will not lack care. . . . In another letter I will tell you at greater length about the honours paid us, and the ridiculous things that have happened to us, and are still happening. The bearer of this has his foot in the stirrup. At first sight these are the rooms of an alchemist with bugs as big as capers, according to Lionardo and Gino, who were the first to hunt them. . . ." [52]

This letter was dated May 16th and is endorsed to the effect that Lorenzo received it on the 17th, so the messenger lost no time.

Lorenzo was at Pisa, where he had gone to meet the Duchess of Ferrara, who was on her way to Naples. Lucrezia sent him some wine and asked for some things in return. She found that, though ordinary provisions were available, luxuries were difficult to obtain. She wrote on May 23 :—

" I am sending you sixteen flasks of remarkably good Greek wine, eight flasks of Poggibonsi marked in ink, and eight flasks from Colle. To us they all seem good. You had better choose. I also send you four plain puddings. I thought it well to do this, as on the arrival of the lady you might need them, and although I am sure you will have provided sufficently, since I had this, and it seemed good to me, I thought you would like me to send it to you. The carrier has to return here, so do not send him back empty. Oranges, biscuits, and fish would be greeted with standards flying. No more. I am well, and hoping much from the Baths, by the grace of God, who I pray will preserve you. In haste on May 23, 1477.

LUCREZIA DE MEDICI at Bagno a Morba.

To the Magnificent Gentlemen Lorenzo de Medici in Pisa." [53]

(Note on the M.S. " received on May 27,").

Villa of Careggi

[*face p. 102*

A few days later she received a letter written by her favourite grandchild, the seven-year-old Lucrezia, who wrote from Careggi :—

" My Magnificent Grandmother. Let me know how you are and when you began your baths. It seems to me a thousand years until you return, and every day I say a Paternoster and an Ave Maria, so that you may return well and happy. Please send me that basket of things you promised me. All we children are here at Careggi, with Mona Clarice, and Mona Bartolommea is here with all her family. Tell Lionardo that they are all well, and commend me to him. We very often go to your fountain, and there we all talk of you. Lorenzo has gone to Pisa. May God be with him, so that he may soon return to us here. Please enjoy yourself for love of me, so that you may return joyful and happy, which seems a thousand years hence. If I can do anything for you, command me. No more. Christ guard you from all ill.

Written on May 24, 1477.

Your LUCHRETIA DI LORENZO DE MEDICI at Chareggi." [54]

This letter is not the unaided production of a seven-year-old child, but shows the hand of the teacher very plainly, though the ideas may have been the little girl's own.

Poliziano was with the family at Careggi, and on May 31 he reported to Lucrezia :—

" Your Piero and Lucrezia and all the other children are well. . . . I have not been able to write because I am at Careggi and have had some difficulty about messengers. Madonna Clarice and Bianca and Nannina and all our party are well. . . ." [55]

Lorenzo was fond of interfering in the matrimonial arrangements of even quite obscure citizens of Florence, and as its head he arranged all the family marriages, often without consulting the parents of the parties concerned. He wanted to strengthen his position by suitable alliances, and saw nothing undesirable in the betrothal of mere children. In June, 1477, he arranged a marriage between his nephew, Cosimo Rucellai, aged eight, and Argentina, the daughter of the Marchese Malaspina, aged five, which gave great satisfaction to everybody. Bernardo Rucellai wrote to his mother-in-law :—

" . . . I write to inform you that Lorenzo has given a daughter of the Marchese Gabrielle Malaspina in marriage to my Cosimo, or I should rather say his Cosimo. . . . We, as you may imagine, could not be better pleased. . . . I am glad to tell you of it, since you are Nannina's mother, and will doubtless be very glad. Do not be surprised because you have heard nothing before, but, as you will hear on your return, the matter was concluded before any of our relatives, or those of the Marchese, could hear about it. . . ." [56]

Lucrezia was much pleased with the news, and immediately wrote to Lorenzo :—

" I am delighted to hear of the marriage arranged between Cosimino Rucellai and the daughter of the Marchese Gabrielle. Quite an unexpected piece of news. . . . We are celebrating it with great rejoicings, and so are all the people of the Bagni . . ." [57]

Lucrezia had nearly finished her course of treatment, and was thinking about her return journey, for she continued :—

" By the grace of God I am well, and have nearly finished my baths. I have decided, if it pleases God, to leave here on the 21st, and to stay the night with Madonna Tita, the widow of Messer Antonio Cortesi, at San Gemignano. She has been here with me for several days and entreated me to do this ; then she sent her son, who left here this morning, to settle about the visit. So, because of her entreaties, and because she is a widow, I have been forced to promise without awaiting thy assent. We shall go quietly and stay little, and on Monday, the Eve of S. John, we shall be at home. I do not see my way to come before as I am still weak from the effects of the baths. . . . Send the horses . . . to arrive here on the 19th, so that they can rest on the 20th, and, as I have said, we start early on the 21st. Seven horses must be sent, nought else is wanted. . . . I have given orders to Maso of Fiesole for the donkeys and mules he is to send. . . ." [57]

Lucrezia did not get well quite as quickly as she had hoped, but she was so anxious to be at home for S. John's day that she decided to cut short her baths and return to Florence. She therefore wrote to Lorenzo :—

" To-day the 18th, the horses have arrived, two days before the time, I suppose by the over-zeal of whoever was charged to send them. It does not matter, although there is a dearth of stabling, straw and oats, but we have sent them where they will be well cared for and fed until we leave, as I said, on the 21st. I cannot leave before as I am very weak and have not yet finished my baths. But to keep my word and be with thee on S. John's day I shall leave although if I remained another eight days it would be more necessary than superfluous. However, now it is settled. We shall not be in Florence before Monday, for the reasons already given. So that if thou hast sent the horses before the time fixed in order that I might be home earlier, forgive me : if I had received a letter from thee urging me to return I should have left at once without considering my own convenience and well-being. Nought else. I commend myself to thee and pray God to keep thee well and happy. Salute the family and tell them I shall be at home on the vigil of S. John, if it pleases God, for I never expected to live so long.

In haste, in haste, on the 18th day (of June) 1477.

Thy LUCREZIA at Bagno a Morba." [58]

When Bagno a Morba became her own property, Lucrezia at once set about making improvements and she soon converted the little tumble-down village into a fashionable health resort. New cisterns were made, and when the first plan was not a success she had it altered and improved, and she also built bath-houses and an hotel as well as a house for herself and her family.

A certain Piero Malegonelle, who was vicar of the neighbouring township of Pomerance, was left in charge, and he wrote several long reports of the work, which give us a good idea of such baths at that time. On September 16, 1477, he reported :—

" . . . There is the same quantity of water for the showerbaths, but we are making a new and a better cistern, with an addition, so that there will be more water. Riccio, the bearer of this, will tell you all about it. This Riccio and his brother are experts in this kind of work, as you know. . . . I think the best thing at these baths is to conduct as much water as possible to the showerbaths, so, as I have to be in the neighbourhood all the winter, which is the best season for seeking it, I will do my best on your behalf." [59]

The work went on apace all through the winter, and in April, just before he left his post, Malegonelle was able to write a most encouraging letter to Lucrezia :—

" . . . I went to the Baths last Friday. I found that the quantity of water had increased rather than diminished, and that it was very hot. The trench has been made as you ordered, underneath the building, from the spring to the showerbaths. There are twelve baths. They have built all except the top part of the cistern according to the design, and in my poor judgment all is well, except that the water entering the cistern by one of the mouths will have to travel twenty *braccia* before it falls. I am afraid the first baths will be too hot to be borne, and the last ones not warm enough. Therefore I would suggest leading the water into the cistern by two pipes, that is to say that when it reaches the old bathroom the pipe would divide into two. It would mean another trench about thirty *braccia* by four and a half in depth ; but this can be done at any time if necessary.

There has been trouble with the embankment of the hill whence the water comes. They have had to dig it out and to put in supports, and to cut away the rock where the water emerges. It is hard rock six *braccia* in length. A channel one *braccio* deep will have to be cut to allow sufficient fall for the water to be carried under the building as far as the baths. They expect to finish it in two or three days. They have burnt the lime and say it has turned out well.

There are about eighty bushels for twenty soldi the bushel. In the fields nearest the trench, on the way to the church, they have found earth that is good for tiles and bricks. There are workmen here to make the tiles and the firing has been entrusted to a Lombard, and they will come to less than forty lire a thousand. They are now in the kiln, and will be very useful to you.

The bathroom is partially built, and seems to be seven *braccia* wide and twenty long. . . . They say they need some of those stones which are made for showerbaths, one for each, and these they say they need urgently.

Riccio has been sent away from the inn, and Giovanni di Pace put in charge. He has begun to receive guests and says that he has enquiries for rooms from Florence and Volterra and other places and that, besides what he already has, he needs all the things on the enclosed list.

The garden is arranged in a way that will please you when you see it." [60]

All these arrangements were not entirely satisfactory, and further alterations were made. On April 28, 1480, one of the doctors resident at Bagno a Morba reported to Lucrezia :—

" In another letter I told you that the spring called 'cooked cheese' now gives about six hogsheads. . . . I also told you that we hoped to find other springs, and as I am anxious . . . to prevent the water from escaping, as it thereby loses some of its power, I have had everything pulled down that was built by Giovanni di Pace. When we got to the bottom we found another spring of water almost in the middle of the bath, and also a small one which gives the same kind of water as the 'cooked cheese,' and together they give twenty hogsheads or more. The water in this bath contains a good deal of sulphur and some alum, and is the very thing for eczema and asthma, and is dissolving and purifying for all the ills of the body, for pains in the joints and nerves, and contains many other virtues, as I will demonstrate to you. The same is true of all the other springs, and especially of the main bath. You must know that I distil this water continually with all possible diligence, and I expect to have finished in three days. . . ." [61]

On April 26, 1478, Lucrezia's younger son, Giuliano, was assassinated in the Duomo by the Pazzi conspirators, and Lorenzo was wounded in the neck, though he managed to escape. Lucrezia was overcome with grief when the dead body of her son was brought back to the Via Larga, but soon afterwards heard that Giuliano had left an illegitimate child. She sought the boy and brought him back with her, and he was educated with Lorenzo's children, and became eventually Pope Clement VII.

A number of those involved in the Pazzi conspiracy were executed, others were exiled, and members of the Pazzi family were excluded from all participation in public life. Their business interests suffered severely, and there is a begging letter from a certain Francesco d' Antonio del Borgo, dated May 27, which gives a glimpse of the affair. Francesco had had a lawsuit with a certain Mona Lisa who owed him money, but could not be induced to pay. He was in a very bad way and appealed to Lucrezia to help him :—

"I do not ask for more than fifteen soldi in the lira on account, but I have nothing. . . . Now I cannot earn, for, as you know, I am with Filippo

Giugni, who was a partner of Renato [Pazzi] : now
we do not work, so how can I live.

My wife has just given birth to a daughter, and
I have nothing in this world to live on or to wrap
her in. I could not have believed that Monna Lisa
would not help me, at least from my own, with
a bit of stuff, or a bushel of flour, or something. . . ." [62]

The problem of the confidential maid was often
a very serious one, and these women sometimes played
a large part in matrimonial differences. When a
girl left home to be married she generally took with
her one of the servants who had attended her from
childhood, and this woman held a privileged position
in the household, where she often made a lot of mischief.
This seems to have been the case in the Torelli household in Milan, where Monna Lisa, the maid, sowed
dissension between husband and wife, possibly in
order to attract her master to herself. The young
bride was Lucrezia's niece, and as she had appointed
this undesirable woman to her household she was
asked to obtain her recall, secretly if possible. Lodovica
Torelli was devoted to her Florentine sister-in-law,
and wrote to Lucrezia :—

" . . . I love Madonna Margherita as much as
if we had been born of the same mother, and when
I see anything unpleasant done to her, I take up
the sword for love of her, and at present it is
particularly necessary that I should do so.

I understand from my sister-in-law that you
gave her Mona Lisa as a maid, but she loves neither
you nor my sister-in-law, nor is she the woman she
seemed, and I will tell you the reason. . . . My father
and brother went abroad and left my sister-in-law
in my house in Milan, together with Mona Lisa.

Since we lived together in the same house, you may be sure I know more about her life than anybody. And to tell the truth I have never seen her do anything which was not beautiful and fine and good. If it were otherwise you may be sure that I, who love Messer Gasparo, could not endure anything that would bring shame on him, for it would reflect on me. But to return to the point. . . . My father and brother arrived here in Milan, safe and sound, and the caresses given by Messer Gasparo to my sister-in-law, cannot be imagined or described. But Mona Lisa, who is the Goddess of Discord, could not bear to see this, and went to my brother and told him more evil of his wife than any human being could imagine, so that there was a quarrel between husband and wife. Things are so bad that if you cannot do anything I am afraid that one day Messer Gasparo will do something so grievous that he will never again be happy, and nor will you. I never saw a more mischievous and lying woman, and I have done my best in the matter, but now I can do no more, and I beg you to do something. Messer Gasparo is devoted to Mona Lisa for love of you, and I again beg you to act secretly, so that it does not appear that I have written.

Madonna Margherita, your niece, who is present . . . begs you to send her thirty-seven *braccia* of pale blue satin to make a cloak and a dress . . . and if you think that the cost is too high, tell her how much it is and she will send the money at once. . . ." [63]

Lucrezia was often asked to mediate in matrimonial differences, and two years later we have a letter from Cornelia de' Martini in Venice, thanking Lucrezia for helping her daughter Francesca. She had married into a Florentine family, but was not on good terms with her new relations, and after her husband's death they refused to restore her dowry. Thus she was penniless and unable to return to Venice as she wished to do. Lucrezia and Lorenzo were therefore asked to intervene.[64]

After the Pazzi conspiracy Lorenzo sent his family to Pistoia, but he later removed them to Cafaggiuolo in the Mugello. This was a delightful place in the summer, but terrible in winter. The great rooms were cold and draughty, and the heating inadequate, whilst outside it rained unceasingly, making the roads impassable so that none could go out and no communications were received from the city. Lucrezia remained in Florence with Lorenzo, and when Clarice addressed a letter to her on December 16, it took two days to arrive :—

" Because of the bad roads, and the rain we have not sent the carrier for the last three days. Now either he or another will come with this, for I am anxious to know how you are, and how Lorenzo is, and all who are with you. I beg you to send me some news and to tell me what is happening. Here, thanks be to God, we are very well, but we are above our heads in water. We stay in the house, and nothing gives us greater pleasure than letters and news from the city. . . ." [65]

The famous humanist Poliziano accompanied Clarice first to Pistoia and then to Cafaggiuolo, for Lorenzo had appointed him tutor to his children. But he was not in the least suited by temperament to teach young children, and life at Cafaggiuolo was a dreary exile to him. He longed for the witty and cultured conversation of the Via Larga, and found no congenial company alone in the country with Clarice, who was not highly educated, but was very devoted to religious observances. He bewailed his lot in his letters to Lucrezia :—

" Our only news is that we are having such continual rain that we cannot leave the house, and have exchanged the chase for ball-playing, so that the children may not miss their usual exercise. We generally play for the soup, the sweet or the meat, and he who loses must not eat any, and very often, when my scholars lose, they pay tribute to Ser Umido.* I sit by the fire in slippers and a great coat, and if you could see me, you would think I was melancholy personified. . . . When we are in town we have some pleasures, if only to see Lorenzo return safely home. Here we are anxious about everything, and I can assure you I am drowned in sloth in this solitude. I say solitude, because Monsignore † shuts himself in his room with his thoughts. I always find him sad and thoughtful, so that my own depression is more refreshing than his company. Ser Alberto di Malerba mumbles prayers all day long with these children, and I remain alone, and when I am tired of study I ring the changes on plague and war, and on grief for the past, and fear for the future, and there is no one to listen to my grumblings. I do not find my Madonna Lucrezia, so that I can unburden myself to her. Our only relief is in letters from Florence. . . ." [66]

The situation at Cafaggiuolo became more and more strained until, in May, 1479, Clarice dismissed Poliziano and turned him out of the house. He took

---

* A Tuscan saying still used when a child cries.
† Gentile Becchi, Bishop of Urbino.

refuge in another of Lorenzo's villas at Fiesole, and when he had been there for some time, busily engaged in study, he wrote to ask Lucrezia whether she could persuade Lorenzo to give him the vacant provostship of Fiesole.[67]

The rest of the family were still at Cafaggiuolo, where Lorenzo found them at the end of May. A case of plague was reported in the neighbourhood, so he at once took them to Trebbio, and wrote to his mother :—

> " You will have heard from Ser Niccolo of the case which has occurred at Castello . . . we have left there and gone to Trebbio, in order to take every precaution. Enclosed is a list of various things which Maestro Stefano has ordered in case anything should happen. . . . Send the things immediately." [68]

The family did not remain long at Trebbio, but soon returned to Cafaggiuolo, where they stayed all the summer. The plague was raging in Florence, and Lucrezia and Lorenzo stayed at Careggi, which was nearer the city and therefore more convenient for Lorenzo, though not so safe as Cafaggiuolo. In July the little Lucrezia, aged nine, wrote to her grandmother :—

> " I must tell you that we are all well, and we hope you are the same, and that God will keep you so. I want very much to see you and beg you to come and see us when you can, for it seems a thousand years since I saw you. Mona Lucrezia mine, please send me a rosary for my Paternosters, made of the palio of S. Giovanni, or rather of that one that was given you at Volterra. Piero and Maddalena commend themselves to you, and Giovanni asks for some sugar-plums, and says that last time you sent very few. . . ." [69]

The question of tutors was always very difficult. It was considered essential that children should be instructed in all branches of learning, but so many of the humanists were men of dissolute lives that it was impossible to allow them to live in the same house as their charges. Even if their personal morality was fairly high, they were mostly sceptics, and were most irritable and touchy individuals, impossible to live with, so that we often hear of the sudden dismissal of the house-tutor. Ariosto sums up the general view in his Seventh Epistle, where he asks Bembo to recommend a tutor for his son and says :—

" The Greek must be learned, but also of sound principles, for erudition without morality is worse than worthless. Unhappily in these days it is difficult to find a teacher of this sort. Few humanists are free from the most infamous of vices, and intellectual vanity makes most of them sceptics also." [70]

Bernardo Rucellai was a man with a rather difficult temperament, so that it was almost inevitable that he should clash with the house-tutor, and in July, 1479, he sent him away at a moment's notice. Nannina Rucellai was much worried by this and appealed to her mother for advice and assistance :—

" I must tell you that Bernardo has sent away the tutor, which displeases me greatly, for I do not know where to send him. The plague is very bad at Figline, where he comes from, and in his own house two of his brothers have died and his father is ill. He has not a penny, and if he ever received anything he has spent it in our house for clothes, and now we pay him with ' Go with God.' This displeases me greatly, but it is no good being born a woman if one wants one's own way. Please ask Lorenzo . . . to give him shelter somewhere until the plague has passed. I do not think he is capable of teaching Piero, but he could teach the little ones and look after them. You could not do me a greater favour for it would show that I have someone who cares about me, as he does not do. If he needs some money for clothes, I will pay it out of my own pocket, for he seems to me very badly equipped. Here I could not give him anything because I had no money. If by chance any small benefice comes into your hands, I should be very glad if you would help him, for I do not want to repay him with ingratitude. . . ." [71]

The plague was again raging on all sides in the summer of 1479, and Bianca de' Pazzi was worried because she did not think that either Lucrezia or Lorenzo was taking suffcient care to avoid infection. They were living at Careggi, but they conducted all their business as usual, and did not refuse to see those who visited them, even if they came from the infected city. Bianca herself was expecting the birth of a child at the beginning of August, and had gone into the country for the event. On July 15, she wrote to her mother :—

" My dearest and most honoured mother. I have had a letter from you which has given me great pleasure, hearing that you are well, especially you and Lorenzo. May God keep you so for a long time. I have not written to you because nothing has happened, and also I have frequently sent to your house, to Marco, for malvasy, and for the book of S. Margaret. I have had all I wanted and have had news of you from him. I would have sent to you, but I thought you were keeping guard because of the plague. We have had it near here, but by the grace of God there is no more, but that is why I have been careful and have not sent to you as I should otherwise have done.

As I told you in Florence, I expect to lie in here, for there you have enough to do, and here I lack nothing if I am not worse than usual, which I do not expect, for I feel well, thanks be to God. I entered into the ninth month a few days ago, and, as I say, I feel well. But if anything should happen Maestro Giorgio is near here, for he has fled from the plague. So do not worry, for I think God will be merciful to me, as is His custom with those who please Him. I hear the family in Mugello is well, which pleases me, and I hear Nannina passed by on the road going to Casentino. I am glad our family is well, for that is no small thing in these times. But I have worried about you, and still do, for you say you have to deal with so many people, and I am surprised that you have not been frightened, but the Lord will not abandon us in everything. But please beg Lorenzo to take as much care of himself as possible, for I hear that he has no fear and goes everywhere, and let him guard against his enemies. Until this sickness is past he should put aside his pleasures, for if he lives he will have greater pleasures than now. I hope God will make up to him the ills he has received, and commend me to him. I commend myself to you and to Lorenzo, together with these children and Guglielmo, for by the grace of God all are well.

Alla Torre July 15, 1479.

Your BIANCA.

To the Magnificent Lady Lucretia de Medici, my honoured mother, at Careggi.'' [72]

When Clarice turned Poliziano out of Cafaggiuolo, he was not abandoned by his patron, but allowed to live in another of the Medici villas at Fiesole, to Clarice's great annoyance. Thence he corresponded with Lucrezia, who was always better able to appreciate him than her sickly Roman daughter-in-law. Besides, she never had to spend many months alone in the wilds of the country with the discontented genius. From Fiesole Poliziano wrote :—

"I send you back by Tommaso your lauds and sonnets and poems that you lent me when I was with you. . . . There is also a little white manuscript book with the poems. Please give it to . . Giovanni Tornabuoni. It contains certain rules his children asked me for. I am also writing to Giovanni and am answering both the children and their master.

I have visited Lorenzo several times, and I cannot tell you how glad he was to see me. Please find out what are his intentions about me. I should be surprised if he let Piero waste time, for it would be a great pity. I hear that Messer Bernardo, the brother of Ser Niccolo, is in the house, but I do not know how his teaching will combine with mine, unless he is there permanently.

I am studying hard. I have not been able to send you the book I promised you, because one copy is in Florence, and the other at the binders, who have had it a long time. As soon as it arrives, I will send it. . . ." [73]

A few days later Poliziano was not quite so sure about Lorenzo, for he wrote to Lucrezia in great haste :—

"I hear that last night Lorenzo was not very well. God knows how worried I was to hear this.

So I am sending Mariotto to you to hear if it is true, and how he is. I would have come myself but I feared to be troublesome. . . ." [74]

Since Clarice and Poliziano had quarrelled irrevocably, the Medici children were without a permanent tutor, and Ser Francesco d' Antonio thought he saw a way of obtaining some benefit for his family. He wrote to Lucrezia to ask her to recommend his son Piero to Lorenzo for the vacant post. When he found that there was no chance of obtaining this he begged to be appointed as " the new vicar of S. Giovanni, who is to be drawn on the coming first of August." [75]

Lucrezia took a considerable interest in the course of events outside Florence, and we often find little bits of news sandwiched by her correspondents between family and domestic details. She, like most important persons at this time, had her regular correspondents in the big cities of Italy, who kept her informed of current happenings. As there were no newspapers all information had to be got from private sources. The rulers of states maintained ambassadors and agents, but there were many men, the forerunners of modern journalists, who collected news and sent it to private patrons. In 1480 Lucrezia's correspondent in Rome was a certain Papinio di Artimino who sent her a series of letters dealing with Roman affairs especially with the taking of Otranto by the Turks. [76], [77]

Lucrezia did not only make use of Papinio as a writer of news, but she also entrusted him with various commissions, for on August 4, after most important news about Otranto, he goes on :—

" I shall have your yarn here by the tenth of this month, for I have had it spun in Naples." [78]

The Turks abandoned first Rhodes, and then Otranto, as Papinio hastened to inform Lucrezia,[79] and on October 4 he continued :—

" On Monday morning a children's school was destroyed, and at first it was thought that twenty children had been killed, but only the master that kept the school perished, which has been regarded as a great miracle." [80]

Lucrezia had never been strong and she died in 1482, on March 25, the day of the Annunciation, fortified by the sacraments of Holy Church. She was buried in S. Lorenzo, and her son was inconsolable. He wrote to the Duke of Ferrara :—

" Besides losing my mother, the thought of which alone breaks my heart, I have also lost a helper who relieved me of many burdens." [81]

and in a letter to the Duchess he describes his mother as :—

" My only refuge from my troubles, and my relief in many labours." [82]

She founded the Cappella dei Chierici in S. Lorenzo, and one of the canons, a certain Francesco da Castiglione, wrote a letter to Lorenzo which shows the high estimation in which Lucrezia was held by her contemporaries. He said :—

" Sometimes her actions, from the political point of view, were more prudent than yours, for you attended only to great things and forgot the less. . . . She advised the most important persons as well as the magistrates, and she also admitted the humblest to her presence and all she sent away happy and contented. . . . She knew how to manage the most important affairs with wise counsel, and how to succour the citizens in time of calamity." [83]

All the authors of Lorenzo's circle spoke most highly of Lucrezia and dwelt on the help she gave her son, and his affection for her, and Giovio says that " Her mind was of a masculine gravity." [84]

In the Archivio Mediceo there is a fragment of Lucrezia's accounts for the years 1474 to 1477.[85] This is not a complete record of receipts and disbursements during those years but merely gives the sums dealt with on her behalf by the Medici Bank in Pisa. There is no kind of differentiation between the items, and payments for household goods, for the repair of house-property and for charity jostle one another on the pages.

Florentine currency was very complicated, any number of different coins being in circulation, so that none but an expert could give any idea of values. But in these accounts, although the various amounts were paid in all kinds of money, they are all made to equal lire, soldi and denari, and we can see that the value of sealed florins and big florins, etc., fluctuated considerably.[86]

Rents were often nominally paid in kind, but commuted for a money payment, and we get items like " On December 18 [1474] we paid to the Chaplains of the Duomo the value of 28 bushels of corn, being the rent for the farm of San Giusto for the year ending in August. . . . lire 84."

On September 16, 1475, the value of 28 bushels of corn was lire 95, soldi 4, and on May 10, 1476, three bushels were worth lire 10, soldi 10, and on May 24, lire 11, soldi 2.

Lucrezia paid large and varying sums for materials

for her own or for household use. On October 31, 1474, she paid 8 soldi to Andrea di Bengni for a piece of bed-ticking he got for her, but there is a note that " she sent a larger sum by Maso da Fiesole." On November 15, she paid 165 lire to Pietro Manzi " in cash for 15 pieces of bed-ticking she had from him for featherbeds." On the following 27th of January she paid " 12 big florins to Pietro del Torto for two pieces of white serge, one fine and one ordinary which Ser Niccolo Michelozzi obtained from him on her behalf last March." In this case the 12 big florins were worth 66 lire 12 soldi. On May 13, 1475, she paid 118 lire 10 soldi in cash to " Buonachorso del Becchaio for linen cloth, most of which was for 81¾ ells of dyed cloth, bought on November 27 last, which was sent to the nuns of S. Agostino on her behalf." In 1475, 5 big florins 11 soldi, which were worth 32 lire 10 soldi, were paid to Giuliano del Torto for a piece of purple camlet, and 4 big florins, equal to 30 lire 12 soldi, for a piece of white serge. On November 8, Leonardo Spini paid Tommaso da Mastino 10 big florins, 2 lire 4 small soldi, on her behalf. This sum, which was equivalent to 57 lire 14 soldi, was paid for 153 lbs. of sugar.

The receipts consist chiefly of the rents of certain farms and some shops. A number of the latter were situated on the Ponte Vecchio, which is interesting because we know that, after the Ciompi rising, the rents of these shops were assigned to Salvestro de' Medici, though he afterwards relinquished them. There are also certain payments from Giovanni di Pace, who had the inn at Bagno a Morba, and there is one item " On November 4, 1477, 6 florins 13 soldi 4 denari from Maestro Piero da Perugia for the rent of his house for a year ending on that day." This sounds like the artist Perugino, though most authorities consider that he did not come to Florence till 1479.

The accounts are fairly complicated in themselves, but they have been considerably simplified, if we may judge from a letter written to Lucrezia by Antonio di Pace in 1470, when he was acting as her agent in Pisa :—

" A few days ago Bernardo Bonsi came and said he had had a letter from Lodovico Masi saying that you wished to sell this year's harvest of corn and wine. I told him that up to the day he left Francesco the goldsmith had collected 112 sacks of corn. . . . The said Francesco sold 110 sacks. . . . to Rinieri Magiolini on September 10 1470. The said Francesco asked me to collect the rest of the rents of the Val di Serchio, and to give grain to the Chaplains of the Duomo and to Federigo del Lante. I have duly collected them, and up-to-date I have received :—

From Giovanni Coraza on September 14, eight sacks of grain.

From Giovanni Coraza on September 18, five sacks of grain.

From Simone da Chierachia on October 2, three sacks one bushel.

From the mother of Giovanni Coraza on Nov. 27, seven sacks

which altogether make one hundred and thirty-five sacks, of which about 25½ sacks remain in the house.

If the Podestà of Librafatta had not had letters from the city I should have collected everything, for there are still 19 sacks to be collected. I have already been waiting two months for Francesco to come, for every day I have been told he would come and settle everything. . . ."[87]

Several items on the accounts relate to linen or other material which had been sent to the nuns of different convents. This was not a present from Lucrezia to the nuns, as would appear at first sight, but was cloth sent them in order to be embroidered or otherwise worked. In 1476 the nuns of the convent of San Piero at Lucca were employed on work of this kind, for their abbess wrote :—

" From your Ser Alberto I received the inquiry for the work being done by my nuns. At that time it was not yet done, but now it is finished and I am sending it to you by the said Ser Alberto. You also ask me what I want in payment for this work. You may rest assured that I will never take any payment, for I regard it as such a great honour that you and Mona Clarice condescended to come and visit me in my house in such a friendly way, and deigned to give me this work to do, which is a sign of great affection and kindness. Therefore I beg that, if these things are well done, you will show it by entrusting other work of the same kind to this house, for I hope that by the grace of God you will always deign to be the protector and defender of this community and convent, which I commend to you as much as I can. And I beg you, for the love of God, not to talk about payment, for it would fill me with shame, for I hope that in your magnificence and benignity you will con-descend to be the defender of this convent, as I most earnestly beg of you. And I beg you also to commend me to Mona Clarice and the magnificent Lorenzo, and I offer myself and my convent to serve you in every possible way.

And if your work is well done I am very glad, but if it is in any way lacking, please excuse us, for it was done to the best of our ability, and we did not know any better.

No more at present. Christ guard you from all ill and keep you in health and happiness.

November 12, 1476.

I am sending you some sugar plums. Please consider the love and goodwill, not the smallness of the present.

> GINEVRA, abbess of the convent of San Piero at Lucca.

To the Most Prudent and Discreet Lady Monna Lucrezia, wife of the late Piero di Medici, who is most honourable." [88]

Unfortunately there is no authentic portrait of Lucrezia, although it has been suggested that she was the original of Botticelli's "Portrait of a Lady," now in the Berlin Museum. But many critics deny this, whilst the medals that have at different times been called "Lucrezia de' Medici" are utterly rejected by the newer criticism.

There is a portrait in the Scuola dei Chierici di San Lorenzo which is supposed to represent Lucrezia, but it is obviously a work of the eighteenth century, though it might have been copied from an earlier original.

Professor Pieraccini, the latest historian of the Medici, denies all these ascriptions, however, and finds Lucrezia among the matrons depicted in the fresco of the Birth of John the Baptist by Ghirlandaio in S. Maria Novella. He bases himself chiefly on the likeness to Lorenzo the Magnificent on the one hand, and to the rest of the Tornabuoni family on the other. But the whole matter is very obscure.

Lucrezia's own direct contribution to contemporary

literature was not very important, but indirectly she is of vital interest to the student of Renaissance poetry. She not only persuaded Pulci to write his *Morgante Maggiore*, but she encouraged and stimulated Lorenzo to write, and her influence may be clearly traced in the letter he addressed in 1466 to Federigo of Naples in defence of the vulgar tongue, and also in the Commentario he wrote on his own sonnets in the style of the Vita Nuova.

Lucrezia's own work consisted of religious songs and lauds, and a number of religious plays, rather like Miracle Plays. Among those that remain to us are the Life of S. John the Baptist and the Story of Judith in *ottava rima*, and the Story of Esther, the Story of Susanna, and the Life of Tobias and the Life of the Virgin in *terza rima*. We also have a *Canzone sulla Natività di Gesù Cristo*, and we hear of some sonnets which are lost.

Lucrezia was hardly a great poetess, though her work is pleasing, and it might have been of greater value if she had written at a time less prolific of genius. Compared with the many poetesses of the next century, her work is more natural and sincere, and less stilted and conventional than that of either Vittoria Colonna or Veronica Gambara.

Lucrezia was a many-sided woman, a devoted wife and mother, a clever politician, a writer and the inspirer of others, and in her many letters she lives for us more clearly than any of her predecessors.

CHAPTER VI

CLARICE ORSINI

THE Italian Renaissance reached its highest development in Florence under Lorenzo de' Medici ; and this pre-eminence did not pass to other cities until the beginning of the decadence. The first flowers of the new spirit sprang up in Tuscany with Giotto and Dante, and the finest fruit was gathered there, at the end of the fifteenth century.

Florence was not only best suited by temperament to lead Italy in the things of the mind, but she was fortunate in her ruler during these epoch-making years. Lorenzo was not only an enlightened patron of art and learning, but was himself a poet and scholar of no mean order. He cannot be classed with the greatest Italian poets, but he stands very high in the second rank, and the encouragement he gave to vernacular literature had very important consequences. He gathered round him other poets, such as Poliziano and Pulci, collected pictures and sculpture, both antique and modern, and did everything in his power to make his native city a centre of light and learning.

His mother encouraged him in all his literary and artistic aspirations, for she was herself a poetess and a woman of wide culture, but unfortunately he did not find the same sympathy in his wife. She came of a pious Roman family, which was still feudal in its ideas, and had not been permeated by the new learning. She was not illiterate, but neither was she clever or cultured, and her husband's court was to her an utterly uncongenial place. It was filled with humanists and artists who discussed everything, and accepted none of the old traditions to which she was accustomed. She could not adapt herself to these new surroundings, and gradually withdrew more and more from the festive gatherings in which Lorenzo delighted, and so alienated her husband, and made herself miserable.

Cosimo had married a member of an old Florentine family, and had sought for nothing better for his son, but Piero wanted Lorenzo to ally himself with one of the great families of the outside world. He thought this would strengthen his position and would also avoid jealousy in Florence. But a foreign bride was not popular, and one cannot help thinking that if Lorenzo had married a Florentine, the course of history might have been different. If his home atmosphere had been more congenial he might have sought less after illicit pleasures, which ruined his health and shortened his life, and if his son had not inherited a large measure of Orsini pride, he might have maintained himself in Florence, and Italy, would have been saved endless misery and bloodshed.

Piero and Lucrezia passed all the eligible damsels of Italy in review as they looked for a suitable bride for their son, and their choice eventually fell on a daughter of the powerful Roman house of Orsini. The alliance was valuable as it gave a connection with the Sacred College through the girl's uncle, Cardinal Latino Orsini, as well as with the extensive military resources of the family.

The chosen bride was Clarice Orsini, the daughter of Jacopo Orsini of Monte Rotondo, and his wife Maddalena, who belonged to another branch of the Orsini. Her father had been Carlo Orsini of Bracciano, and she was the sister of Cardinal

Orsini. The girl was still very young, being only about sixteen when the negotiations were begun, and the match seemed suitable in every way. But Lucrezia felt that it was necessary to go to Rome to see the girl for herself before the final arrangements were made.

She left Florence in the middle of March and immediately on her arrival in Rome she dictated a letter to Piero :—

" On the way I wrote to you several times and told you about the roads. I arrived on Thursday, and was received by Giovanni with the greatest joy you can imagine. I have had yours of the 21st and it gives me great pleasure to hear that the pains have entirely ceased. Nevertheless every day seems a year to me until my return, which will be a joy for us both.

On Thursday morning, going to S. Peter's, I met Madonna Maddalena Orsini, the sister of the Cardinal, with her daughter, who is aged fifteen or sixteen. She was dressed in the Roman fashion with a cloak, and clad thus she seemed to me very beautiful, big and fair, but as the girl was covered I could not see her to my satisfaction. It so happened that yesterday I went to see the said Monsignor Orsini, in his sister's house, which is next to his own. After I had greeted him suitably on your behalf, his sister came in with the girl, who was dressed in a tight Roman dress, without a cloak. We stayed talking a long time, and I looked carefully at the girl. As I said, she is fairly big, and fair, and has nice manners, though she is not as sweet as our girls. She is very modest and will soon learn our customs. Her hair is not fair, for there is none such here, but it is reddish and she has plenty of it. Her face is rather round, but it does not displease me. Her throat is graceful, but a little thin, or rather delicate. We could not see her bosom, as it is the custom here to wear it entirely covered, but it seems good. She does not carry her head erect, like our girls, but holds it a little forward which I think is due to shyness. Her hand is long and graceful. Altogether we consider that the girl is quite out of the common, but she is not to be compared with Maria, Lucrezia and Bianca.* Lorenzo himself has seen her, and you can hear how he liked her. I think that whatever you and he are agreed upon will be right, and I will give my consent. Let us leave it to God to guide us aright.

The girl is the daughter of Signor Jacopo Orsini, of Monte Rotondo, and her mother is the sister of the Cardinal. She has two brothers. One is a soldier and is in favour with Signor Orso ; the other is a priest and a sub-deacon of the Pope. They have half of Monte Rotondo ; the other half belongs to their uncle, who has two sons and three daughters. Besides this half of Monte Rotondo they have three other castles belonging to their brothers, and, as I hear, they are well-established. And every year they will be better off because, besides being nephews of the Cardinal on the mother's side, and of the Archbishop, of Napoleone and the Cavaliere, they are also their cousins on the father's side. For the father of this girl is the second cousin in the direct line of these gentlemen, who love him greatly. And this is what I have found out on the matter. If you prefer not to enter into negotiations until my return, you can do as you think best.

* Piero's daughter.

PLATE VII

Clarice Orsini. Picture formerly ascribed to Botticelli. Known as La Bella Simonetta, in the Pitti Palace, Florence

[*face p. 130*

I think of leaving here on Monday week. I will tell you by what road, and will be home by the time agreed. May God conduct me safely, and keep you well. I am not writing to Madonna Contessina as there does not seem any need. Commend me to her and embrace the girls and Lorenzo and Giuliano.

Your LUCREZIA.

In Rome, March 28, 1467." [1]

This description of Lorenzo's bride seems to agree with the portrait in the Pitti Gallery of a girl with reddish hair who pokes her head forward. This was formerly ascribed to Botticelli and called " La Bella Simonetta." The critics now agree that it does not represent her, and is not an authentic work by Botticelli, and to me it seems much more like Lorenzo's querulous consumptive wife than the beauty adored by Giuliano.

The only actual portrait of Clarice is a medal ascribed to Bertoldo, inscribed " Claricia Ursinia Magnif. Laur. Med. uxor," but the authenticity of this has also been questioned.

Piero was afraid Lucrezia might go too far in these negotiations before he had had time to weigh the advantages and the disadvantages of such an alliance, but she wrote with her own hand to reassure him :—

" As I told you in the letter written by the hand of Giovanni, we saw the girl easily without fuss, and if matters should come to nothing you are not involved, for there has been no discussion. The girl has two good qualities, she is big and fair ; her face is not beautiful, but it is not common and she has a good figure. Lorenzo has seen her, ask him if she pleases him. There are so many other advantages, that if she pleases him we may be content. Her name is Clarice." [2]

Some days later, just as she was preparing to leave, Lucrezia wrote once more :—

" I have had your letter by Donnino, which tells me what you have decided, and I am glad. For I think that when I am back and have told you everything, you will be satisfied, especially as she pleases Lorenzo. We have not seen her again, and I do not know if we shall do so, for there is no reason. You say I speak coldly. I do so on purpose, but I do not think there is a more beautiful girl of marriageable age here at present. . . ." [3]

Lucrezia returned to Florence at the beginning of May, after being delayed by illness at Foligno, but the marriage negotiations continued for over a year longer. At last, at the end of 1468, everything was satisfactorily settled, and the contract signed. Cardinal Orsini then wrote to Piero with his own hand :—

" With great joy we have signed what Giovanni Tornabuoni brought us from you. I hope, thanks be to God, that this will conduce to the well-being of your house and ours, for it pleases us old people and also the youth and the maiden, and indeed all. We should be glad to see our nephew Lorenzo, or *saltem* his brother, at the feast of the Nativity. We should give him a magnificent, a quiet or a middling reception, according to your wishes. . . ." [4]

Clarice's dowry was six thousand Roman florins, in money, jewels and dresses, and it was agreed that, according to Roman custom, this sum should return to her family if she died childless or intestate. It was also customary in Rome for the bridegroom to settle a sum equal to a quarter of her dowry on the bride, but the Orsini agreed to waive this, as it was not usual in Florence.[5]

Lorenzo had seen Clarice when he was in Rome in 1465, on his way to Naples, and he appears to have liked her. But he did not take any particular interest in the question of his marriage, but regarded it purely as a matter of state, to be arranged by his parents.

He was at this time enamoured of a Florentine lady, Lucrezia Donati, in whose honour he arranged a tournament, but he would not take the trouble to write to his bride in Rome. He did once write to her mother, who replied on behalf of her daughter :—

> " I am very pleased with your letters, and I am as happy about you as about any of my other sons, for as such I regard you. It grieves me that there should be delay in seeing you, and Clarice will find the waiting hard. But since such a virtuous cause keeps you, I encourage you to the joust, and hope you will do yourself honour. For the women of the house of Orsini are as happy in the success and honour of their husbands as in their presence. If Clarice knows the day of the joust, I believe she will fast the day before, for your sake, so that God may keep you safe and grant you the victory." [6]

Lorenzo's relations were most anxious to interest him in his bride, and Francesco Tornabuoni, who was also in the Medici Bank in Rome, wrote to him at the beginning of January :—

> " There is not a day passes without my seeing your Madonna Clarice, who drives me wild, for she improves daily. She is beautiful, and has all the good qualities and an admirable mind. About a week ago she began to learn to dance, and every

day she has learnt a new dance. It has hardly been shown to her before she knows it. Maestro Agnolo asked her to write to you with her own hand, but she would not do so on any account. I also begged her so much that she said that for love of me she would do it, but she also said that you seemed very busy with this tournament, since Donnino came without bringing any letters from you to her. Since you cannot visit her personally, at least do so frequently by letter, for this pleases her greatly. . . ." [7]

Lorenzo at last mended his ways and wrote to Clarice, who sent a very stilted reply :—

" I have received a letter from you and have understood all you write. That you liked my letter rejoices me, as I am always desirous to do what pleases you. Then you say that you write but little ; I am content with whatever is your pleasure, living always in hope for the future. Madonna, my Mother, sends you her blessing. I beg you to commend me to your and my father, to your and my mother, and to the others as you deem right. I always commend myself to you.
At Rome, the 28th day of January, 1469.
Your CLARICE DE URSINIS." [8]

Francesco Tornabuoni was very interested in this marriage and was continually visiting the Orsini house. As soon as he had news of the tournament he hastened to Clarice, and then wrote to Lorenzo :—

" To-day we received letters from Giovanni Tornabuoni telling us how you jousted and that you were unhurt and had great honour. As soon as I heard this I went to tell your Madonna Clarice, and showed her the letter from Giovanni, which gave her more pleasure than I can say. For four days she has not been very happy for she always feared for you in the joust and also she had a slight headache. When she heard the news her headache left her and she is now quite happy. I will say nothing about Madonna Maddalena, for it would be impossible to tell you how pleased and happy she is. She has only one wish left, which is that you should come here this Lent, for she wants you to see your goods before you take them home, for they improve every day.

Enclosed is a letter from her. Madonna Clarice did not want to write, but asked me to write for her and say that she has a very great secret to tell you. She will not confide it to anyone, nor send it in a letter in case it should go astray. She is always talking about you, and says that now the joust is over you have no more excuse for delay. She commends herself to you and begs you to commend her to the Magnificent Piero and to Madonna Contessina, and Madonna Lucrezia, and to Bianca, Nannina and Giuliano.

Yesterday I bought some purple cloth from London for a dress in Romagnol fashion, for Madonna wishes her to be dressed thus during this Lent. I do not think it will suit her badly, and she wants to go and visit all these relics to pray for you.

Here they do nothing but talk of your magnificent display, especially in your person, and they say you acted as well as possible. No paladin ever did as much as you, and everyone is greatly pleased, especially your friends. Messer Giovanfrancesco, the son of the Marquis of Mantua, commends himself to you, and he rejoices greatly and says he is always anxious to please you.

There is no more to say now, except that I always commend myself, and may God keep you from all evil, and grant you happiness.

> Your FRANCESCO DI FILIPPO TORNABUONI in
> Rome." [9]

This joust was a great tournament organized by Lorenzo in honour of Lucrezia Donati, to celebrate his forthcoming marriage with Clarice Orsini. This seems a little incongruous, but it was quite according to the customs of chivalry, which governed a tournament such as this. The Provençal Courts of Love had laid it down that love and marriage were incompatible, and it was not thought strange that Lorenzo should honour one lady while betrothed to another.

The tournament took place on February 7, 1469 with the utmost splendour, but Lorenzo made a very bald entry in his *Ricordi* :–

> " To follow the custom and do like others, I gave a tournament on the Piazza S. Croce at great cost, and with much magnificence ; I find that about ten thousand ducats were spent on it. Although I was not a vigorous warrior, nor a very hard hitter, the first prize was adjudged to me, a helmet inlaid with silver, and a figure of Mars as the crest." [10]

Lorenzo first became enamoured of Lucrezia Donati during the marriage festivities of his friend Braccio Martelli. He sent her violets and vowed to arrange a tournament in her honour, which was duly done in 1469. It inspired Luigi Pulci's poem *La Giostra di Lorenzo dei Medici*, which gave Póliziano the idea for his much more famous *Giostra*, written for Giuliano's tournament several years later.

Lorenzo's tournament was held in the Piazza of S. Croce, which was richly decorated for the occasion, and eighteen knights entered the lists. Besides Lorenzo and Giuliano these included Guglielmo and Francesco Pazzi, Jacopo Bracciolini, Braccio de' Medici Piero Vespucci, Carlo Borromeo, Carlo da Forme and Benedetto Salutati.

Lorenzo and Giuliano were accompanied by a great procession headed by nine trumpeters and two pages bearing Lorenzo's red and white banner. Then came two squires, fully armed, who represented Federigo of Urbino and Roberto Sanseverino, and rode at the head of twelve nobles on horseback. They were followed by Giuliano, whose costume had cost eight thousand ducats. He wore a tabard of silver brocade, a silk doublet embroidered with silver and pearls, and a black velvet cap adorned with three feathers worked in gold thread, and set with pearls and rubies.

Five mounted pages and a number of drummers and fifers immediately preceded Lorenzo, who rode a fine horse presented to him by Ferrante of Naples, which was caparisoned in Lorenzo's colours, white and red velvet, adorned with pearls.

Lorenzo's surcoat was also red and white, and his scarf bore his motto " Le Tems Revient," and was embroidered with roses, some full blown and some withered. This was one of his favourite devices, which we find many times in Botticelli's pictures, especially in the Birth of Venus.

His black velvet cap was studded with rubies, diamonds and pearls, and carried a feather of gold thread spangled with precious stones. His shield was adorned with the fleur de lys, the Royal arms of France, which had been granted to the Medici by Louis XI. In the centre of the shield was the famous Medici diamond, known as " Il Libro," which alone was worth two thousand florins.

On reaching the Piazza Lorenzo dismounted, and exchanged his surcoat for a tabard of Alexandrian velvet with gold fringes and gold lace, and put on a helmet adorned with three blue feathers. He then mounted another horse, presented to him by Borso d'Este, and after vanquishing four of his adversaries, he was adjudged the victor.

Clarice, away in Rome, worried considerably about this tournament, but there was little need, for it was more an occasion for sumptuous display than a real exhibition of prowess. She prayed and fasted to secure Lorenzo's victory, but it was almost a foregone conclusion.

After the joust was over she wrote another stilted little letter to Lorenzo :—

"I have had a letter from you which pleased me greatly, since it told me about the tournament in which you gained so much honour. I am very glad you have been satisfied by a thing which gives you so much pleasure, and if my prayers have been heard, it is an especial joy to me, for I am so anxious to please you. I beg you to commend me to my father Piero, to my mother Lucrezia, and to Madonna Contessina, and to everyone else you think good. I commend myself to you. No more.

In Rome February 25, 1469.

Your CLARICE DE HORSINIS." [11]

Clarice and Lorenzo had been formally betrothed, but now it became necessary to make arrangements for the actual marriage. Lorenzo somewhat offended Rinaldo Orsini by not communicating direct with him on the subject[12], and the whole family were grieved because Piero would not let his son come to Rome before the wedding. On March 4, Maddalena wrote :—

" How glad I should be to see you before sending my daughter, I cannot express, but I am sure the Magnificent Piero knows best. . . . At all events I hope you have the wish to know me and all your relations here. . . . Clarice is well. . . ." [13]

Piero definitely decided that Lorenzo was not to go to Rome, and Filippo de' Medici married Clarice by proxy, after which she set out for Florence. Piero had originally intended to send his cousin Pierfrancesco to fetch her, but he was unwilling to undertake the journey, so Giuliano went instead, at the head of a brilliant company of gentlemen.[14]

When she arrived in Florence Clarice was sumptuously lodged at the house of Benedetto degli Alessandri, where she rested after the journey and prepared for the wedding.

The festivities began on Sunday, June 4th, when she left the Alessandri palace on horseback for the Via Larga. She rode in a magnificent procession, preceded by fifers and trumpeters, and surrounded by " the youths generally in attendance on marriage festivities, well-clothed," and followed by two knights on horseback with their retainers.

A stage had been erected for dancing in front of the Medici palace in the Via Larga, and when she arrived and was preparing to dismount, she was greeted by thirty young damsels and matrons, richly dressed. They were accompanied by more youths attired for dancing, the whole preceded by trumpeters, whilst thirty more maidens awaited her in the house. The bride herself was dressed in white and gold brocade, with a magnificent hood on her head.

The first ceremony consisted in the customary hauling up of an olive tree through the window, accompanied by music, and this was followed by a banquet and dancing. Sunday and Monday were spent in festivities in the Via Larga, but on Tuesday Clarice went to mass at S. Lorenzo and then watched a tournament in which a mock fort was attacked. Afterwards she returned to the house of the Alessandri for the night, this custom being a legacy from ancient Rome, when a wife returned to her father's house in order to safeguard some of her rights, and not pass entirely into her husband's power.

Clarice must have had the majority of her wedding presents before she left Rome, but we hear that in Florence she received " about fifty rings, costing from ten to fifty or sixty ducats each, one piece of brocade, a sweatmeat dish of silver, and many other such things and a small book of the Offices of Our Lady, in gold on blue vellum, covered with crystal and worked silver, which cost about two hundred florins."

There were five banquets in all, to which two hundred persons were invited every day, whilst many others were regaled when the principal guests had finished.

The bride sat in the garden under the loggia, with about fifty maidens ; in the loggie round the courtyard sat seventy or eighty of the principal citizens ; in the ground floor hall the thirty-six young men who danced, whilst Madonna Lucrezia entertained the elder women on a balcony in the great room upstairs. There is no mention of Lorenzo in the whole account of the festivities, and we do not know whether he sat with the young men, or with the principal citizens. Forty men of mature age were engaged in marshalling the company, and the writer of the letter which describes the feasts was much impressed with the efficiency of the service, from which we may surmise that there was apt to be considerable confusion at these great banquets. He said "each man knew his service and his place and did naught else."

Although the Medici entertained practically the whole city on this occasion, they were studiously modest in the actual food provided. "As an example to others not to exceèd the modesty and simplicity suitable to marriages, there was never more than one roast." Two banquets were served daily. In the morning the guests received "a small dish, then some boiled meat, then a roast, after that wafers, marzipan and sugared almonds and pineseeds, then jars of preserved pineseeds and sweatmeats." At the evening meal they had "a jelly, a roast, fritters, wafers, almonds and jars of sweetmeats," but on Tuesday, which was a fast day, the roast was replaced by "sweet and succulent vegetables on trenchers." These trenchers were placed one between every two guests, with a carver in attendance. The wines drunk were malvasy, trebbiano and ordinary red wine.

To our modern ideas, this does not seem a particularly modest meal, but if we compare it with the Tudor banquets of the next century, we are impressed with its frugality. All through Florentine history, efforts were made to regulate the amount that might be spent on weddings, but without success.

Our author, Piero Parenti, tells us especially that "of silver plate there was but little," but he goes on to say that there were silver vessels on the tables in which the glasses were put to keep cool, whilst the salt-cellars, the forks, the knife-handles, the bowls for the fritters, almonds and sugar-plums, and the jars for the preserved pineseeds were all of silver, as were also the jugs and the basins used for the washing of hands.

The tables were all covered with the finest white

damask, laid in the Florentine fashion, and, though there were no sideboards, there were tall tables in the middle of the courtyard, round Donatello's statue of David. These were also covered with tablecloths and held four great copper basins for the glasses.

Besides the two hundred invited guests, it was reckoned that more than a thousand people were fed, and at least a hundred barrels of wine were drunk every day, for "every respectable person who came in was at once taken to the ground floor hall, out of the large loggia, to refresh himself with fruit, sweetmeats and white and red wine." On the other hand "the common folk were not invited," though a great many persons were entertained at the house of Cosimo's illegitimate son, Carlo de' Medici.

We get most of these details in a letter addressed by Piero di Marco Parenti to his uncle, Filippo Strozzi, in Naples.[15] The latter had been allowed to return to Florence a short time before, but his business affairs still kept him a good deal in the South. On his return to Florence he had married a wife, but left her behind with his mother. The young girl, for she was no more, was among those bidden to the wedding, but she had not the clothes suitable to such an occasion, and was very unwilling to go. But an invitation from the Medici was rather like a Royal command, so Fiammetta pleaded illness in order to be excused. Filippo, however, thought she ought to go, and on May 6 his brother Lorenzo wrote to him :—

" I hear you have decided to send her to the wedding. She does not want to go at all, but Mona Lucrezia insists on her coming. So I tell those who ask that she is going. But she would prefer to plead illness, so you must decide. You know how difficult it is not to obey. . . . You must send four hundred florins at least, and without delay, for the time is getting short." [16]

Mona Alessandra her mother-in-law was not at all willing to let Fiammetta go to the wedding, and on May 8 she wrote to Filippo herself :—

" I told Lorenzo to tell you how Mona Lucrezia has asked Fiammetta to the wedding, before the baby was born. She replied that she was about to bear a child and might be in labour. When the baby had come Lucrezia sent again, and said she wanted her at all costs, and would take no refusal. Fiammetta does not want to go, and I do not think she ought, firstly because you are not here, and secondly because, if she goes, it will be necessary to spend several hundred florins. For they are all making dresses and cloaks of brocade and she would need the same, and also she is badly provided with jewels. . . . The invitations are for June 4, but they say the festivities will go on until S. Giovanni, which is a long time to provide dresses for." [17]

The celebrations did not last as long as Mona Alessandra feared, and Fiammetta did go after all, for Parenti says that among the thirty richly dressed matrons who greeted the bride, was " your Fiammetta, one of the two handsomest there."

A full account of all these gay doings was at once despatched to Rome, where it gave great satisfaction,[18] but a few weeks after the wedding Lorenzo had to leave his young bride and go to Milan.

A son had been born to the Duke, Galeazzo Sforza, and he asked Piero to stand godfather, but as his infirmities did not allow him to go in person, he somewhat unwillingly sent Lorenzo in his stead.

Clarice knew that her husband would not be a good correspondent, so she asked his former tutor, Gentile Becchi, Bishop of Arezzo, to send her an account of their doings once a week. In his letter of July 18, 1469, we can follow the journey from day to day.[19]

On leaving Florence on Friday they lunched at Prato with Carlo de' Medici, and then went on to Pistoia, where Lorenzo stayed in the Bishop's Palace. On Saturday they lunched at Pescia with the Vicar, a certain Baptista Nasi, and then spent some time with the Grand Master of Altopascio. They got to Lucca that evening, but went right through and dismounted at the inn of the Corona, outside the Pisan gate. Lorenzo had intended to leave early the following morning, but the citizens were so grieved that he had refused to stay in the town itself that he had to postpone his departure until after lunch.

On Sunday morning, after attending Mass in the cathedral, he went to the Signoria and spoke to the assembled citizens, and as soon as he came back to his lodgings, presents of all kinds began to arrive. He gave presents in return and entertained some of the citizens to lunch, after which he proceeded on his journey, passing by Chiesa, Mazarosa, and Capezano, and reached Pietra Santa that night, where he lodged at the inn of the Campana, outside the gates. Here he supped in an arbour overlooking the sea, in company with many leading citizens, and the following morning he rode sixteen miles to Sarzana, where he was greeted by the Marquis of Fosdinovo, who had married Clarice's sister, Aurante Orsini. After lunch he went to look at the fortress of Sarzanella which had recently been purchased by the Florentines, and paid various visits. The next day he lunched at Villa Franca and slept at Pontremoli, and reached Milan on the Saturday, having taken eight days on the journey.

Whilst he was in Milan Lorenzo wrote two short notes to his wife, neither of which is particularly interesting, since it gives no news. On June 22, he wrote :—

"I have arrived safely and am quite well. This, I believe, will please you better than any other news, if I may judge by my own longings for you and home. Be good company to Piero, Mona Contessina and Mona Lucrezia, and I will soon come back to you, for it seems a thousand years till I can see you once again. Pray to God for me, and if there is anything here you want, let me know before I leave.

Your own LORENZO DE MEDICI." [20]

Nearly a month later he wrote :—

"I wrote you a letter by the hand of Messer Gentile because I was unable to do so myself. This is to tell you that I am well and will return quickly, an it please God. Be good company to Piero and Mona Lucretia, and tell Nannina I will bring back Bernardo quickly and well. Salute all the rest of the family from me, and take care of yourself. No more by this.
In Milan, July 24, 1469.

Your LORENZO." [21]

Lorenzo's journey to Milan was a great success, and when he presented the Duchess of Milan with "a necklace of gold with a large diamond which cost nearly a thousand ducats," the Duke desired him to stand godfather to all his children.

Clarice complained that Lorenzo was not a good correspondent, but she does not seem to have been much better herself, for her family in Rome had to depend on others for news of her, which did not please them at all. On July 26, 1469, her sister Gracellina wrote reproachfully :—

" . . . Considering your great love for me, you might have left everything else in order to answer me, for you know that I have no greater joy in the world than to have good news of you, of Lorenzo, and of the whole family. Please comfort me for your absence with some letters." [22]

Lorenzo was still very young, hardly more than a boy, but greater responsibilities were soon to be thrust upon him. On December 2, 1469, Piero died, and although his son was barely twenty, the leading citizens came to him and asked him to take charge of the state. This was a serious undertaking for so young a man, but Lorenzo knew that if he did not rule in Florence, his family would not be able to live there. If they were not supreme they would be speedily exiled by their opponents.

Clarice quickly settled down to married life, and on August 4, 1470, she presented her husband with a little daughter, named Lucrezia after her grandmother, and on February 15, 1472, Piero was born. In March of the preceding year she had given birth, prematurely, to twin boys, at five or six months, of whom Lorenzo says "they lived long enough to be baptised." Maddalena was born on July 25, 1473, and in the following year there was another child whose name we do not know, who was buried in 1475. Giovanni was born on December 11, 1475, Luigia in 1477, Contessina in 1478 and Giuliano on March 12, 1479.

This large family kept Clarice well occupied, so that she had no time to interest herself in politics like Lucrezia, even if she had wished to do so. But she was always anxious to obtain appointments for various preachers and other ecclesiastics who appealed to her pious soul. In March, 1472, Agnolella Orsini wrote to her from Rome asking her to persuade Lorenzo to get a certain Maestro Bartolommeo di Padova appointed as a special preacher at the cathedral. She seems to have had no doubt of Clarice's influence with her husband, for she says :—

" . . . You need have no doubt of his acceptance, for I have already spoken to His Reverence, and he says he is willing." [23]

Lorenzo, however, would not make the suggested appointment, and Clarice ignored the letter. But Agnolella was not easily discouraged, and on April 10 she wrote again :—

" If Lorenzo has made other arrangements since I wrote on Monday in Holy Week, I beg you if possible to rearrange matters, for I was the first to ask, and am very surprised at receiving no reply from you, for I hoped that the matter was arranged." [24]

In the middle of April Clarice went to Rome to attend her brother's wedding, which was afterwards postponed. They did not travel in haste, but by slow stages, and Clarice was much gratified at the honours paid her as Lorenzo's wife throughout Tuscany. They went by Figline and then turned aside to Levarne and spent the second night at Arezzo, where they received many presents and were sumptuously entertained. The following day they lunched at Castiglione with the Podestà and spent the night at Cortona. From there Clarice wrote a letter to Lorenzo, which ends :—

"If you have any news which you do not think it necessary to keep secret, please let us have a line, we shall be most grateful for it." [25]

Clarice stayed first at Sabina and then at Monte Rotondo with her kinsfolk, and on May 5, she entered Rome accompanied by about eighty horsemen, an imposing cavalcade. [26]

Her Roman relations were always very anxious that she should use her influence with Lorenzo on their behalf, but the young wife knew that her husband did not depend on her in politics or business, and did not take much notice of what she said. However, her relatives were so insistent that on May 11 she wrote to Lorenzo :—

"A few days ago, by request of Signor Virginio, I wrote to you recommending a certain Messer Alfonso from Lisbon, a friend of his. Now by request of Mona Francesca and Mona Isabella I should do the same, but since I think to write once on one subject is enough I will not repeat myself." [27]

Whilst she was in Rome Clarice went to visit Zoe Palaeologa, the daughter of the Despot of the Morea, who had been driven from his territories in 1461. He had taken refuge in Rome, bringing with him the head of S. Andrew. He died in 1465 and his three children were educated under the supervision of Cardinal Bessarion. Zoe afterwards married a Muscovite Grandduke, but she must have been very stupid, for after ten years' residence in Rome she still had to talk through an interpreter. She was immensely fat, and if we may judge from Pulci's letter to Lorenzo it would seem that the party visited her more as an entertainment than anything else. He gives a detailed description of her, and sums it up as " . . . a noise in the middle and fat everywhere." She was a great talker, and Clarice told her through the interpreter how beautiful she was. " They talked of many things until the evening. But there was no mention of eating or drinking, neither in Greek, nor in Latin, nor in the vulgar tongue. She went so far as to tell our Madonna that the dress she wore was mean and tight, for her own was plump and swollen, and must have consisted of at least six pieces of crimson satin, enough, I should think, to decorate the cupola of S. Maria Rotonda." [28]

In the middle of June Clarice left Rome and returned to Florence by way of Siena, bringing her mother with her. From Siena she wrote to Lucrezia :—

" This is to tell you that to-day, being the 20th, we arrived safely in Siena at the eighteenth hour, grace be to God ; and my mother, Mona Maddalena is with me. Please have a room prepared for her. If Lorenzo is away in the country I should be glad to have her in mine. . . ." [29]

Maddalena Orsini did not remain very long in Florence, and on her return to Rome she wrote to her daughter telling her to ask Lorenzo to confer a certain benefice on a priest whom she favoured. Clarice did not find it easy to influence Lorenzo, but her mother was very peremptory with her :—

" I beg you earnestly that you will remind Lorenzo several times that we recommend the said Girolamo to him . . .'

and then as a postscript she adds :—

" Item. My daughter, you will be blessed if you take good care of Girolamo in this matter." [30]

In 1473 Clarice accompanied Lorenzo to Pisa together with Lucrezia and Nannina Rucellai, but in 1475 Lorenzo went there alone, and as he very seldom wrote to his wife, she depended on his companions for news of him. Poliziano went with him on this occasion, and as he and Clarice were still on good terms, he sent her interesting accounts of Lorenzo's doings. He had gone there in order to hawk, which was one of his favourite sports, and Poliziano's letter tells us how the days were spent :—

" I did not write yesterday to Your Magnificence because Lorenzo sent me to Lucca. Now that I have returned I at once take up my pen so as to keep my promise. Lorenzo is well and of good cheer. Yesterday, though there was a little wind, he went hawking, but their luck was not good, as they lost Pilato's nice falcon, the one called Il Mantovano. This morning we also went into the country, but the wind again spoilt the sport. We saw some fine flights, however, and Maestro Giorgio made his peregrine falcon fly, and it returned most obediently to the lure. Lorenzo has fallen completely in love with it. He is not far wrong, for Maestro Giorgio says that he has never seen a better nor a finer one, and he thinks he can make it into the best falcon in the world. While we were abroad Pilato returned from the shore with his lost falcon, so that Lorenzo's pleasure was doubled. If I knew what to write I should not be sorry. Just now I can only tell you about this hawking, because we do nothing else, either in the morning or the afternoon. This evening I hear that Lorenzo intends to hunt roedeer on Monday, and then to return at once to Florence. Pray God we may find you with a boy in your arms. I commend myself a thousand times to Your Magnificence.

Pisa, December 1, 1475.

Please make my excuses to Madonna Lucrezia for not writing to her, but I do not know what news to give her except this that I have written to you. Please commend me to her.

Your servant, AGNOLO DA MONTEPULCIANO." [31]

Lorenzo was very anxious to re-establish the prosperity of Pisa, and spent a good deal of time there. In April, 1476, he went there again with Poliziano, who wrote to Clarice from San Miniato al Tedesco on April 1 :—

" After we left you yesterday we came as far as San Miniato, singing all the way, and sometimes speaking of sacred things, so as not to forget that we are in Lent. At Lastra we drank zappolino, which was much better than I had been told. Lorenzo shines and causes the whole company to do likewise. Yesterday I counted that he was accompanied by twenty-six horse.

Last night, when we arrived at San Miniato we began to read a little S. Augustine. But this reading resolved itself into making music and coaching and directing a young dancer here. Lorenzo is just going to hear Mass. I will finish another time. . . ." [32]

Lorenzo spent some time at Pisa, for on April 19 he was still there, and Poliziano wrote Clarice a letter full of obscure family allusions :—

" Lorenzo laughs at the spots on my clothes and recommends your specific. . . . I have written this with great difficulty, for I have a very bad headache, and my stomach is out of order. God grant that it is nothing more. I have gone without my supper this evening and hope this will do me good, for I suspect a little fever. But this is beside the point. Lorenzo is well and happy, and so are the rest of the party." [33]

During the summer months Clarice took the children to one of the Medici villas, to escape the great heat. They most often went to Cafaggiuolo in the Mugello, but Lorenzo could not stay there with them, as business and politics kept him in the city. But he paid visits to his family at fairly frequent intervals, though Clarice sometimes felt rather neglected. On one occasion when he did not come as expected she wrote :—

" We are sending you by the bearer seventeen partridges, which your falconers took to-day. I should have been glad if you had come and enjoyed them with us here. We have expected you for the last three evenings up to the third hour, and were very surprised that you did not come. I am afraid something out of the ordinary must have detained you. If there is anything new, please let me know, for in any case it would be better to be together, rather than one in Florence and the other in Lombardy. We expect you to-morrow in any case, so please do not let us wait in vain. The children are all well, and so are all the rest. I commend myself to you and beg you to come and bring Madonna Lucretia.

Cafaggiuolo, August 20, 1476." [34]

In the spring of 1477 Clarice was expecting a visit from her brother, Organtino, who was a soldier fighting in the south. But her mother wrote and told her that he had not long enough leave to come to Tuscany just then, but hoped to do so later.[35] Her Roman relations very seldom visited her, and she must have been greatly disappointed.

In the summer Clarice took the children to Cafaggiuolo as usual, and in September Lucrezia was there with her, but Lorenzo was at Dicomano. The little Giovanni, who was not quite two years old, was taken ill, and the whole family were very worried over what seems to have been only a minor infantile ailment, possibly mumps. Poliziano wrote to Lorenzo on September 4 :—

" Both Madonna Lucrezia and Clarice think the child is improving, although he cannot suck, but he eats soup quite well. I think he has a little catarrh in his tongue rather than in his throat, and that is what makes it hard for him to suck, and I think his neck is a little stiff, since he has difficulty in turning his head. But he does not seem to be very weak, and except for the trouble about sucking there does not seem to be anything wrong, and he has got very little thinner. I have not been able to find out what is going to be done, nor when we shall leave, but I think that, if nothing further happens, we shall stay until to-morrow. In fact to me, to Madonna Lucrezia, and to Fracassino, who has just come in while I am writing, the child does not seem to have anything much the matter with him. Madonna Clarice is still worried because she fears that he will get too weak if he does not suck. . . ." [36]

On April 26, 1478, the dastardly Pazzi conspiracy

came to a head, and Giuliano was murdered in the Duomo, and Lorenzo was wounded, though he managed to escape into the Sacristy. All the murderers and their confederates were eventually caught and slain and Lorenzo became stronger and more popular than ever before.

But the Pope and the King of Naples declared war on Florence, saying they did so only out of hatred for the Medici, who ought to be expelled from the city. The Signoria replied by appointing twelve trusty men to form a bodyguard for Lorenzo, but he felt that his wife and children would be safer away, especially as the plague was very prevalent. He considered that in time of war the various Medici villas were not very safe either, so he sent his family to Pistoia, to live in the house of his friend, Andrea Panciatichi. They were accompanied by Agnolo Poliziano, who was to act as tutor to Piero, now about seven years old. But the famous humanist was an irritable genius, not built for domesticity, nor probably for the teaching of the very young. Clarice was proud and rather overbearing, and in very delicate health, whilst the lack of a first-rate education in her youth was not compensated by any special intellectual ability. The haughty Roman disliked the clever scholar, and though this natural antipathy was not very obvious in the busy life of Florence, when they were almost entirely alone in the country, they inevitably got on each other's nerves. Poliziano had the true Italian dislike of country life, except in the great heat of summer, and he pined for the congenial company and movement of the city. There are many letters both to Lorenzo, and to other friends, in which he complains of his exile, and alludes to Clarice's dislike of him, which culminated in May, 1479, when she turned him out of the house.

Clarice and Lorenzo never seem to have corresponded very much when they were separated, and often depended on third persons for news of each other. Soon after she arrived at Pistoia Clarice wrote :—

" In order not to give you more to do than you have already, I caused two letters to be written to Ser Niccolo, telling him that we were well. I also asked him to tell me how you were, for I cannot be happy without news of you. He has not written anything so far, so I wanted to write this to you to tell you that we are all well and contented, by the grace of God. Please have letters written often, telling me how you are, and whether the plague continues, and any other news that is going about, for we are all anxious. I have told the bearer of this that he is not to return without an answer. The house is comfortable, and we are well-guarded. . . ." [37]

A few days later Clarice was not so satisfied as to their safety, and wrote again to her husband, and also sent him a present :—

" I am sending you a hundred little birds that have been given me, and a pheasant. I have kept some for ourselves. . . . No guard is kept here, and everyone is allowed to enter, which makes me rather suspicious. . . ." [38]

Poliziano was not enjoying his position, and being possessed of the artistic temperament when he had had a difficult time, he at once sat down and wrote to tell Lorenzo all about it. Afterwards he was sorry, as the following letter, dated August 24, shows :—

" I hope you have not been worried by the letter I wrote this morning, which was inspired by passion, only caused by my lack of patience. . . .

Madonna Clarice sends you three pheasants and a partridge. She says you must take as much care as if they had been sent by enemies for we do not know who the bearer is, nor whence he comes ; he is the father of your boy who broke his leg, Cavallaro di Pistoia.

Piero is well, and I take the greatest care of him, and all the others are also well. We manage as well as we can, but I get all the kicks ; however *te propter Libyae, etc.*

I am anxiously awaiting news that the plague has ceased, both because I fear for you, and because I want to return to serve you. I had hoped and wished to stay with you, but since you, or rather my bad luck, has given me this position in your service, I will endure it. . . ." [39]

In the absence of reliable news, rumours of course were rife, and Clarice was worried and thought Lorenzo was making light of his troubles for her benefit. She felt very lonely, and thought she would like the company and protection of Giovanni Tornabuoni, for on August 26, Poliziano wrote to Lorenzo :—

" Madonna Clarice would be glad, if you do not need him too much there, if you would send Giovanni Tornabuoni back here, for she is lonely without him . . . and for every reason she thinks that his presence here is desirable.

I look after Piero and exhort him to write, and in a few days I think you will be very surprised, for we have here a master who teaches writing in fifteen days, and he does marvels at his work. The children play about more than usual, and are quite restored in health. . . . I would have liked to serve you in some greater thing, but since this has fallen to my lot, I will do it gladly." [40]

Although Clarice did not write very often, Poliziano reported to Lorenzo at least every second day, though he often found it difficult to find anything to say. On August 28, he wrote :—

" Madonna Clarice does not write, as there is no cause, and she does not wish to trouble you." [41]

Two days later, however, there is quite a long letter from her :-

" We are all well, thanks be to God. I send you a pheasant and a hare, for it seems a shame to eat them all ourselves.

I wish you would come and spend an evening here for many reasons, especially because I cannot believe your business keeps you so tied there as you would like me to think.

I asked Madonna Lucrezia for a black dress of mine, which is short and without a train. She writes that you have the key and I must tell you where it is. It is in the cupboard next to the Library, the middle one.

Giovanni is always asking what news we have of you, and all the time he says ' When will Loencio come ? '

I commend to you Ser Benedetto da Ceparello, so that you may help him to get away from the rebel officers, for he writes that he is in great straits, and as you know, he is one of our adherents. In the same way I commend to you the affairs of my relative Giovan Francesco dal Pian di Meleteo, and I commend myself to you.

Pistoia, August 30, 1478.

CLARICIA DE MEDICIS.

To the Magnificent Laurentio de Medicis. Florence." [42]

Poliziano's next report is dated August 31, when he said :—

"... Piero does not study much, but every day we go about the place and visit the gardens of which the city is full, and sometimes we go to the library of Maestro Zambino *, where I have found one or two good little things, both in Greek and Latin. Giovanni rides every day on his pony and is followed by all the people. Madonna Clarice is very well, but she takes no pleasure in anything, except the good news we receive from you. She goes out very little. We lack nothing, and we do not accept presents except salad, figs, a flask of wine, or a few small birds, or things of that kind. These citizens would bring us water in their jars, and we are so well treated by Andrea Panciatichi that we are all indebted to him. Everything is well looked after here, and a guard is already placed at the gates. Take care of yourself and win, and when you have time come and see us here, for the whole family awaits you with clasped hands. . . ." [43]

The whole party were extremely anxious for a visit from Lorenzo, for Poliziano mentions it again on September 2 :—

" We are awaiting your coming with the greatest anxiety." [44]

But during the next few days Clarice changed her mind and was greatly relieved when Lorenzo did not come to meet the Duke of Ferrara, who was in command of the Florentine forces, at Pistoia, as he had intended, for she feared that the enemy might try to capture him on the way. On September 6 she wrote :—

" I am very glad (though there is nothing I want

* A certain Canon Sozomeno died in 1458 and left his library of more than 150 Greek and Latin volumes of his native city of Pistoia.

more in this world than to see you) that you did not come to meet his Lordship. But I beg that later, when you conveniently can, you will come and see us one day. . . ." [45]

Clarice was about eight months with child, and at the beginning of September she and her household were very worried lest something should go wrong. She had symptoms of a miscarriage, but prompt measures were taken and this was averted. We have very full details of her indisposition in the various letters received by Lorenzo at this time. On September 7 Poliziano wrote :—

" Since last night Madonna Clarice has not been feeling very well. She is writing herself to Madonna Lucrezia, and says that she fears she may have a miscarriage, or else may suffer in the same way as Giovanni Tornabuoni's wife.* After supper she lay down on the couch, and this morning she rose late, lunched well, and afterwards lay down again. The women of the Panciatichi family are with her, including the mother of Andrea, who is a very wise woman. Andrea tells me that she says that Madonna Clarice is not without danger of miscarrying. I thought I had better tell you everything. But all these women say they do not think things will go badly, and to see her, she does not look ill. . . .

I will note carefully what happens and will do my duty to the best of my ability and will tell you all." [46]

As soon as Clarice became unwell, the family doctor, M. Stefano da Milano, was sent for, and his arrival considerably relieved Clarice's mind.[47] He found that things had not gone too far to be remedied, and she was soon well again.[48] She was kept in bed for some

* Giovanni Tornabuoni's wife died in giving birth to a premature child, who was born dead.

days with hot fomentations on her back, but in spite of having some fever she ate well. We hear that on one occasion she supped off two poached eggs and some sugar cake soaked in white wine. [49, 50]

After Clarice's recovery and the departure of the Duke of Ferrara, life at Pistoia settled down again to its customary routine. But the differences between Clarice and Poliziano grew steadily worse, as we can see from the tutor's letters to Lorenzo. On September 20, he wrote :—

"... I only write to give you news of your family. By the grace of God they are all well, and Piero is still learning to write, and is becoming quite a good scribe, so that I hope he will soon relieve me of this burden of writing *sine argumento* as I do, for I am ashamed of it. ... Madonna Clarice is cheerful and quite well again. As far as I am concerned I will not lack diligence, nor goodwill, nor loyalty, for I know how much I owe you, and I love Piero and your other children almost as much as you do, who are their father. If sometimes something hard happens I will force myself to bear it for love of you. ..." [51]

The next day Piero wrote, to show his progress in penmanship and Poliziano, in a covering letter,[52] explained that the child had written and composed it himself. But the tutor's hand is visible all the same, when a child of seven writes :—

" I write this letter to tell you that we are well. Although I do not yet know how to write well, I will do my best for the present. I will try and do better in future. I have already learnt many verses of Virgil, and I know nearly all the first book of Theodoro † by heart, and I think I understand it. The

† The Greek Grammar of Theodoro Faza, which was very frequently used at this time.

Master makes me decline and examines me every day. Giovanni sometimes comes to Mass with the Master. Madonna Clarice and the others are well. I commend myself to you.

Pistoia, September 21, 1478." [53]

At the end of September Clarice's third daughter, Contessina, was born, and soon after Lorenzo decided that the family would be better at Fiesole. He himself still remained in Florence, for on October 18 Poliziano wrote to tell him that the family were all well and to ask permission to come to Florence for a short time, as there was some difficulty about some books he had borrowed from the library of the Badia :—

" They have been asking me for them since before I went to Pistoia. When I came back I could not return them, for there are several books, and I could not send a porter back with them when I was with the children, for such were Madonna Clarice's orders. They are in the box, and in order to return them I must come to Florence for half an hour. I beg you to allow me to do so, for without your permission I will never leave Piero. The children could stay with Monsignore for that short time. . . ." [54]

Lorenzo decided that Fiesole was not suitable for the family and in November they all moved to Cafaggiuolo in the Mugello, where they spent the winter. This was no doubt because the villa was almost a fortress, surrounded by high walls, and could be well guarded when necessary. But, like all Italian villas, it was really built for the summer only, and must have been terribly cold and damp, and the state of the roads made communication with the city very difficult. Poliziano and Clarice got on each other's nerves more than ever, until in the spring matters came to a head.

In her own way Clarice felt the discomforts of her exile quite as much as the humanist. She was parted from her husband at a time full of anxiety, and constrained to live in a cold draughty house with no visitors from the outside world, and very little news and the constant fear of attack. On December 16, she wrote to her mother-in-law :—

> " On account of the bad roads and the rain we have not sent the carrier for three days. . . . We are all quite well, but in the water above our heads." [55]

At this time she wrote to Lorenzo to intercede for a servant he had dismissed :—

> " Please either keep him with you, or find him a place, for since he has shown himself faithful to you, it would be contrary to your nature not to pardon him for an error. . . . His mother was so glad that he should be in your service, and now she is so unhappy, for she fears that her son, if he is not with you, will get into bad ways and bring sorrow upon her." [56]

The war with Naples and the Papacy dragged on and became increasingly unpopular in Florence, until at length Lorenzo felt that he must stake everything on a bold coup. As a boy he had been very friendly with the Duke of Calabria, and he now decided to test the strength of that old friendship. He left Florence secretly and went to Naples, where after protracted negotiations, he made a satisfactory peace. Unfortunately we have none of the letters which must have passed between Lorenzo and his wife at this time, only a short note which his chancellor, Niccolo Michelozzi, sent to Clarice and Lucrezia, reporting that peace had been concluded.[57]

Clarice and the children remained at Cafaggiuolo, though apparently she went away for a short time in the early spring. The situation became daily more strained. On April 6, Poliziano wrote to Lorenzo :—

" Our Piero is writing to you about the affairs of Cafaggiuolo. I must tell you that his last letter to you was not, as were the previous ones, first shown to me for correction, but was written entirely by himself, at one sitting. We had discussed the subject of the letter at table, but the words and the composition are both his.

I am training him in such a way that I do not doubt that he will come up to our expectations, though you fear his impetuosity. As to Giovanni, you will see. His mother has changed his reading to the psalter, of which I do not approve, and has taken him away from us. When she was away it is incredible what progress he made. He could already find all the letters, and some words in the book by himself.

I have no other daily prayer to God than that I may some day be able to show you my fidelity, diligence and patience, which I would gladly do, even at the expense of death. I omit much, so as not to burden your busy mind. Farewell, and remember us all.

From Cafaggiuolo, April 6, 1479." [58]

Some days later there is another letter from Piero, which shows considerable progress :—

" I have not written to you recently because there has been nothing of importance to tell you. But yesterday there arrived at the port of Cafaggiuolo three ships very well armed. They came from Mozzate and offered to help us. We received them well. We do not know what to do. Please send us a bloodhound, the best that can be found. No more. The whole family commends itself to you, I especially. I beg you to guard against the plague, and to remember us, for we are small, and we need you. We are all well, thanks be to God, and Giuliano also. I attend to my studies. The Master commends himself to you.

In Cafaggiuolo, April 16, 1479." [59]

The youngest of the Medici children, Giuliano, was born on March 12, 1479, and at the end of April he was ill, though the trouble does not seem to have been serious. On April 25, Clarice wrote both to Lorenzo[60] and to Lucrezia[61] to reassure them, and the thing soon passed off, but Giuliano was never strong.

At last the long-standing quarrel between Poliziano and Clarice came to a head, though we do not know what was the actual cause of the final rupture. Clarice ordered the tutor out of the house, and he took refuge at Careggi, whence he wrote to Lorenzo :—

"I am here at Careggi, having left Cafaggiuolo by order of Madonna Clarice. I beg you to allow me to tell you the reason and the way of my departure by word of mouth, for it is a long story. I think that when you have heard my tale you will agree that I was not wholly in the wrong. Out of respect for you, and so as not to come to Florence without your orders, I am here and I await your pleasure, for I am yours whatever the world may say, and if I have been unlucky in your service, it was not because I did not serve you with all the devotion I possess . . .

Careggi, May 6, 1479." [62]

Clarice and Lorenzo had very little in common, but Poliziano was his dearest friend, so that in their quarrel he sided rather with the humanist than with his wife. Although he did not insist on Poliziano's return to Cafaggiuolo, he allowed him to live at his other house at Fiesole, and befriended him as much as ever. The original mistake had been his, in thinking that a genius would make a good tutor.

But his wife was still very angry, and since he did not come to Cafaggiuolo she wrote him a furious letter on May 28 :—

> " I hear that the plague is worse than usual. All the prayers of your wife and children beg you to take care of yourself, and if you could with safety come here for this festival, it would cheer us greatly. I leave it all to your prudence.
>
> I should be glad not to be turned into ridicule by Franco in the same way as Luigi Pulci, nor to hear that Messer Angelo can say that he will stay in your house against my will, and that you have given him your own room at Fiesole. You know that I said that if you wished him to remain I would be content, and though he has called me a thousand names, if it is with your approval, I will endure it, but I cannot believe that it is true. . . ." [63]

Lorenzo hastened to Cafaggiuolo to appease his irate wife, and finding that there had been a case of plague in the neighbourhood he took the whole family to Trebbio, whence he wrote to his mother.[64] He did not remain more than three or four days in the country and was not able to make peace between the disputants, for on his return to Florence he wrote to his wife, who had been behaving in a very exasperating manner :—

> " Monna Clarice. I have been much annoyed that the books have not been handed to Messer Agnolo, as I requested you through Ser Niccolo, and that Messer Bernardo has not come here to bring them. Send them on receipt of this, for I wish him to have them all, and if Niccolo has any of them, let them be sent here this evening without fail.
>
> LORENZO." [65]

165

The family were now established at Gagliano, near Trebbio, which was healthy, but where many domestic necessities were lacking. On June 2 Clarice wrote to Lucrezia :—

" We are now all well in Gagliano, where you know there is nothing but the walls. . . . I would like you to send me various things from Florence, for I have nothing for the use of the family. Please send two pairs of forks, four pairs of sheets for ourselves and four pairs for the servants, and two tablecloths. . . . Please send me twenty braccia of linen cloth so that I can make shirts for these children. . . ." [66]

Some of the household had been quarantined at Fagna, but as they had not shown any signs of the disease by June 9, Clarice thought they must be safe, though the family doctor, M. Stefano, still seemed rather doubtful. But she was very anxious to have some of the children's clothes from there, and wrote to ask Lorenzo's opinion. [67]

Lucrezia was at Careggi, but Clarice wanted her to come to Gagliano on a visit, and wrote on June 15 :—

" You want to know where and how we are in Gagliano. We are in the old house on the right as you enter, and we have arranged things so that, if you care to come here at any time, there will always be a room ready for you . . ." [68]

Clarice got her own way, for Poliziano was never again appointed house-tutor to her children, but a little later Piero went to stay with him at Fiesole, while the rest of the family remained at Cafaggiuolo, whither they had soon returned. During this time the little boy wrote a number of letters to his father, most of them asking for presents of some kind, especially for a pony which had been promised him. It is impossible to judge how spontaneous these letters were, but there are pieces of family news and naïve requests interspersed with pompous sentences obviously copied straight from the book, whilst some are written entirely in Latin " to show the writer's culture."

Clarice was getting very tired of the loneliness of Cafaggiuolo, and was most anxious to return to Florence, for on October 2, 1479, she wrote :—

> " I am sending you these two hares, which were caught by La Turcha early this morning, so please think of me and of your family in the Mugello when you eat them. I am very anxious to come to Florence, and if it is healthy, as you say, and unless you write to the contrary, I shall come on Monday with the whole family. . . ."[69]

Although Clarice did not take the same interest in public affairs as Lucrezia, she had her correspondents who sent her news, especially when she was away at the Baths.[70] In 1480 she was at Bagno ad Aqua when she heard of a domestic contretemps which made her write in great haste to Lucrezia :—

> " I hear from Pisa that the priest Benedetto, or rather Penechio, has pawned, if not sold, certain linen shirts, and I know not how many towels. He says he received them from you as a gift in order to sell them, but I do not know if this is true. These things were in my room at Pisa, so please let me know at once whether you gave them to him or told him to sell them, or else I shall have a very bad opinion of him. . . ."[71]

Clarice was always ailing, but she does not seem to have gone to the Baths as often as Lucrezia. Probably, being consumptive, not rheumatic, she did not derive any particular benefit from them. However in 1480 she was at Aqua, and in May, 1485, she and Lorenzo went to Bagno a Morba together. On their return journey they parted at Capitulo, and Lorenzo went to Pisa, whilst Clarice returned to Florence. We get an amusing account of the journey in a letter from Matteo Franco to Ser Piero Dovizi da Bibbiena.[72]

When Clarice's party reached Monte Castelli they were somewhat alarmed to see a party of twenty-five soldiers with shields and pikes coming towards them. However, they turned out to be an escort which had been sent to meet them, and in whose company they descended into the plain. Here they were greeted by a number of old women with faces wrinkled like chestnuts, who offered them cakes and wine. They drank on horseback and then went on to Monte Guidi. Here they met a priest in a great state of agitation, with his frock tucked up, who ran about begging them to visit him. This they did not do, nor did they enter the town of Casoli. Shortly after passing there they were joined by two of the party who remained behind, and had met Nannina, Lorenzo's sister, at Casoli in a litter, on the way to Casentino. She was very sorry not to see either Lorenzo or Clarice, the latter was equally grieved at having missed her.

The party spent the night at the little town of Colle, in the house of the brother of Antonio da Pela, who seems to have been a terrible chatterer. He had filled his house with about thirty-five of his relations whom he wanted to present to Clarice. After a while Franco intervened, as she was tired, and after they had all rested they went to see the paper works for which Colle was famous. Their supper consisted of " crisp cakes, puff pastry and trebbiano wine, salad and pickles, boiled chicken and kid, and then roast pigeons and I know not how much chicken, almond paste and boxes of sweets."

Before supper a deputation from the township of Colle waited on Clarice, and brought her presents of corn, wax, marzipan, wine and sweatmeats. They begged her to commend them to Lorenzo, for they had been much impoverished during the war of the Pazzi conspiracy when it had withstood a two months' siege. Clarice promised to do all she could for them, but refused to accept their presents.

In the evening she received a Sienese ambassador who had come to meet Lorenzo, as he did not know he had gone to Pisa.

On the following day they went by Tavernelle to Passignano, where they lunched on boiled liver and kid, broad beans, curds and good wine, and where they remained the rest of the day, inspecting the church and the surroundings.

The day after they heard Mass in the early morning and started on the San Casciano road. At Fabrica a horseman met them saying he had been sent by Piero to ask which way they were going, as on the previous day he and Giovanni had ridden as far as Impruneta to meet them. On hearing that they were going by San Casciano, he hurried off to tell the children. Near there they met Jacopo Salviati and Tommaso Corbinelli, and at the Certosa they were greeted by Piero, Giovanni, Giuliano and Giulio, who threw themselves into their mother's arms. Giuliano, who was six, asked, with a long face, " Oh, oh, where is Lorenzo ? " and to tease him they said " He has gone to Poggio to find you," and the little boy nearly cried.

In November, 1487, Clarice went to spend the winter in Rome, hoping that her native air would bring her some relief. She was accompanied by her favourite daughter, Maddalena, who was betrothed to Franceschetto Cibo, the Pope's illegitimate son. The marriage took place on November 20, but Clarice remained in Rome until the following May, when Piero came to fetch his bride, Alfonsina Orsini. The negotiations for this latter marriage had been somewhat protracted, and by the beginning of April Clarice felt that she was merely wasting time, and wrote to Lorenzo suggesting that she should return home. Lorenzo was very anxious to get the matter settled and would not hear of his wife's departure, whereupon she replied :—

"... I will be patient and stay here until the matter is settled. When I spoke of wishing to return it was because I desired to see you and the family again, not because I am in want of anything, nor that I cannot endure that desire for your benefit and convenience. As for the expense, I think I have arranged so that it will be all right, but if it is necessary to economise more, I will do so gladly as soon as I see that I must stay longer. ...

I am as usual, always between the two, sometimes well and sometimes the opposite. But on Monday and Tuesday and to-day up till now I have felt fairly well, without that blessed stomach trouble which does not let me rest. ..." [73]

While she was in Rome Clarice received a letter describing the wonderful presents sent to Lorenzo by the Sultan of Egypt. These included a lion and a giraffe, which, as Armstrong says, " became the most popular character in Florence." There were also " a fine bay horse, strange animals, sheep and goats of various colours, with long ears down to their knees, and tails trailing on the ground nearly as big as their bodies ; a large beaker of balsam, eleven sable-skins, aloe-wood . . . great vases of porcelain . . . cloth of various colours in one piece, fine dimity which they call turban cloth, cloth treated with gum which they call sexe, great vases of sweetmeats, dried plums and ginger. . . ." [74]

Clarice persuaded the Pope to let her beloved Maddalena accompany her back to Florence, and the whole party returned in the middle of May. The marriage festivities were interrupted by the death of Lorenzo's third daughter, Luigia, which followed almost immediately on that of Bianca de' Pazzi, his sister.

The bridal party therefore went to Careggi without entering Florence and remained there until S. John's Day, when wonderful festivities took place.

Clarice was very ill, but the doctors did not think she was in immediate danger, and since Lorenzo was also in very bad health they sent him to Filetta to take the baths on July 21. On July 29 Ser Piero Dovizi wrote to Lanfredini in Rome :—

> " I do not know what to tell you about Madonna Clarice. For a day or two she is better, and then she is worse again, so that she slowly approaches dissolution." [75]

She died suddenly that day, in Maddalena's arms, and though Lorenzo had never been a very devoted husband, he was sincerely grieved, as may be seen in his letters, especially the one addressed to Innocent VIII.[76]

Lorenzo was dissuaded by his friends from returning to Florence at once, and Clarice was buried in S. Lorenzo on the day of her death, without any pomp. Three days later, on August 1, a solemn funeral service was held, which was attended by the whole city. But her death was not regarded as very important by the foreigners in Florence, since it had no political significance. She had never influenced her husband in public matters, and the remarks of Messer

Aldovrandini, the Ferrarese ambassador, sum up the general attitude :—

> " I wrote that Madonna Clarice was ill. She died three days ago, but I did not send the news at once, as it did not seem to me of much importance. Now that I am despatching the courier with letters from Naples, I inform your Excellency." [77]

From first to last Clarice was the foreign bride, who was unhappy in her adopted country, and took no interest in the life of the city, nor in the favourite pursuits of her husband. She was truly pious, and though not uneducated she could not make friends with the sceptical poets and humanists who frequented the Medici palace, where she always felt out of her element. She is the least attractive of the Medici women, perhaps because she was not a Florentine, and in the fifteenth century Medici and Florence were one.

CHAPTER VII

THE YOUNGER GENERATION

CLARICE and Lorenzo had at least seven children, without counting the twins who died at birth in 1472, and the unknown child that was buried in 1475.

The three sons all played their part in Italian history. They were Piero, the ruler of Florence, who was expelled in 1494, and drowned in the Garigliano in 1503 ; Giovanni, who became Pope Leo X, and Giuliano, Duke of Nemours, who was in many ways the best of the three, though unfortunately he had not the strength to withstand his Papal brother, who had the brains of the family.

Clarice's eldest child was Lucrezia, born on August 4, 1470. She was always the elder Lucrezia's favourite, and several of her childish letters to her grandmother have survived.[1]

When Piero was eight years old he wrote a letter to his father which gives a charming picture of the little family :—

> " Giuliano thinks of laughing and naught else ; Lucrezia sews, sings and reads ; Maddalena knocks her head against the wall without hurting herself ; Luigia can already say a few words ; Contessina makes a great noise all over the house. . . . "[2]

Lucrezina, so-called in her childhood to distinguish her from the elder Lucrezia, was also her father's favourite, and was the only one of his daughters present at his deathbed.

She was married to Jacopo Salviati on September 10, 1488. Her husband was a cousin of the Archbishop Salviati who was hanged for his share in the Pazzi conspiracy, and Lorenzo arranged this marriage in order to re-establish cordial relations between the two families. After the expulsion of the Medici in 1494 the Salviati were allowed to remain, and Lucrezia became one of the leading conspirators on her family's behalf. She made no secret of her sympathies, but when cross-examined by the magistrates, said that it was only natural for her to wish for her brother's success. After the Medici restoration, her husband, Jacopo, did his best to dissuade his kinsmen from assuming despotic power, but without effect.

On the accession of Leo X, Lucrezia took up her abode in Rome, in the Medici palace in the Piazza Lombardi, where she remained until she had to vacate it in favour of Margaret of Austria, the widow of Duke Alessandro. She was a lady of somewhat fiery temper, with many protégés, for whom she sought preferment. Slanderous tongues said she trafficked in such things, but even if this is untrue, her anger knew no bounds when her demands were refused by the Pope.

The three Medici sisters were all in Rome, claiming the best of good things from their brother, and the scenes they made in the Vatican became common gossip. Alfonsina Orsini wrote to her son on February 19, 1514 :—

" I want to tell you a story that has been going round lately. Mona Lucrezia, as you know, had been promised the Priory of Capua by the Pope, and when it was given to Giuliano Ridolfi she was much grieved, and as she is not accustomed to suffer

things which displease her, she could not bear this,
but went to the Pope and complained at length.
First she complained of His Holiness, and said that
everybody wished her ill, and spoke evil of Madonna
Maddalena and of you, and said particularly that
I mocked and derided her, and that you caused
Jacopo a thousand annoyances. . . . The Pope
told me all these things, and told them also to
Madonna Maddalena, for a few days ago Contessina
made such a fuss in the house that all the Palaces
and Banks are full of it. It was about some accounts,
and Contessina persisted and would not be quiet.
This is known to the Cardinals and everybody, for
it was overheard by outsiders." [3]

Lucrezia was with Leo X when he died, and she at
once took away with her all the valuables she could
lay her hands on to save them from being pillaged
by the Roman mob, an action which did not increase
her popularity.

She had altogether eleven children : Pietro, who
died young ; Caterina, who married Francesco Nerli
of Montemurlo ; Lorenzo, a humanist and author
who married Costanza Conti of Rome ; Maria, who
married Giovanni delle Bande Nere ; Gianbattista,
who married Costanza Bardi ; Bernardo, who was
made a Cardinal by Pius IV ; Luigia ; Alamanno ;
Francesca, who became the second wife of Ottaviano
de' Medici ; Giovanni, who was made a Cardinal
by Leo X in 1517 ; and Elena, who married Giacomo
Appiano, Lord of Piombino.

Cardinal Giovanni Salviati was an important man,
but Benvenuto Cellini always called him " Il Cardinale
Bestia," and described him as looking " more like
an ass than a human being," and he seems to have
inherited his mother's temper.

175

Lucrezia kept up a copious correspondence with all her children and many grandchildren, and was profuse with good advice on every detail of their lives.

In 1527–8 Jacopo Salviati took refuge at Orvieto during the sack of Rome, and Lucrezia joined her daughter Maria, born 1492, who was in Venice with her young son Cosimo. Thence she wrote some letters to her husband which are documents of true diplomatic value. After leaving Venice Lucrezia lived in Cesena for a while, but she ended her life in Rome, where she founded a chapel in S. Maria sopra Minerva, and completed the tombs of Leo X and Clement VII, which had been left unfinished on the death of Cardinal Ippolito de' Medici.

All through her long life she seems to have enjoyed the best of health, for there is no record of any illnesses except in 1512–13 and 1530, and on December 6, 1543, at the age of seventy-three, she was able to write to her daughter Maria :—

" During the last few days I have had a little catarrh, but it did not trouble me as much as I expected, and now, by the grace of God, I am well and have risen. . . ." [4]

She lived to be over eighty, but the exact date of her death is unknown, though it must have taken place after 1550. She was buried in her own chapel of S. Maria sopra Minerva, where her tombstone may still be seen.

Clarice's third daughter, Luigia, born in 1477, is a very shadowy figure, and has been confused with her own niece, the daughter of Piero and Alfonsina, who was also called Luigia, and died in 1494. The elder Luigia died in 1488, just after her betrothal to Giovanni de' Medici, one of the other branch of the family. After the fall of the Medici, calumny suggested that she had been poisoned at the instigation of her brother Piero, who disliked the match. There is, however, no evidence for this, and Pieraccini thinks she was probably consumptive, like her mother and her brother Giuliano.

The youngest daughter was Contessina, who was born at Pistoia in 1478. When he was at the Baths in 1489 Lorenzo wrote to her :—

" My Contessina. I hear that you ask about me every hour, how I am and when I shall return, so I write to tell you that, by the grace of God, I am very well, and I hope, if it pleases God, to return as well as ever I, was. I shall come back soon, and in a few days I shall be there to see you. Take care that I find you well and cheerful, so pray to God for me, and caress Alfonsina and stay with her, and tell her from me to make much of the baby. I hear that Monsignore and the other children went away early. They did not do well to leave you all alone, but I shall soon be back, and they can stay in the country by themselves. . . . Salute your Piero and Niccolo and all the others from me when you see them." [5]

She was betrothed to Piero Ridolfi at a very early age, and in a letter of 1490 addressed to Lorenzo we read :—

" . . . Contessina is at Casa Ridolfi, and is as pale as usual, or even more so. When you return I will tell you the opinion of one who knows her affairs, which will not displease you." [6]

In the same year she went to the baths of Vignone with her brother, Piero, who wrote to his father :—

" Contessina is well ; she has already had three syrups and is purging herself." [7]

Her marriage took place on May 24, 1494, and on the expulsion of the Medici from Florence in the same year Contessina and her husband were allowed to remain, though after the execution of her father-in-law, Niccolo Ridolfi, in 1497, as a Medicean conspirator, the possessions of the Ridolfi family were confiscated, and the young couple lived in poverty for a time.

Contessina had three sons, Luigi, Niccolo and Lorenzo, and two daughters, Emilia and Clarice, as well as two other children who died in infancy.

Luigi was a very ordinary man, who married the granddaughter of Piero Soderini, the Gonfalonier, and in 1512 he took part in the coronation procession of Leo X. A certain doctor Gian Giacomo Penni was present during these festivities, and wrote a long and interesting letter of description to Contessina in Florence.[8]

Lorenzo was a man of considerable talent, but the most important member of the family was Niccolo, who was made a Cardinal by Leo X, and also greatly favoured by Clement VII. He was Archbishop of Florence and Salerno, and held many other sees at different times, including that of Vicenza, where he built the front of the beautiful episcopal palace. He kept a splendid court and collected gems and antiques, and was one of the most cultured men of his generation. Only his unexpected death on January 20, 1550, prevented his election to the Papacy on the death of Paul III.

Soon after the accession of Leo X Contessina went to Rome, and she died there on June 30, 1515, and was buried in the church of S. Agostino, though no trace of her grave remains.

Clarice's favourite child was her second daughter, Maddalena, who was born on July 25, 1473. Lorenzo once described her as " the eye of her mother's head."

PLATE VIII

Maddalena Cibo.   Portrait by unknown artist.

[face p. 178

She was beautiful and accomplished, but she inherited her mother's consumptive tendency, and though apparently destined to great things, her life was not happy.

When she was a child at Cafaggiuolo, in 1479, Maddalena dictated a letter to her grandmother, Lucrezia:—

> " I would like you to send me a doll, if you can, for I should like to have one like Lucrezia, and I will make it a pretty dress. Please also send some sweets." [9]

But for this one glimpse we do not catch sight of her until negotiations are begun for her marriage. Lorenzo was very anxious to get his second son, Giovanni, made a Cardinal, and he therefore suggested to Innocent VIII that he would marry his daughter, Maddalena, to the Pope's illegitimate son, Franceschetto Cibo, and give her a magnificent dowry.

Maddalena was barely fifteen, and Franceschetto was forty years old, dull, heavy and uninteresting, and an inveterate gambler, but at least he was not such a profligate as the Papal nephews of the previous reign.

The negotiations for the marriage took some time, as, though Lorenzo was prepared to give his daughter a handsome dowry, the Pope did not seem inclined to make a corresponding settlement on his son. Innocent was not an exemplary pontiff, but at any rate he did not despoil the Church for the benefit of his family as his predecessors had done. Lorenzo, however, did not want a pauper for a son-in-law, and, though he himself was probably the most high-minded statesman in Italy at the time, he had no scruples about asking for a settlement for Franceschetto.[10]

The negotiations were carried on by Lanfredini, Lorenzo's agent in Rome, and in March, 1487, the marriage contract was drawn up, whilst the betrothal was solemnised in May. The bride's dowry consisted in four thousand ducats in cash, the reversion of the Pazzi palace in Florence, and the Pazzi villa at Montughi, and Lorenzo's own estate at Spedaletto, and, of course, a magnificent trousseau. Lorenzo also bought the county of Anguillara, and had some difficulty in finding all the money, for the Pope had hurried matters in the end, and the dowry was extremely large. The average sum given to a wealthy Florentine girl at this time was fifteen hundred ducats, whilst Lorenzo only gave his other daughters two thousand.[11]

Franceschetto Cibo was born in Naples in 1449, when his father was only seventeen years of age. The name of his mother is unknown, but he had a younger sister, named Teodorina, who married into the Genoese family of Usodimare. Francesco himself remained in obscurity until his father's accession to the Papacy, but he then became Governor of Rome and Captain-General of the Church, and was given the right of legitimising bastards. Later in life Leo X made him Governor of Spoleto, while the Emperor Frederick III made him a Count of the Empire. His possessions were scattered among many Italian cities, and he thus acquired the citizenship of Venice, Florence, Pisa, Volterra and Viterbo.

He was both stupid and avaricious, and spent his nights in debauchery, on one occasion gambling away fourteen thousand ducats to Cardinal Raffaelle Riario in one night.

Although Maddalena was formally betrothed in May, 1487, she was still so young that Lorenzo wished to postpone the marriage for a time. But in October he wrote to Lanfredini :—

" My wife Clarice has half decided to visit her relations to see what effect the Roman air will have, for, as you know, this does not suit her in winter. A short time ago you spoke of a wish that Maddalena should come there. If this is still the case she could conveniently accompany her mother. These are at present our own ideas, which you can tell to the Pope and Signor Francesco, and if they agree, it shall be done, otherwise not." [12]

On November 4 Maddalena and her mother, accompanied by Piero, by Jacopo Salviati and by Gentile Becchi, Bishop of Urbino, left for Rome, where the marriage was solemnised with great pomp and circumstance. Just before she left Lorenzo wrote a letter of good advice to Maddalena, in which he said :—

" Remember the sacredness of the place where you are, and what the Roman people expect of you. Consider that, while it is shameful to neglect your duties, it is honorable to perform them well, and do not forget that your first duty is to please the Pope and to cherish your husband." [13]

On arriving in Rome the party was met outside the gates by the bridegroom, accompanied by various members of the Papal household, and most of the Florentine colony. They were conducted to the Leonine city where Franceschetto had a house which had been built by his uncle Maurice. At the head of the procession rode the Papal servants, the retainers of the Medici and those of the ambassadors. Then came Franceschetto riding between Piero de' Medici and Jacopo Salviati, followed by Maddalena between the Archbishop of Cosenza and the Bishop of Oria, and Clarice between the Bishop of Roveredo, who was acting as the Milanese ambassador, and the Bishop of Volterra.

On November 18 the Pope entertained the bridal

couple at a sumptuous banquet, and gave Maddalena a jewel valued at eight thousand ducats, and another worth two thousand to his son. The actual marriage took place on November 20, after which most of the Florentines returned home. Clarice remained in Rome all through the winter, and when she thought of returning to Florence in the spring, she wanted Maddalena to accompany her, for she was a sick woman, and felt that her daughter was very young to be left alone in Rome. Lorenzo therefore wrote to Lanfredini :—

" I hear what you say about Clarice, which grieves me, though her illness is no news to me. I have written to tell her the reason why Piero may be delayed for a little while, but she need not consider this if she thinks it better to return, though I should have liked her to wait for Alfonsina. I should like Maddalena to accompany her, for she is but a child, and her husband's house is in disorder, and it would be a comfort to Clarice. . . . If Signor Francesco would like to come and visit this place at the feast of San Giovanni, or at any other time . . . I should be glad. . . . It seems that in this matter, and the others that concern his son, His Holiness is acting very coldly, and so far he has had great difficulty in getting the little he has. I am sorry, not only for the sake of Signor Francesco, but because my daughter has to be stinted. . . ." [14]

Most of Maddalena's Florentine friends and servants had returned home after the wedding, but a few faithful retainers remained with her. Among these was Matteo Franco, who was nominally appointed as her chaplain, but who seems to have performed the most diverse functions. On the journey to Rome he acted as paymaster. caterer and courier for Clarice, who said :—

" I will not allow any man to have the spending of my money but Franco ; and I will eat nothing but what has passed through his hands."

Among Franceschetto's possessions was the little township of Stigliano, thirty miles from Rome and eight from Bracciano, and seven hundred metres above sea-level. This little place was noted for its mineral springs, and was largely patronised by the Roman nobility, though it had been allowed to get into a very bad state of repair. On his marriage Franceschetto decided to give the income from the Baths to Maddalena, but as it was not great, he sent Franco there to put matters in order, for he thought him the best business man in his entourage. Maddalena was anxious that Franco should accompany her back to Florence, to act as her chaplain and secretary, but her husband would not hear of this, but kept him to look after Stigliano. We get an account of his labours in a letter to his friend, Ser Piero Dovizi :—

" I have already built the bridges, churches and hospitals, for there was nothing, and I have arranged these Baths in the Tuscan fashion. The place is filthy, so that Bagno a Morba is a Careggi in comparison. The air is accursed, the men are Turks, and everything is of the worst. Day and night I struggle with bandits and soldiers and thieves ; with poisonous dogs, lepers, Jews, madmen, fools and Romans." [15]

But all this work bore good fruit, and visitors came from far and near, as many as a hundred or a hundred and fifty in a day, so that Franco hoped to make a profit of at least four hundred ducats for his adored young mistress.

After considerable discussion Franceschetto allowed

Maddalena to return to Florence with her mother, though he would not let Franco accompany them. Piero came to Rome to fetch Clarice, and took his bride, Alfonsina Orsini, back with him. Magnificent festivities had been arranged for May 22 in Florence, but these had to be postponed owing to the sudden death of Luigia de' Medici, which took place just before the arrival of the bridal party. Therefore, instead of going to the Via Larga, they went straight to Careggi, where they remained for a month. In the middle of June Franceschetto Cibo joined his wife, and the feast of San Giovanni was celebrated with all the magnificence that had been customary before the Pazzi conspiracy. The city was sumptuously decorated, and a wonderful " Trionfo " was staged for the benefit of the populace, whilst Franceschetto was knighted with the ancient pomp and ceremony.[16]

He was accompanied by a large retinue of Roman gentlemen, who were entertained by various leading citizens, though Cibo himself was Lorenzo's guest. He was much struck with the simplicity that prevailed in the Medici palace, and feared that his friends would get a bad impression of Florentine hospitality. They, however, reassured him, saying that they were magnificently entertained. He therefore put the matter before Lorenzo, who explained to him that it was the Florentine custom to entertain guests and strangers in a splendid manner, but that as he was now a member of the family, he was treated without ceremony.[17]

Clarice was very ill, and most anxious to keep her favourite daughter by her side, so Lorenzo persuaded the Pope to send his son on a mission to Perugia, and allow Maddalena to remain in Florence with her mother. She was with her when she died, and did not leave for Rome until September 4, when she was accompanied by a certain Madonna Maria de' Medici. Piero and his great-uncle Giovanni Tornabuoni, accompanied her as far as Aquapendente, but after that she was left almost without any Florentine friends. She was not happy in Rome, for although she adored her spend-thrift husband, he neglected her, and her health was not good, and she was very often pregnant.

She had at least seven children : Lucrezia, born in Rome in 1489, who died three years later ; Clarice, a cripple, born in 1490, died 1492 ; Innocenzo, born in Florence on August 26, 1491, who later became a Cardinal ; Lorenzo, who married Riccarda Malospina and through her obtained the Marquisate of Massa and Carrara ; Caterina, who became the famous Duchess of Camerino ; Ippolita, who married the Count of Caiazzo, and Giambattista.

All through her life in Rome Matteo Franco was Maddalena's most devoted servant. He was not only her chaplain, her secretary and her man of affairs, but he nursed her when she was ill, and wrote to Florence complaining of her husband's neglect and asking Lorenzo to make his son-in-law behave properly.

We have a series of letters from Franco to his friend, Ser Piero Dovizi, written during one of Maddalena's pregnancies, full of the most intimate medical details, and giving an account of the treatment and diet advised by the doctors. Invalids were always fed on pounded chicken, but Franco says that Maddalena got tired of it, which is hardly surprising if she had no variety.[18]

The summers of 1490 and 1491 Maddalena spent in Florence, when two of her children, Clarice and Inno-cenzo, were born. After the death of Pope Innocent she and her husband went to live first at Anguillara, and then in Florence, but as they were not well received by Piero, they moved to Pisa, where they remained after the expulsion of the Medici from

Florence. They also spent some time in Genoa, but they were very poor, and in 1497 Franceschetto tried to sell to the Venetians a fragment of the True Cross. In order not to seem to be trafficking in Holy Things, and in order to preserve his dignity, he said :—

" I wished to present the Signory with this sacred relic, but in recompense I desired a present, not a payment of money." [19]

After the death of Pope Alexander VI, Maddalena and her husband and children returned to Rome, and on the accession of Leo X her son Innocenzo was made a Cardinal, and her husband governor of Spoleto. He died on July 25, 1519, and she followed him to the grave on December 1 of the same year, and was buried in S. Peter's.

Lorenzo himself had married one of the Roman Orsini, but the marriage had not been a great success, so that it is surprising that he should seek a bride for his son from the same family. In 1488 he wrote to Lanfredini, possibly in a moment of irritation :—

" The brains of these Orsini citizens are of a strange and peculiar nature . . . they are greedy and ambitious, and if not kept in order by necessity, they are unstable." [20]

But Lorenzo's foreign policy was based on the Neapolitan alliance, and he therefore sought a wife from there for his son. He could not aspire to a member of the Royal family, but found a girl who was greatly favoured by the King. This was Alfonsina, the daughter of Roberto Orsini, who had been Grand Constable of Naples, and had been generally known as the " Cavaliere senza Paura." He had been twice married, his first wife bearing him five daughters, and his second, Caterina d' Amerigo di San Severino, two girls, Maria and Alfonsina. The latter was born in 1472.

The alliance was valuable politically, in cementing the friendship with the Neapolitan Court, but it also had its financial side. The Neapolitan Orsini were deeply in debt to the Medici, but this was remitted at the time of the marriage.

Before the matter was finally settled Lorenzo gave his brother-in-law, Bernardo Rucellai, the Florentine ambassador in Naples, instructions to see the girl and report. He wrote :—

> " She does not seem to be particularly good or bad, but I rather dislike her throat, which is somewhat thick at the back. If it were in proportion it would not matter. . . . She does not displease me, for if she is only thirteen years of age, as our friend tells me, she is not small. Her arms, which are usually a guide to the legs, are good, and also her hands. She seems to be straight, but about this and her height I will tell you another time. Her skin is good and she has a good natural colour. Her eyes are light, but not unpleasantly so ; she has a good nose, and her mouth, though a little heavy, is not enough to destroy her charm. . . ." [21]

The negotiations, as usual, took some time, but eventually the dowry was fixed at twelve thousand ducats, though popular rumour increased it to thirty thousand. The marriage, by proxy, as befitted a semi-Royal bride, was celebrated with great pomp in the Royal Palace of Naples in February, 1488. The King and Queen and the whole Court were present, and Ferdinand, partly out of compliment to Lorenzo and partly out of affection for the bride, put off the mourning he wore for his son.

In May Piero went to Rome to meet his wife, and

spent some time there in festivity, after which they returned to Florence. Great rejoicings had been prepared for their arrival, but these were cut short by the sudden death of Luigia de' Medici, and Alfonsina was taken straight to Careggi.

For the feast of San Giovanni, however, Lorenzo laid aside his mourning, and a magnificent ball was given in honour of the bride, which was attended by all the ambassadors of the foreign Powers.

Alfonsina had three children: Lorenzo, born on September 2, 1489; Clarice; and Luigia, who was born in 1493 but died young.

Piero was proud and headstrong, but he was also a fool, and possibly, without his wife's influence, he might not have made himself so well-hated by the Florentines. His ancestors had striven for power without showing it, but he wished to be a tyrant without having the necessary means at his disposal. He was not content to be the first citizen of a republic, but wanted to rule in name as well as in fact. In this he was supported by Alfonsina, who was not only proud herself, but had been brought up in the feudal atmosphere of the Neapolitan Court. When the Florentines began to murmur at Piero's high-handed doings, his wife counselled him not to conciliate the grumblers, but to assert himself. But she tried, on occasion, to dissuade her husband from his more foolish actions, and it was without her knowledge that he yielded the fortresses to the French King.

When the three Medici brothers were forced to flee, Alfonsina herself remained in Florence, and begged Charles VIII to restore her husband and son to their native city. The King was quite willing to do this, and bade Piero return under his protection, but the latter, acting on the interested advice of his Venetian hosts, refused the invitation.

In the treaty signed by Charles and the Signory of Florence on November 26, 1494, it was agreed that Alfonsina's dowry should be restored to her, and that her infant son, who had been smuggled out of the city in a basket and taken to Urbino, should be allowed to return to Florence.

Piero met Charles in Rome, but did not accompany him to Naples. Instead he tried to re-enter Florence. He collected a small force and was joined in Siena by Alfonsina, who had escaped from Florence disguised as a nun. But the attempt was abortive, chiefly owing to Piero's incompetence and mismanagement. Henceforth he gave himself up to a life of debauchery, though his wife still worked for a return from exile. Another attempt was made in 1497, but this also ended ignominiously.

Piero was drowned in the Garigliano in 1503, but Alfonsina was not greatly troubled thereby. What little affection she may originally have had for him was killed during the years of futile plots and debauchery in exile. After her husband's death she was allowed to return to Florence to claim her dowry, but she continued to live in Rome. There, in 1508, she arranged a marriage between her daughter Clarice and Filippo Strozzi the younger.

Piero's brother, Cardinal Giovanni, was now the head of the family, and with the help of the Pope and of Spain he was able to re-establish the Medici in Florence in 1512, and his young nephew, Lorenzo, became almost the head of the State.

Alfonsina was not content with this, but desired the Dukedom of Piombino and the rule over Siena for her son, and at the same time she strove to arrange a marriage which should bring the family both political advantages and wealth. Position without money she despised, as she showed in her remarks on the marriage of Giuliano with Filiberta of Savoy. She brought no dowry because she was the niece of the French King, and his alliance and friendship were supposed to be sufficient, much to Alfonsina's disgust. She wrote to her son :—

"... the dowry will be 100,000 ducats, which His Holiness will have to pay, for all the other brides of this house have received 100,000 ducats from the Duke of Savoy, and now Giuliano gives her the same in order to get her, and in my opinion he is a great simpleton." [22]

At the same time she discussed the possibilities of a marriage between Lorenzo and one of the nieces of Raimondo da Cardona. She was greatly in favour of this because she hoped that the bride would bring her husband

" a state in the Kingdom [Naples] with an income of 10,000 ducats, and lands bearing the title of Duke and Prince, and one of the seven Royal offices, which have a good income and great dignity." [23]

Lorenzo was in Florence, acting as the head of the State, but Alfonsina remained in Rome, whence she kept up a copious correspondence with her son. She may almost be said to have ruled Florence by letter.

Piero had been a great lover of tournaments and feats of arms, and in 1514 Lorenzo wished to emulate his father and organise a tournament on a splendid scale. But Alfonsina would not allow him to take part himself because she feared he might be injured. She made her secretary tell him that

" she recommends that you should rather engage others in the contest and stand by and enjoy the entertainment ; thereby consulting your own safety and preserving the hopes of your family." [24]

In 1516 the Pope called on Florence to supply him with seven hundred armed men to fight against Francis I of France. Alfonsina managed to get the command of this force for Lorenzo, but she was shrewd enough to see that the Spanish alliance was unpopular in Florence. Lorenzo went to Bologna on August 16, 1516, leaving Florentine affairs in his mother's hands. Two days later she wrote to him :—

"I beg you to consider that the King is in Italy with eighty thousand men, and that this city is most devoted to the French crown. I also remind you that because Piero was obstinate and insisted on his own opinion we spent nineteen years away from home."

Francis had made himself supreme in Italy almost without striking a blow, and it behoved Florence to make peace with him. The Pope asked Alfonsina to select the Florentine ambassadors to the King, but as she also wished Lorenzo to send him a private envoy who should arrive before his colleagues, she managed to detain them for several days in Florence.

Alfonsina watched the progress of the war anxiously and even sent Lorenzo advice as to its conduct. When negotiations for peace were begun after the battle of Marignano, she was considered sufficiently important to be furnished with a copy of the proposed terms, but these did not meet with her unqualified approval, and she expressed her views in her usual distinct manner. It was eventually arranged that Francis and Leo should meet and settle all outstanding questions in person. Alfonsina was very anxious for this meeting to take place in Florence, whilst Lorenzo preferred Bologna, and much correspondence passed between mother and son on the subject. Alfonsina was far-seeing and invariably knew her own mind, but she did not seek to impose her will by force, but by persuasion. She is not an attractive character, but she compels our admiration for her statesmanlike qualities and her inflexibility of purpose.

Bologna was eventually chosen for the meeting-place of Pope and King, but as Leo signified his intention of passing through Florence, enormous preparations were made for his reception, whilst Alfonsina now conceived the idea of getting her son made Duke of Urbino. On November 3, 1515, she wrote to him :—

"It will be enough for me if the Pope will come here and stay a month or so, and that you will be here too, for thus we may pass the time happily, and the King's friendship may last, so that we may yet obtain a state, and my idea would be Urbino."

Alfonsina had some difficulty in persuading the Pope to attack Urbino, for the scheme was opposed by Giuliano, who could not forget the kindness shown him by the Duke during the years of his exile. But soon after his death a Papal army invaded the state, the Duke fled, and Lorenzo was proclaimed as his successor.

Alfonsina was overjoyed, and although she remained in Florence she regulated all her son's actions, for she was the better statesman of the two. The Copialettere of her secretary, Goro Gheri, has come down to us, and shows the interest she took in everything, down to the smallest detail.

Even the Dukedom of Urbino did not satisfy Alfonsina, who wanted to make of Lorenzo another Cæsar Borgia, to rule over the whole Romagna. On Giuliano's death he was made Captain-General of the Church, but did not receive any other new titles, much to Alfonsina's disgust.

The question of Lorenzo's marriage was also much to the fore. Various brides had been proposed at different times, and Alfonsina was most anxious for the daughter of Gonsalvo da Cordova because she had a large dowry. She told her son that though Gonsalvo had only " blood of medium nobility," he could boast of the " nobility of valour " and he was wealthy, a virtue which, in her eyes, covered a multitude of sins. For, after her love for her son, the love of money was the ruling passion of Alfonsina's life. In one place she quotes S. Jerome as saying that " love comes from the dowry."

The Pope, however, veered from a Spanish to a French alliance, and this wealthy bride was not for Lorenzo. He was now Captain-General of the Florentines, Duke of Urbino, Prefect of Rome and Governor of Fano, but he was not popular with his subjects, partly owing to his own tyrannical ways, and partly because he so often left his mother, and her secretary, Goro Gheri, in supreme authority.

Francesco Maria della Rovere, the rightful Duke of Urbino, went to war to recover his patrimony, and after a preliminary defeat he was largely successful. Alfonsina remained in Rome, but she was in daily correspondence with her son, so that she almost conducted the campaign, which was, however, disastrous for the Medici. At the siege of Monforte Lorenzo was wounded in the head and not expected to live, but a successful trepanning operation at Ancona saved him, and he soon recovered. His mother was kept in ignorance of his condition until he was out of danger.

Since the French alliance was now in force, Lorenzo asked the King to find him a wife, and Francis offered him one of the daughters of Jean d'Albret. But the Pope was more in favour of a marriage with Madeleine de la Tour d'Auvergne, the daughter of Jean, Count of Auvergne and Boulogne, and Jeanne, the daughter of the Duke of Vendome.

The bride was a beautiful girl of seventeen, nearly related both to the King of France and the Bourbons. Her dowry consisted of an annual income of six thousand gold ducats, as well as another five thousand derived from the County of Dives, and the Dukedom of Valentinois. The presents received by the young couple were sumptuous, and were valued at more than thirty thousand ducats. Included among them was a state-bed composed of tortoise-shell, mother-of-pearl, and other costly materials, and all together thirty-six horses were required to convey the gifts and the bride's trousseau to Paris.

Lorenzo appointed Vettori as his proxy and the marriage was solemnized on January 25, 1518. In honour of the occasion Alfonsina held magnificent receptions in Florence, which were attended by all the citizens, and on March 22 Lorenzo set out for France. Immediately on his arrival he stood godfather to the young Dauphin, and on May 22 he married Madeleine amid great pomp and rejoicing. The young couple remained at the French Court until August, when they left for Florence. They rested for a few days at Poggio a Cajano and Cafaggiuolo, and on September 7 they made a solemn entry into the city. They were accompanied by all the leading citizens, including the Florentine Cardinals, Cibo and de' Rossi; and Madeleine, who, magnificently dressed in the German style, was the cynosure of all eyes. On her arrival at the palace in the Via Larga she was graciously received by Alfonsina, and grand festivities were held. According to Soriano, the Venetian ambassador in Rome, the whole journey to France cost at least two hundred thousand ducats.

Soon after her son's return, Alfonsina became seriously ill, and suffered acutely from a gastric ulcer for four months. After that she seemed well again, but it was probably a recurrence of the same trouble which killed her, less than two years later.

Lorenzo did not remain long in Florence but went to Rome, leaving his young wife in the care of his mother, though he kept up a copious correspondence with her during his absence.

On April 15, 1519, Madeleine gave birth to a daughter in the palace in the Via Larga, but died herself a few days later, on April 28. Alfonsina was present at the birth of the child, and carried it to her son, who was very ill with fever in another part of the palace. The baby was named Caterina, and in fullness of time she became Queen of France.

Lorenzo had led a dissolute life, both before and after his marriage, so that he was worn out with disease when still quite a young man. In addition to this he contracted consumption, possibly by infection from his uncle Giuliano. During his illness he turned against his mother and became utterly unreasonable and violent. He insisted on riding from Careggi to Poggio a Cajano, where he arrived more dead than alive. His mother summoned all the best doctors in Italy, and followed him, but he received her very badly, and promptly had himself carried back to Florence, where he died on May 4.

After his death Alfonsina had nothing left to live for. In June, 1519, she spent some time at Vallombrosa, and then went to Rome, where she died on February 7, 1520.

Alfonsina was the masculine woman, and in a sense the evil genius of the Medici family. But for her Florence might have been spared many troubles, but one cannot help admiring her resolute character and her statesmanlike ability. Lorenzo was a fool, like his father, and but for his mother, he would never have been able to maintain himself in Florence or Urbino.

CONCLUSION

CONTESSINA the housewife, Lucrezia the help-meet, Clarice the foreign wife, Alfonsina the clever but unsympathetic ruler—thus they pass before us during a hundred years of Medicean history. They did not directly help to shape events, but they influenced their men folk, and the glimpses we get of them through the mists of time are not without interest. We see them looking after their households, concerned about their children, going to the Baths, taking part in festivities and helping the poor and afflicted.

It has been said that the future lies in the hands of women, but a true understanding of the life of the past can only be obtained by a study of the women who flit shadowily through the pages of history.

NOTES

CHAPTER I

[1] Ross & Erichsen, *The Story of Pisa*. London, 1909.

CHAPTER II

[1] There has been much controversy about this work, which has been ascribed both to Leo Battista Alberti and Agnolo Pandolfini, and it is probable that the one re-wrote and slightly altered the work of the other. But for the present purpose the question of authorship is immaterial.

[2] *Della Famiglia di L. B. Alberti*. Milan, p. 229 *et seq.*

[3] Quoted by W. Boulting, *Woman in Italy*. London, 1910, pp. 150–151.

[4] I. del Lungo, *La Donna Fiorentina del Buon Tempo Antico*, Florence, 1906.

These instructions for female behaviour were very common all over Europe during the Middle Ages, and a large number of them have been collected and analysed in A. A. Hentsch *La Littérature didactique du moyen âge, s'adressant spécialement aux femmes*, Cahors, 1903.

[5] I. del Lungo, *op. cit.*

In another place Sacchetti says :—

" The most skilful painters and sculptors count as nothing against women, neither their faces nor their limbs remain as God made them. Some of their dresses are cut low enough to show the armpit ; then in a jump their collars stick above their ears. Girls that once went about in a modest way have cut their hoods down to a cap now, and wear a collar with all sorts of little beasts dangling down into their bosoms. As for sleeves, they are as fat as mattresses. Was anything more destructive or useless ever invented ? Can a woman lift a glass with these things on, or remove anything from the table without soiling both sleeves and tablecloth, not to speak of upsetting the vessels ? They squeeze their waists in too, cover their arms with their tails and their throats with their hoods. But to talk about these women, beginning with the train, is never to come to an end. Then they pile their hair high enough to reach the roof. Some curl it, some plaster it down, others powder it ; it is enough to make one sick.''

CHAPTER III

[1] A large eighteenth century tome entitled *Chronologica Series Simulacrorum Regiae Familiae Mediciae Centum apud Jos. Allegrini*, Florentia, 1761, contains portraits of all members of the Medici family. These include Lisa Donati from the Orsini Museum and Giacoma Spini from Cafaggiuolo, but it is most improbable that these are reproductions from authentic portraits.

[2] *Purgatorio*, Canto xxiv. (Cary's Translation).

> ". . . he whose guilt is most,
> Passes before my vision, dragg'd at heels
> Of an infuriate beast. Toward the vale
> Where guilt hath no redemption, on it speeds
> Each step increasing swiftness on the last ;
> Until a blow it strikes, that leaveth him
> A corse most vilely shattered."

[3] *Paradiso*, Canto iii.

> " I from the world, to follow her, when young
> Escaped ; and, in her vesture mantling me,
> Made promise of the way her sect enjoins.
> Thereafter men, for ill than good more apt,
> Forth snatch'd me from the pleasant cloister's pale."

[4] Janet Ross, *Lives of the Early Medici, as told in their Correspondence*. London, 1910, p. 6. The letter is quoted from Cavalcanti, *Istorie Fiorentine*.

[5] These two younger sons are mentioned by Litta, but not by Marsuppini.

[6] W. Bode, *Florentine Sculptors of the Renaissance*, Eng. Trans. London, 1908, p. 23, n. 2. " From Brunelleschi's *Denunzia de' Beni*, as well as from Buggiano's for the year 1433, we learn that the former held in trust for his adopted son a sum of 200 gold florins, the remuneration for various works in marble, among which are mentioned an altar and a tomb commissioned by Cosimo de' Medici. That this altar was the ornate one in the Sacristy of S. Lorenzo, C. Von Fabriczy correctly surmised, but that he failed to recognise the tomb under the table of the Sacristy as that of Cosimo's parents was entirely due to a constantly repeated tradition, nowhere confirmed, that made it the work of Donatello. Yet this sarcophagus, by its clumsy outlines, and its uncouth, bloated putti, is particularly characteristic of Buggiano's methods—strongly influenced by Donatello, certainly, whom Buggiano followed closely in those early days of his career."

CHAPTER IV

[1] Quoted by E. L. S. Horsburgh, *Lorenzo the Magnificent*. London, 1908, p. 68.

[2] B. Felice, *Donne Medicee avanti il Principato*, Rassegna Nazionale. Dec., 1905, *et seq.*

[3] Quoted by K. D. Ewart, *Cosimo de' Medici*. London, 1899, p. 46.

[4] Quoted by Ewart, *op. cit.* p. 57.

[5] Ross, *op. cit.* 31.

[6] *Archivio Mediceo avanti Principato*, filza xi., n. 233 (mod. 228).

[7] *Ibid.*, cxxxviii. 21.

[8] *Ibid.*, cxlviii. 3.

[9] *Ibid.*, xvi. 8 (mod. 9).

[10] *Ibid.*, viii. 336 (mod. 355).

[11] G. Pieraccini, *La Stirpe de' Medici di Cafaggiuolo.* Florence, 1925, p. 37.

[12] *Archivio Mediceo avanti Principato*, ix. 537.

[13] B. Felice, *op. cit.*

[14] Ross, *op. cit.*, p. 47. The Florentine year began on March 25, which fact is liable to lead to chronological complications.

[15] *Archivio Mediceo avanti Principato*, Av. v. 274 (mod. v. 520).

[16] *Ibid.*, Av. v. 278 (mod. v. 524).

[17] *VII Lettere di Contessina Bardi de' Medici ai figliuoli Piero e Giovanni.* Florence, 1886.

[18] *Archivio Mediceo avanti Principato*, ix. 262 (mod. ix. 263).

[19] *VII Lettere, op. cit.*

[20] *Ibid.*

[21] *Ibid.*

[22] *Ibid.*

[23] *Ibid.*

[24] *Archivio Mediceo avanti Principato*, c. ins. viii., n. 53.

[25] *Ibid.*, xvii. 124 (mod. xvii. 118).

[26] *Ibid.*, cvi. ins. 21, n. 7.

[27] *Ibid.*, ix. 147 (mod. 150).

[28] *Ibid.*, ix. 152 (mod. ix. 155).

[29] *Ibid.*, cxxxvii. 68.

[30] *Ibid.*, cxxxvii. 70.

" I am writing to you by Agnol Tani to tell you that Piero has sent several masters to Fiesole to see if that wall cannot be mended, since he understood that it was to be done without you. They have in fact opened the foundations to see what could be done, and Piero says he wants to understand the whole matter very well before they do anything, for he says such things must not be done in a hurry. The stuff from Careggi arrived the same day. Oh, if I could have written that I had seen a line from your hand. Cosimo and the others are well, and Cosimino is so without doubt. About myself I say nothing, for I am as well as may be. No more now. May Christ guard you.

August 3, 1455.

GINEVRA.

To Giovanni di Coximo de Medici in Milan."

[31] *Ibid.*, cvi. ins. 13, n. 6.

[32] *Ibid.*, vi. 239.

[33] *Ibid.*, vi. 289 & 289 *bis.*

[34] *Archivio Med. Mediceo avanti Principato*, lxxxv. 6.

[35] *Ibid.*, ix. 382.

[36] *Ibid.*, cvi. ins. 21, c. 9.

[37] *VII Lettere, op. cit.*

[38] *Archivio Mediceo avanti Principato*, xvii. 352.

[39] *Ibid.*, x. 413.

[40] Quoted by Ewart, *op. cit.*, p. 205.

[41] Fabroni, *Magni Cosmi Medicis Vita.* Pisa, 1789.

[42] Baccini, *Le Ville Medicee di Cafaggiuolo e Trebbio.* Florence, 1897.

[43] B. Felice, *op. cit.*

[44] Baccini, *op. cit.*

[45] *Archivio Mediceo avanti Principato*, xxi. 248.

" It is a just thing to apply to those in whom one has firm hope. I have heard that your son Lorenzo has been chosen as ambassador to His Holiness the Pope, and as I have two sons of almost the same age, and as I always wish to do that which will please you, I am sending one to you, begging that he may take him with him as a page, or a servant or a relative, or in any other way he thinks fit. And since there is no better way of approaching the son than through his mother, I send him to you, begging you to ask him to take him if he is taking any outsiders. If his party is complete, I beg you to give him as a page to your Giuliano, or whoever you like, so that he may learn manners through your help, for he is apt, and if he remains here, he is wasting time. I am sorry to trouble you, but it grieves me to see him apt and to be unable to help him unless you are moved to pity and compassion for him. I beg you for the love of God not to abandon him, for he is good and wishes to do well, and God will give you grace and reward you for me. I know that you are informed as to my condition, so I will not remind you of it, and you need not consider his lineage, for I know you will not put him in anything but an honourable position. I give him to you entirely, and, since you would accept the gift of a dog, so all the more you must accept the gift of a person. I beg of you to do with him exactly as you please. May the Almighty keep you in happiness.

In Vernio September 21, 1471. Your ALEXANDER DI VERNIO.

To the Magnificent and Generous Lady Contessina wife of Cosimo de' Medici, honoured as a mother. Florence."

CHAPTER V

[1] C. Guasti, *Lettere di una Gentildonna Fiorentina del secolo xv ai figliuoli esuli.* Florence, 1877, p. 23, n. 1.

[2] *Archivio Mediceo avanti Principato*, xvi. 30 (mod. 32).

[3] *Ibid.*, lxxx. 109.

" My wise and honourable sister. You know how much I love you for many reasons. I have written you ever so many letters, and have not had a reply to one of them. Then Piero left here and I sent you another by him. Thinking that you knew we were all well, I told you there was no need of an answer. So if I have delayed in writing, you must not think it was from forgetfulness for I love you all more than I can say. But I have sent you so many letters without receiving an answer that I thought they did not please you. So every day I have been wondering about you and everybody, but as I knew you were all well, I put off writing. We are all well here, and so are all your people. Cosimo's hand pains him, but he looks well.

When you get this, I think Piero will have arrived. I commend myself to him, and to Giovanni and to everybody. Bless Lorenzo and Bianca and Nannina from me and kiss them. Vagia commends herself to you, and Mona Ginevra. I have no more to tell you. May Christ keep you happy.
January 5, 1450 (1451) in Florence.

MARABOTTO DI F. TORNABUONI.

To the Virtuous Lady . . . Luchrezia, wife of Piero di Chosimo de Medici in Volterra.''

⁴ G. Levantini-Pieroni, *Lucrezia Tornabuoni*. Florence, 1888, p. 29.

⁵ B. Felice, *op. cit.*

⁶ *Archivio Mediceo avanti Principato*, xvii. 158.

⁷ B. Buser, *Beziehungen der Mediceer zu Frankreich*. Leipzig, 1879.

⁸ *Archivio Mediceo avanti Principato*, xiv. 52 (mod. 54).

'' My Magnificent father and lord. . . . Lorenzo is well, but your absence is always in his mind. So far we are well on with Ovid and have read four books of Justin, both history and fable. Do not ask how he enjoys his present studies. In all other matters he is obedient, and since you are not here the fear of transgressing makes him more diligent. Your breviary, which was beginning to take such a long time, is getting on ; the delay will be compensated by its beauty and I will take great care of it. I commend myself to you.
From Florence, September 5, 1461.   Your GENTILE.

To the Magnificent Piero Cosme Medicis, my father and lord at Balnea Corsiniana.''

⁹ Levantini-Pieroni, *op. cit.*, p. 37.

¹⁰ B. Felice, *op. cit.*

¹¹ C. Guasti, *Lettere di una Gentildonna Fiorentina, op. cit.*, p. 396.

¹² L. Landucci, *Diario Fiorentino*, ed. by I. del Badia. Florence, 1883.

¹³ Tenhove, *Memoirs of the House of Medici* (English trans.). London, 1797.

¹⁴ *Archivio Mediceo avanti Principato*, xvii. 565.

¹⁵ *Ibid.*, xx. 306.

¹⁶ *Ibid.*, xxiii. 126.

¹⁷ Levantini-Pieroni, *op. cit.*, p. 49.

¹⁸ *Archivio Mediceo avanti Principato*, xvii. 585.

'' We are at Castiglione Aretino, and as it is about the eighteenth hour we are just leaving for Arezzo, which we shall reach without fail to-night. Mona Lucrezia has been much better for the last two days, and Maestro Girolamo and she have both informed you continually of the progress of her illness. It seems to me that she looks as if she was getting on well, and though she does not confess it, she rests better when asleep, and has less pain than usual, and less fever. We are travelling very slowly in order that she may have as little discomfort as possible. This will be sent by Bartolomeo, one of our men at Quinto, who lives at Bevagnia, and further on in those parts, where he has the name of a valiant constable. He is popular in that place, and, having heard how things were going, and of our needs, has offered himself. He is coming to you with this to see if you will make him a constable. I commend him to you as much as possible, for I understand he is a worthy man, and as I say, here he is esteemed and popular. You can speak to him and if you find him suitable, you can make use of him. He has been most helpful in Madonna Lucrezia's affairs, and has accompanied her with all his men. No more. May Christ keep you happy.

In Castiglione, May 15, 1467.   Your NICCOLO TORNABUONI.

To the Magnificent and Generous Gentleman Petro Cosme de Medicis. Florence."

[19] *Archivio Mediceo avanti Principato,* cxxxvii. 225 (old Misc. 76)·

[20] *Ibid.,* lxxx. 7.

[21] *Ibid.,* xiv. 218.

[22] *Ibid.,* xxi. 53.

"I wrote to you a few days after Lorenzo came, that it would be wiser to take him away from there, even though I thought it was imagination. From him, and from the doctor's letters, and from yours to Mona Contessina, we understand that you are better, and you seem to have benefited considerably, so I hope for your recovery. It certainly should be so, and I might say it could not be otherwise, considering the prayers and orations which have been and are being said in the appointed places, some of which are known to you, and some not. It seems difficult to believe, though by the grace of God it is true, that prayers are offered for you by those who do not know you, and whom you have never known. It is a marvellous thing, more divine than human, and I truly and firmly believe that, owing to the prayers that are being said, the matter cannot but end well, and we shall receive grace from God. But, as you in your wisdom know, we remain all the more His debtors, and may He make us grateful and able to do our duty. Have faith and obey the doctors, and do not budge one jot from their orders, and bear and suffer everything, if not for yourself and for us, for the love of God, Who is helping you. Do not do anything besides what you are there for. Do not worry about us, for we are well, and lack nothing, and similarly . . . (*) come to a good conclusion, and return in better health than you went . . . (*) prosperously and well, so that we have good hope of peace. If God be willing, Giovanni Tornabuoni will leave to-morrow for Rome. Please note. Do not trouble to write if you cannot. No more.

In Florence, October 1, 1467.   PIERO DI COSIMO DE' MEDICI.

To the Magnificent Lady Lucretie de Medicis."

(*) The manuscript is torn here.

[23] *Ibid.*, xxi. 54.

[24] *Ibid.*, lxxx. 9.

" I have had your letter and I am very sorry that since I wrote to you the pains have returned, but I am glad to hear from your letters that they did not last long, so that perhaps this time they will have left you altogether. May it please God that this is so, and remains so. I wrote and told you that Giovanni was leaving, which he did on Saturday, but he did not go to you, because he was in a great hurry, so he did not do what I told you. I have remained here for the reason I gave you, and I may have to stay so long that I shall not be able to return to see you there, as I would like to do, as you have not much longer to stay. May it please God to let you return as you and we wish. We are all well, and especially Piero, and we are longing to see you, and we hope to see you soon in good health. I commend myself to you.

In Florence, October 14, 1467.   Your LORENZO DE' MEDICI.

To Monna Lucretia, wife of Piero de' Medici at Bagno Amorbo."

[25] *Ibid.*, xxi. 31.

[26] *Ibid.*, cxxxvii. 229.

[27] *Ibid.*, xiv. 155.

" Jesus.

To my magnificent sir, my worshipful benefactor, recommendation. By the grace of Almighty God, to whom be all praise and reverence, the magnificent Monna Lucretia continues to improve and is willing to do the veriest tittle of what is recommended for her health. She does whatever is necessary, and prays to God for good weather, so that all may go as you wish.

From Bagno, November 4, 1467.   BENEDICTUS.

To the Magnificent Gentleman Petrum Medicem Cosmi filium, my benefactor."

[28] Levantini-Pieroni, *op. cit.*, p. 53.

" My Lucrezia. As I know you will read the letter I am writing to Niccolo I shall not write at length, especially as you are just returning, which I desire greatly. I enclose a letter I have just received from the Illustrious Madonna Duchess. You will see from it what she says. Show it to Messer Benedetto. You see how much we are obliged to her. We must give infinite thanks to our Lord God, and also to her in due time. No more at present. May Christ grant you health.

In Florence November 13, 1467, at the 8th hour.

PIERO DI COSIMO DE' MEDICI."

[29] *Archivio Mediceo avanti Principato*, xvi. 266.

[30] *Ibid.*, xxi. 71.

" I hear that the parish of Brozi is vacant owing to the death of the priest last winter. Lorenzo, you know that Bartolomeo da Saminiato, who is here with me, is faithful, and how much we may count on him in everything. So I beg you and pray you to do your best with whoever it may concern so that Messer Domenico the parish priest of San Cervagio di Val d'Elsa, the brother of the said

Bartolomeo, may have this parish. We will offer to give annually to the said priest for his life whatever is necessary and seems best to you. This would give me great pleasure, and I am sure that if you will attend to this with your usual diligence, the desired conclusion will be attained. I am well, and hope to be better, as you will hear from Niccolo. Commend me to Mona Contessina and to Piero, and may God preserve you all.

At Bagno a Morba di Volterra, the last day of May, 1468.

LUCRETIA DE MEDICI.

To my honourable and beloved son Laurentio Petri Cosme de Medicis. Florence."

[31] Levantini-Pieroni, *op. cit.*, p. 54.

" By Francesco the sawyer I wrote to you on the 25th of last month. Since then I have not heard from you, and have nothing to say. As you will have seen by that letter, as well as by this, by the grace of God I have been getting better and better, and am now well. Now the time of return approaches, but as I lost three days by my journey to Volterra, it seems best to me, an it please you, to postpone my return. I had thought of leaving on the 7th, but now I think of leaving on the 10th or 11th without fail. I have quite given up the idea of returning by Volterra, owing to the plague which has been doing damage there for the last four days, so I shall come by Colle. This we have decided among ourselves, and if I hear no more from you before the time for our departure approaches I will send the boy to tell you about the horses and mules. Comfort all the family on my behalf. I commend myself to you a thousand times. May Christ keep you happy.

On July 2nd at Bagno a Morba. Your LUCREZIA DE MEDICI.

(Kept until the 2nd of the month.) "

[32] *Archivio Mediceo avanti Principato*, xxx. 394.

[33] *Ibid.*, lxxxv. 42.

" Mona Lucretia mine. Although I am sick with a tertian fever, for the sake of charity, for the love of God and of truth, I will try and write to you.

We have been employing a young German, aged thirty-six, a perfect master of linen-weaving, who had a workshop in Poggibonsi with seven looms. He is not only an upright man, but holy in his life and conversation, as he shows in his face and in his speech to all who know him. And now he has been arrested for bigamy. The truth is that, sixteen years ago, in his own country, he married a wife. Before the year was out, one morning, in Antwerp, where they lived, she ran away in anger on to a ship, and went to Libya. Piero sought her for some time, but did not find her. So he came to Italy and has been in Florence, San Casciano and Poggibonsi all this time. During this time his wife took two husbands, who died. His mother heard of his wife's death, and wrote and told him. Thereupon, seven years ago, in Poggibonsi, he married a good and well-brought up girl, who presented him with three children, two of whom are the most beautiful boys I have ever seen, and a girl of six months. This wife died two months ago. In December last his first wife passed through here. She was not dead but pretended to be going to Rome with a lot of Germans. She spoke with him, and in the presence of those Germans, she made him give her a document in which he recognised her as his wife, and he promised to go back to her in September, and he swore to this. Being anxious to destroy him, as soon as she had the document, she denounced him, for she is dying of jealousy. But since he is an excellent man, and has been misled in several ways by the woman, who ran away and married, and of whose death he had heard from his mother, it would be only kind to help him and to save his life, for every reason, but especially for love of those poor babes. Everybody has come to plead for him, including the Commune of Poggibonsi, etc. So, if you wish to do a great kindness and acquire much merit, I beg you to persuade Lorenzo to write a strong letter to the Vicar, which I think will be enough. I commend him to you for the love of God, for he does not deserve death on account of this woman, who, as well as everything else, has been a prostitute. Have patience with my long letter. You will hear further details from these Religious, whom you can trust. No more, except that may God keep you in health and happiness. I commend myself to you as much as possible, and beg you to remember what I have written.

In Certaldo, July 31, 1471.

Your servant FRANCESCO DI SER ANTONIO, notary.

To the Magnificent and Generous Lady Ma Lucretia, wife of the late magnificent Piero de Medici in Florence, who is such a great lady."

[34] B. Felice, *op. cit.*

" During the last few days Lorenzo d' Abramo brought me a letter from you which was most pleasing to me. In this you recommend the said Lorenzo as a debtor of the Commune, and further state that you have paid twenty-five florins for the dowry of that girl from Bibbiena about whom I spoke to you. Later I had a letter from Ser Niccolo, your chancellor, telling me that you had arranged matters for me with Pierantonio Cennini, the Captain in the mountains. I thank you as much as in me lies both for the one and for the other. firstly for having arranged matters for me, and secondly for your charitable act, and I shall place both with the many great and infinite obligations I bear to you. Since I am unable to repay you in the slightest degree, I pray to God, who rewards all good deeds, that He will confer gifts on you and on your generous son. As I have written at other times, I would wish to serve you, and nothing could give me greater pleasure than to receive a command from you.

June 5, 1472.   FRANCESCO DI ANTONIO, notary."

[35] *Archivio Mediceo avanti Principato*, lxxx. 23.

" Magnificent and greatly honoured lady. I commend myself humbly to you. I should never forgive myself if, before leaving here, I did not write you a few lines, commending myself as usual, and offering myself to you. Although for the next six months I shall be away, I shall always be with you with all my heart and soul, and I shall pray and entreat the Lord that He will keep you and your magnificent and generous sons in health and happiness. I shall especially ask the Holy Friars of Monte di Vernio to pray for you when I pass by there on Tuesday on the way to my Vicariate. Please do not fail to ask me if there is anything I can do for you, for I shall be most happy and shall regard it as a singular grace.

I have left with Madonna Bice the record, which I sent you, of those thirteen big florins due to me. Arrigo was to collect them and send them, as I told you at Careggi. When you have received them, please ask Arrigo how much he wants for the work he did for you. I know that I am presumptuous, but I do it from love and faithfulness and so I ask your pardon. No more. May the Lord keep you in health. I am always at your service.

From Bibbiena, August 28, 1472.

Your servant FRANCISCHUS SER ANTONII, notarius.

To the Magnificent Lady Lucretia de Medici, my most singular Lady in Florence."

[36] *Archivio Mediceo avanti Principato*, Av. f. i. 100 (mod. i. 274).

" Magnificent Lady, beloved as a sister, greeting. In my great calamities I apply to you in the hope of help, and beg that you will give me your assistance and kindness, for I am truly the most unfortunate of queens. Please ask your sons to order their Bank to pay us the provision assigned to us by Holy Church in money and not in cloth, for neither I nor those who are with me are accustomed to this kind of trade. You will be performing a pious act, and we shall always be most grateful to you. Farewell. We commend ourselves to you.

From the City, January 18, 1472."

[37] *Ibid.*, lxxxv. 80.

[38] B. Felice, *op. cit.*

" I wrote from the Mugello to Lorenzo Ubaldini about a little church of which he is the patron, asking him to present it to Ser Lorenzo del Riccio da Barberino, who, as you know, is most faithful to us. Now I hear that you have written to ask for it for the god-father's brother. Thus the matter is in suspense, and it has not been conferred on either the one or the other. Therefore I beg you, for love of me, to do me this favour, since I was the first to ask, and so to arrange by a letter that the first man shall obtain the living. No more.

August 7, 1473."

[39] *Archivio Mediceo avanti Principato*, xxix. 675.

" Your Magnificence knows how this community has always been and still is an adherent of your house, and thus we shall always be all our lives. This is one of the things which gives us and our friends courage in our necessities, and especially to those who need to apply to Your Magnificence, by whom we have always been well received and helped. Now we hope all the more because of our faith in your illustrious house which increases daily, so that if you were to seek for it you would find the name of your house written in the hearts of great and small in this community. Now, Magnificent Madonna, after these long and tedious words we must apply to your aforesaid Magnificence.

The matter is this. Several months ago, one Ser Michele, a priest, was taken by the Lords of the Mint because of some money which he is said to have coined, and after torturing him they put him in the Stinche. Thus you will understand that he has already atoned for his sins, and is purged of them. Here we have some of his relations, men of substance, who are anxious for the honour of the world to release him from such misery. We should be glad to oblige them in this matter, and we apply to you to beg that you will arrange for his release from his misery, so that he may not die in this shame. By doing this you will confer a great favour on this community, and we shall always be greatly obliged to you. We therefore commend him greatly to you, and offer ourselves to Your Magnificence.

From Galatea, August 23, 1473.

Your most faithful servants, the SYNDIC-GENERAL,
      STANDARD-BEARERS AND ANCIENTS of Galatea.

To the Generous Lady Lucretia de Medici, our most singular lady.''

[40] *Ibid.*, xxix. 822.

'' I have not written to you before because I know that anything I may write has been written to you already. Nevertheless you may be glad to hear of our well-being, and to rejoice in it and give thanks to God by words and deeds, as said S. Paul to the Ephesians in the Epistle for next Sunday. . . . (Here follow Biblical quotations in Latin, interspersed with comments in Italian.)

First, Mona Contessina is well, and Giuliano the same. I have been to see Mona Bianca many times. She is well, and her children are coming to spend three days with Mona Contessina, to her great joy. Lucrezia has a little eczema, but otherwise she is well, and is well cared for by Mona Nanna, and Lucrezia obeys her like the clever little thing she is. Piero's complexion is good, and he is happy and joyful, by the grace of God, and often comes to the door leading to Terzola, and calls everybody saying ' Granny, Father, Mother ' in a way that would make you laugh if you saw it. Maddalena is well also, and every day, when I come back from Casa Tornabuoni, I go and stay with her a little, and I say to the wet-nurse ' Go for a little walk,' for this pleases her and she gets some exercise and keeps well, so that her milk comes better. She is very pleased and says ' I will pray to God for you.' In truth she is most diligent.

Cosimino, the son of Mona Nannina is well, but he does not want to read, and says ' I did not come into the country to read ' and Mona Contessina is not pleased. After All Saints it will be better.

Galasso comes to me every morning to read, and then returns in good time, because of the children's love for him. I have great trouble with him, more than with the others, but it does not seem a weariness to me, for I do it willingly for the love of God, for the love of Lorenzo, of Mona Clarice, and of you, for you know I am yours. None the less, with the help of God, I have made him learn by heart the Salve Regina and part of the Introito, and we are proceeding slowly with the Psalter. Ser Mazante has gone to the other life. May he rest in peace. I know you have had many petitioners, but when something comes to you of small value, re-member me, for I want to be a little out of the ordinary, and if you will promise me, you know I will look after your affairs well.

All your relations are well. Mona Bartolommea (*) and Mona Francesca (†) often go to see Mona Contessina and the children. All the men commend themselves to you, and I commend myself to you, and beg you to commend me to Lorenzo, and Mona Clarice and Mona Nannina. No more. May Christ guard you from evil deeds.

September 25, 1473.

Your CRISTOFANO D' ANTONIO DI MASO,
priest at Renini in Florence.

To the Noble Lady Lucretia, wife of the late Piero di Cosimo de Medici, to whom much honour is due. Pisa.''

[41] Pieraccini, *op. cit.*, p. 103.

[42] L. Pulci, *Lettere*, ed. by S. Bongi, Lucca, 1886.

'' On my return I did not find our Madonna Contessina, which grieved me sorely. I would like at least to have seen her. I pray that God may give peace to her soul, and preserve all the others, all of whom I exhort to patience.

The bearer of this is your great friend, Andrea Ughi. Urbano Cattani, who refused to wait any longer, took him to-day to give sureties for 600 Lire at the Palace of the Podestà, besides taking away his vineyard. Therefore he is very unhappy, and some evil may befall Urbano. I beg you to write to Urbano to ask him to withdraw the accusation and refer the matter to you or to Messer Piero Vespucci, who is his great friend, and does not wish to ruin those who are worthy men and your good friends. On your return here you will hear his reasons. He will receive 22 soldi in the Lire, and I will see that Messer Piero speaks to him as well. I would like this letter at once, and well written. This I beg you to do for love of me, and of your poor friend, and to avoid the scandal which I am sure will follow, and it will be a good deed done. And if Urbano is ungrateful, and forgets the benefits he received from Lorenzo, who had him restored when he had been admonished, and refuses to do this, I will speak to Jacopo Guicciardini for you, for it is their business at the Monte to find a remedy. No more. I commend myself to you, and will come and see you. May Christ guard you. Florence, October 26, 1473.''

[43] *Archivio Mediceo avanti Principato*, Av. f. i. 474 (mod. i. 273).

[44] *Ibid.*, lxxxv. 112.

[45] *Ibid.*, lxxx. 38.

[46] *Ibid.*, lxxxv. 148.

[47] *Ibid.*, lxxxv. 152.

'' Some days ago I sent you a letter by Frate Giovanni, telling you about the river, and explaining at length how the lake could be made. I offered you my services and begged you to give me your commands about this or anything else. So far I have had no reply or acknowledgment. Now the time for the appointment of the Captain of Bagnio approaches, a position which I should like to hold for many reasons, but particularly in order to make this lake for you. I am writing to Lorenzo to ask him to favour me under

* Wife of Leonardo Tornabuoni. † Wife of Giovanni Tornabuoni.

the circumstances, and I beg you to do the same, as you have always done. I am writing to Baldinaccio to ask him to remind Lorenzo, and to beg his help at the drawing. The office is a small one, but since it is near home, and I could help you with the lake, I would go there gladly. If this is impossible, will you help me with the Vicariate of Certaldo, which will be drawn a few days later. I once went there, with Andrea Carducci by your help, as you know. I am writing to Ser Mariano to attend the drawing, and give notice to Lorenzo. If this letter of mine seems presumptuous to you, I ask your pardon, for love and faith cause me to write it. No more. I always commend myself to you, and pray God to keep you in health and happiness. At your service.

In Bibbiena, May 25, 1475.

FRANCISCHUS SER ANTONII notarius.

To the Magnificent Lady Lucretia de Medicis, my most singular mistress. Florence."

[48] *Archivio Mediceo avanti Principato*, lxxxv. 160.

" My dearest Mother. I hear that Monna Lisa, the mother of Giovenco de Medici, and Monna Francesca, his widow, together wish to sell, or rather, have sold, certain pieces of land bought by the said Giovenco in the township of Treschi near Volterra, but the contract is not yet signed. Therefore I urgently beg you to write to Monna Lisa and Monna Francesca saying that you want this land yourself, and requesting them to meet your wishes rather than those of anyone else. I want you to buy this land for me, for I desire it greatly for many reasons, which I will tell you when I see you. But do not say who you want to buy it for, until we return to Florence, which I hope, please God, will be in fifteen days from now, and then you shall hear why I do this. I only beg of you to do as I ask, for you could not give me a greater pleasure than to do this small commission for me. And tell them not to say that you have asked them to sell to you, but only to reply that they do not wish to close with any offer at present, for any reason that seems good to them and you. No more now. I commend myself to you, and may Christ keep you happy and in good health. Here, by the grace of God we are all well, and hope to hear the same of you.

October 17, 1475.   Your BIANCA, alla Torre.

To the Magnificent Lady Mona Lucretia di Piero di Cosimo, my most beloved mother."

[49] Pieraccini, *op. cit.*, p. 88.

" I am writing to you because I hear that Francesca, Giovenco's widow, wants to sell the farm of Magugnace, and that your Madonna Lucretia is going to buy it. If you do not want it, please arrange that the rents may provide dowries for poor girls, or be otherwise used for charitable purposes, as you may think best. By the grace of God we are all well, and hope to hear the same of you.

At Trebbio on October 20, 1476.   Your GINEVRA."

[50] *Archivio Mediceo avanti Principato*, xxxiii. 516.

" Martino da Cataccione, my great friend, has asked me to write to you on his behalf, because he is banished from Florence owing to a difference he had with his brother. Owing to the trust I have in you I have undertaken to ask you to favour him in this affair. I shall be for ever obliged to you for this as for everything else I owe you, and I always commend myself to you. I beg you to do him this favour, so that he may be with his wife and children instead of going to the bad by wandering about the world. It would be a pious act. The Magnificent Lorenzo has promised to help him, so I beg Your Magnificence not to abandon him, for Cataccione is your slave.

From Pisa, July 3, 1476.   GALASSIUS DE PISISDE SABAUDIA.

To the Honourable Lady Lucretia de Medici, Florence."

Galasso of Savoy was probably a member of the house of Savoy, but he was not the Duke, as Levantini-Pieroni states. The reigning Duke was Filiberto II, Il Cacciatore, 1472–1482.

[51] I. del Lungo, *Letterine d'un Bambino Fiorentino—pubblicate per nozze Bemporad-Vita*. Florence, 1887.

[52] *Nonna, Mamma e Nipotina. Lettere femminili di Casa Medici*. Florence, 1892.

[53] *Archivio Mediceo avanti Principato*, xxxiv. 133.

[54] *Nonna, Mamma e Nipotina, op. cit.*

[55] Poliziano, *Prose Volgari inedite*, ed. by I. del Lungo. Florence, 1867. Letter iv.
" The family are all well. Lorenzo has told us of the honours paid to Madame of Ferrara at Pisa, and in order not to repeat that which I expect you know already, I will only say that she left very well content.
Here we speak again of the affairs of Milan, and of Signor Ruberto You will have heard that when he had come to Milan with Messer Obietto the Duchess heard of some of their plans. Donato del Conte, who was one of the conspirators, was sent for and imprisoned. Whereupon Signor Ruberto and his family took up arms and caused a tumult, together with some of the Duke's brothers. When he saw that he was not succeeding he fled, and Messer Obietto with him, and to-day they say the latter has been taken. There is no more news of Signor Ruberto. The Duke's brothers begged for Madonna's pardon, saying that they acted thus in self-defence. It is said that Signor Ottaviano was drowned in his flight.
There is also the case of Messer Antonio Ridolfi who, on his return from the Genoese coast, was attacked by some soldiers of Pietra Santa and Emilia, and they skirmished for some miles. Finally Messer Antonio's mounted bowmen did valiantly, and wounded and killed and slew some of the soldiers. Thus they gained honour, and Messer Antonio arrived here safe and sound.
Your Piero and Lucrezia and all the other children are well and commend themselves to you. I have not been able to write because I am at Careggi, and have had difficulties about messengers. Madonna Clarice and Bianca and Nannina and all our party are well. I commend myself to you.

Florence, the last day of May, 1477.   Your servant ANGELUS POL."

[56] *Archivio Mediceo avanti Principato*, lxxx. 49.

" As my duty is, I write to inform you that your Lorenzo has given in marriage to my Cosimo, or rather I should say, his Cosimo, a daughter of the Marchese Gabrielle Malaspina. This connection, as you will understand, is most suitable in every way, and is much grander than we might have expected. These, Madonna Lucretia, are the benefits which Lorenzo has conferred upon us, which show that he regards us as his loving relatives, and my sons as his own. We, as you may imagine, could not be better pleased, not only because of the good position and quality of the Marquis, but because of the affection which we see daily increasing in Lorenzo. I am glad to tell you of it, since you are Nannina's mother, and will no doubt be much pleased. Do not be surprised because you have heard nothing before, but, as you will hear on your return, the matter was concluded before any of our relatives, or those of the Marquis, could know about it. May it please God to give you that pleasure which you desire, and to send you back soon greatly benefited by the baths. Nannina and I commend ourselves to you.

In Florence, June 6, 1477.   Your BERNARDO RUCELLAI.

To the Noble Lady, my beloved Mother-in-law, Lucretia de Medici."

[57] Ross, *op. cit.*, p. 182.

" To-day I have received a letter in thy name which has caused me much rejoicing, particularly as thou sayest thou art well, and also the others. I am delighted to hear of the marriage arranged between Cosimino Rucellai and the daughter of the Marquis Gabrielle. Quite an unexpected piece of news. Coming from so good a source it must be good ; and having been settled by so excellent a person, excellent. We are celebrating it with great rejoicings, and so are all the people of the Bagni. To so fortunate and good a beginning may God grant a joyous and happy ending, *et suffit*. By the grace of God I am well, and have nearly finished my baths. I have decided, if it pleases God, to leave this on the 21st, that is Saturday week, and to stay the night with Madonna Tita, widow of Messer Antonio Cortesi, at San Gemignano. She has been here with me for several days and entreated me to do this ; then she sent her son, who left this morning, to settle about the visit. So because of her entreaties, and because she is a widow I have been forced to promise without awaiting thy assent. We shall go quietly and stay little, and on Monday, the Eve of S. John [23rd June] we shall be at home. I do not see my way to come before as I am still weak from the effects of the baths. But should any necessity arise for me to come sooner, let me know and I will leave all. Send the horses, if it suits thee, to arrive here on the 19th, so that they can rest on the 20th, and, as I have said, we start early on the 21st. Seven horses must be sent, nought else is wanted. May Christ keep you all. I commend myself to thee.

In haste on the 8th day of June, 1477.   Thy LUCREZIA.

I have given orders to Maso of Fiesole for the donkeys and mules he is to send."

[58] Ross, *op. cit.*, p. 183.

[59] *Archivio Mediceo avanti Principato*, lxxxv. 203.

" Beloved as a mother. Being here at the baths, and finding that things have been going as I have long desired, it has seemed my duty to rejoice with you, not only for your own pleasure, but for the general good, since in no other way would the thing be able to come to perfection. May God grant you His grace and permit you to enjoy it for a long time.

There is the same quantity of water for the showerbaths, but we are making a new and better cistern with an addition, so that there will be more and better water. Riccio, the bearer of this, who comes to visit you, will tell you all about it. This Riccio and his brother are experts in the work, as you know. I commend them to you as much as possible, for they seem to me the right people for the place. I think the most important thing at these Baths is to conduct as much water as possible to the showerbaths, so, as I have to stay near here all the winter, which is, I think, the best season for seeking it, I will, if you wish, do my best on your behalf, as my duty requires. I have no more to say, except that I offer myself to you as much as I can, and commend myself to you, and pray that you may be preserved in all happiness.

From Bagno a Morba, 16 September, 1477.

> Your faithful PIERO MALEGONELLE.

To the Magnificent and Generous Lady Monna Lucretia, wife of the late Piero de Medici, my most honoured mother, in Florence."

[60] *Archivio Mediceo avanti Principato*, xxxiv. 312.

[61] *Ibid.*, xxxiv. 320.

[62] *Ibid.*, lxxx. 40.

"Jesus. May 27, 1478.

Mona Lucrezia. I have been several times to Filippo Giugni who arbitrated for you in the affair between me and Mona Lena, and he tells me that Messer Piero da Sant'Agnolo will not give his award, and that on the day of the judgment he went into the country, I know not for what reason. I do not ask for more than fifteen soldi in the lira on account, but I have nothing. I have now been away from my house and from Florence for three years, more or less on your behalf, and without any pay, and I cannot earn, for, as you know, I am with Filippo Giugni, and you know he was a partner of Renato ; now we do not work, so think how I can live.

I must also tell you that my wife has just given birth to a daughter, and I have nothing in this world to live on or to wrap her up in. I could not believe that Mona Lena would not help me at least from my own, with a bit of stuff, or a bushel of flour, or something. I commend myself to you for the love of God, and I should be glad if you would send here to Varlungho, to the hovel in which I live, which belongs to the General of Vallombrosa, so that you may see my poverty, and where I keep my wife, for I am sure that when you know this you will pity me and my wife, for I want you to be certain that there is not a case more deserving of charity in the world.

I also beg you to adjust our difference, which is a great evil. I see my property taken away while I die of hunger. Since my possessions have been taken away I have wished to lose my life, and have fought hard against this wish. Do not allow this wrong to be done to me. If I had not a wife I could go away from here, and should not have to fight with those who have my things, and would follow all the wishes of Mona Lena.

I will cease, in order not to weary your reverence. I will ask Bernardo Giugni what he will give me to-day for your house, and I will do the same every day, and if through you I can earn anything, I commend myself to you for the love of God.

Your most faithful servant FRANCESCO D' ANTONIO DEL BORGO, in the shop of Filippo Giugni at San Martino.

To the Wise and Worthy Lady Mna Luchrezia, wife of the late Piero di Chosimo de Medici.''

⁶⁸ *Ibid.*, lxxxv. 213.
'' Although I have had no intercourse with you, the relationship, the kindness, and the love you bear to your niece, Madonna Margherita, my sister-in-law, makes me love you as a mother. Therefore I have been moved for various reasons to write this letter, and if I have not done my duty before, I beg you to pardon me. The reason for this letter is first to show you the love I have for you in my heart, and if there is anything you would like from here, if you will be kind enough to tell me, you will find the truth of what I write. I regret my other reason for writing, as it will grieve you, but I think that you are the person who can deal with the matter most successfully, so I am writing to you, but I beg that I may never be discovered.

As I said above, I love Madonna Margherita, my sister-in-law, as much as if we had been born of the same mother, and when I see anything unpleasant done to her, I take up the sword for love of her, and at present it is particularly necessary that I should do so.

I understand from my sister-in-law that you gave her Mona Lisa as a maid, but she loves neither you nor my sister-in-law, nor is she the woman she seemed, and I will tell you the reason. I think you know that my father and brother went abroad and left my sister-in-law in my house in Milan, together with Mona Lisa. Since we lived together in the same house, you may be sure that I know more about her life than anybody else. And, to tell the truth, I have never seen her do anything which was not beautiful and fine and good. If it were otherwise you may be sure that I, who love Messer Gasparo, could not endure anything that would bring shame on him, for it would reflect on me. But to return to the point. By the grace of the Lord, my father and my brother arrived here in Milan, safe and sound, and the caresses given by Messer Gasparo, my brother, to my sister-in-law, cannot be imagined or described. But Mona Lisa, who is the Goddess of Discord, could not bear to see this, and went to my brother, Messer Gasparo, and told him more evil of his wife than a human being could imagine, so that there was a quarrel between husband and wife. Things are so bad that if you cannot do anything, I am afraid that one day Messer Gasparo will do something so grievous that he will never again be happy, nor will you. I never saw a more mischievous or lying woman, and I have done my best in the matter, but now I can do no more, and I beg you to do something. Messer Gasparo is devoted to Mona Lisa for love of you, and I again beg you to act secretly so that it does not appear that I have written.

Madonna Margherita, your niece, who is present, commends herself to you, and begs you to send her thirty-seven *braccia* of pale blue satin to make a cloak and a dress, which will show her that you love her, and if you think the cost is too high, tell her how much it is, and she will send the money at once.

Here there is nothing more except that I commend myself infinitely to you, and beg you to command me as a good daughter, for I will obey you always as a mother, and that which I have written I have written for a good purpose, so I beg you to keep my secret, as I hope you will.

From Milan die x 1478. LODOVICA TORELLA COMITISSA, *manu propria*."

[64] *Ibid.*, lxxxv. 241.

"Jesus 1480.   January 21.

I am writing these few words to ask you to help my daughter, Francesca, as you have always done. If you do not help her she will be abandoned by everyone there, for those who should help her keep her there unwillingly. We have new proofs of this every day, and I do not know how poor Francesca bears all that is done to her. I promise you, Madonna Lucrezia, that when we have her dowry, we will act differently, for we do not want her to be stinted, and we will do as you and Lorenzo advise in the matter. For we hear every day of the increasing love and compassion you have for her and her children, and I thank God that He has granted her this mercy, for you take as much trouble about her affairs as if they were your own. She and her children will always have cause to pray to God for you, since you have done such a pious act, and I do not doubt that God will help and prosper you in every good thing. For I do not doubt that without your help she would be still worse treated, for they are not relatives but enemies who have been the cause of all her ills, both men and women, in deeds and words. Pardon me, Madonna Lucrezia, if I write too much, but the passion I feel at seeing my daughter treated as she is by her people, makes me say more than I intended. But I hope to be able to act differently with your counsel, and that of Lorenzo, and to take her away from all these troubles, for since they have her dowry I do not want her to stay there, and they keep it so that she cannot do otherwise. But I have hope in God and in you that we may get it, and for this I pray you most earnestly.

I say no more. I commend myself to you, and if you want anything from here, tell me, for I shall always do everything gladly. By the bearer of this I am sending you a Venetian purse for your grandson Piero, the son of Lorenzo, and though the present is very small, I beg you to accept it as an act of love, and tell Lucrezia I will bring her something more beautiful when I come, but I beg you earnestly to tell me before I leave if she wants anything particular, for I will do everything gladly. I commend Francesca to you, please recommend her to Lorenzo, and myself also, and Roberto does the same. May God preserve you in His grace with all the others.

From Your CHORNELIA DE MARTINI in Venice.

To the Magnificent and Generous Lady Lucretia de Medicis, most honoured. Florence."

[65] *Nonna, Mamma e Nipotina, op. cit.*

[66] Poliziano, *Prose Volgari, op. cit.* Letter xxi.

"Our only news is that we are having such continual rain that we cannot leave the house, and have exchanged the chase for ball-playing, so that the children may not miss their usual exercise. We generally play for the soup, the sweet or the meat, and he who loses must not eat any, and very often when my scholars lose they pay tribute to Ser Umido. There is no other news to send you. I sit by the fire in slippers and a greatcoat, and if you could see me, you would think I was melancholy personified. And that is what I seem to myself, for I can neither see nor do anything that pleases me, for I am so oppressed by our affairs, and sleeping and waking they haunt me. Two days ago we were all on wings, for we heard there was no more plague with you ; now we are again in the depths, for we hear there is still a little here and there. When we are in town we have some pleasures, even if only to see Lorenzo return safely home. Here we are anxious about everything, and I can assure you I am drowned in sloth in this solitude. I say solitude because Monsignore (*) shuts himself in his room with his thoughts, and I always find him sad and thoughtful, so that my own depression is more refreshing than his company. Ser Alberto de Malerba mumbles prayers all day with these children, and I remain alone, and when I am tired of study I ring the changes on plague and war, grief for the past and fear for the future, and there is none to listen to my grumblings. I do not find my Madonna Lucrezia, so that I may unburden myself to her. Our only relief is in letters from Florence, especially from Malerba, who has just sent us some news. I must say he generally sends us good tidings, and for a short time we believe everything, for we are so anxious that it should be true. However, these plums soon turn to sloes, but, as far as I am concerned, I arm myself with good hope, and take hold of the smallest thing, so as not to be utterly overwhelmed. I have no more to tell you, and I commend myself to you.

From Cafaggiuolo, December 18, 1478.   SERVITOR ANGELUS."

[67] *Ibid.*, Letter xxiv.

"I am ever conscious of the good work you are always doing on my behalf, and I thank you in my old way, that is to say I will do so in spirit, since I cannot do so in fact.

Just now Tommaso and Madonna Maria (†) and the youngsters of Anton di Taddeo, to all of whom I owe a great deal, are worrying me every day to write you a line about that provostship of Fiesole. I know that this is not the time to ask for anything, partly because of the storm, and partly because I might be told ' You already have enough.' They reply that I must apply to you, and put myself in your hands, and in this I cannot err. To be brief, if I ever needed help, now is the time because, besides the daily exhortations of my sister, I have been deprived of the hopes I was building on Piero, and besides I want somehow to be able to repay Lorenzo in part as far as possible : you will understand. And after all, this is not a troublesome matter, and it is an easy thing for you to give. It would be most convenient to me for several reasons, especially as

* Gentile Becchi, Bishop of Urbino.   † Poliziano's cousin and sister.

I understand there is a very pretty little bit of land attached. Please, Mona Lucrezia, help me a little if you can, for I believe the place itself, if it could speak, would ask for nothing better than to belong to one of your household, and you know there is no one more devoted to you than I am. Speak a word to Lorenzo if it seems good to you, or show him this letter. God knows I am accustomed to patience. I have had to ask for it so often, but he has had compassion on my needs, and has made up his mind to overcome my bad luck, which God grant may succeed. Commend me to him, and to yourself always.

Fiesole, May 25, 1479. V. M. Servitor Angelus Politianus."

⁶⁸ *Archivio Mediceo avanti Principato*, xxxvii. 389.

⁶⁹ *Nonna, Mamma e Nipotina, op. cit.*

⁷⁰ Quoted by J. A. Symonds, *The Renaissance in Italy.* London, 1912. Vol. iv., p. 452.

⁷¹ *Archivio Mediceo avanti Principato*, lxxx. 70.

⁷² *Ibid.*, cxxxvii. 435 (old no. 73).

⁷³ Poliziano, *Prose Volgari, op. cit.*, Letter xxv.

" I send you back by Tommaso your lauds and sonnets and poems that you lent me when I was with you. These ladies took the greatest pleasure in them, and Madonna Lucrezia, or rather Lucrezia, learnt by heart nearly all the writings of *the* Lucrezia, including many sonnets. They write that they all commend themselves to you.

There is also a little white manuscript book with the poems. Please give it to your and my good Giovanni Tornabuoni. It contains certain rules his children asked me for. I am also writing to Giovanni, and am answering both the children and their master. Please give him the letters, and commend me to him, for I greatly value the place he shows that I hold in his affections.

I have visited Lorenzo several times, and I cannot tell you how glad he was to see me. Please find out what are his intentions about me. I should be very surprised if he let Piero waste time, for it would be a great pity. I hear that Messer Bernardo the brother of Ser Niccolo, is in the house, but I do not know how his teaching will combine with mine, unless he is there permanently, which would show that the bubble had burst. But I do not believe it, and I beg you to discover Lorenzo's ideas, so that I may know whether to arm myself for a joust or for battle. I think you can do this easily, and I shall always be ready to comply with Lorenzo's wishes and orders, for I am certain he knows me well enough, and will give me an honourable position, as he has always done, and as my faithfulness and service merit.

I am studying hard. I have not been able to send you the book I promised you, because one copy is in Florence, and the other at the binder's, who has had it a long time. As soon as it arrives I will send it. I commend myself to you and beg you to commend me to Lorenzo.

Fiesole, July 18, 1479. V. M. Servitor Angelus Politianus."

⁷⁴ *Ibid.*, Letter xxvi.

" I hear that last night Lorenzo was not very well. God knows how worried I was to hear this. So I am sending Mariotto to you to hear if it is true, and how he is. I would have come myself, but I feared to be troublesome. If you see that there is nothing to be done for me, I beg you to let me know, for nothing is too great for me to acquiesce in it. I commend myself to you.

VOSTRO SERVITOR AGNOLO at Fiesole."

[75] *Archivio Mediceo avanti Principato*, lxxx. 74.

" A few days ago I wrote to you about my son Piero, who wishes to come and serve you as tutor to the children, now that Maestro Agnolo has left, and I could have no greater grace from God, for I hoped you would have been well served by him, as I think would have been the case.

I write this in my usual faith, for having lost a year, I am hoping to be appointed as the new vicar of San Giovanni, who is to be drawn on the coming first of August. Wherefore I beg you to help me and speak to Lorenzo in my favour, and I beg you to send a line on this matter to Ser Mariano, to ask him to see to it.

No more now, except to offer and commend myself to you and Lorenzo, whom may God keep well and happy. With this will be a letter to my brother Ser Giuliano, at the printers', please send it when somebody is going to Cafaggiuolo.

In Vergareto, July 18, 1479. Your servant,

FRANCISCHUS SER ANTONII DE BIBBIENA notarius.

To the Magnificent Lady Lucretia de Medici, a most singular lady. Caregio."

[76] *Ibid.*, xxxviii. 10.

" I wrote to you at length about the happenings here by means of the courier of the Duchess of Milan. This is only to tell you, so that you may know, that yesterday, the 11th of this month, His Holiness the Pope proclaimed a league with the Venetians, and there was much pleasure and rejoicing here. To-morrow, please God, I shall have the terms of the League, and I will send them to you by the first messenger. I have no more to say. I commend myself to you always, and also Count Pier Noferi da Montedogli. Farewell.

From Rome, May 12, 1480.

Your servant PAPINO DE MACTHEO DE ARTIMINO CANCELLARIUS.

To the Honourable and Worthy Lady Lucretia de Medicis in Florence, my most singular lady."

[77] *Ibid.*, lxxx. 88.

" In my last letter I wrote that I hoped that the discords of Italy might be settled, for the ambassadors of our most serene League had found His Holiness the Pope well disposed, and Count Girolamo the same. And by this I renew these statements, and may it please God.

This is only to tell you that to-day Messer Anello, the Royal [Neapolitan] ambassador received a letter from H.M. the King enclosing one for His Holiness sent by the Grand Master of Rhodes, asking for help. For on May 27 the Turks encamped before Rhodes, and surrounded the walls by land with seventy thousand Turks, and also put many galleys on the sea. They have placed artillery before the town in such a way that, if he does not rapidly receive

217

help, he will have to surrender, for he cannot see how to resist such an army. His Holiness was much troubled by this news, but I do not know whether he will be able to give any help.

Signor Ottaviano, the brother of the Duke of Urbino, has been here. He is leaving to-day, and going to Urbino. Last night the ambassadors of the King of Hungary arrived, and were met with great honour by all the envoys of our League. There is no more to say except that I commend myself to you. Farewell.

June 30, 1480.

Your Servant PAPINUS DE ARTIMINO CANCELLARIUS.

To the Magnificent and Worthy Lucretia de Medicis, my most singular benefactress. In Florence."

[78] *Archivio Mediceo avanti Principato*, xxxiv. 367.

"For some time I have not written to Your Magnificence. This is only to tell you that to-night there are letters from His Majesty the King [of Naples] saying that the Turkish fleet has arrived in Puglia and has already taken more than twenty villages and castles, and more than fifteen hundred souls, who have been tortured in a most cruel manner. Now it is said they have camped at a place called Otrototo [Otranto], and there they have landed ten thousand infantry and four thousand cavalry and have planted several cannon, and have already begun to bombard the walls. Here it is the general opinion that by this time the port will have been lost. A great deal has been made of this news here, and it is regarded as a very sad thing. May God provide for our wants ; this I think will make men forget the affairs of Italy.

Besides there are letters saying that His Majesty the King freely yields all our castles, and has given them to Messer Giovan Baptista Bentivogli, to hand them over to the Florentines, which is good news.

I shall have your yarn here by the tenth of this month, for I have had it spun in Naples, and by what Benedetto Salutati writes, you have been well served'. If you wish me to send it as soon as I have it here instead of waiting for my return, let me know, for I will do whatever you write. I think we shall remain here all September. I have no more to say at present, except that I commend myself to Your Magnificence, and if no friend of yours has been made Vicar of San Giovanni, I beg you to remember me, for I should do you honour. Farewell.

From Rome, August 4, 1480.

Your PAPINUS DE ARTIMINIO CANCELLARIUS.

To the Magnificent Lady Lucretia de Medici, my singular benefactress. Florence."

[79] *Ibid.*, lxxx. 91.

"This is to inform you that this morning at six o'clock Count Antonio, the nephew of His Holiness, passed from this life and died, and was greatly honoured at his burial. Now His Holiness is sick. He was taken ill yesterday at the twentieth hour. There is no other news except that we had letters from Naples yesterday, saying that the King is hastening his preparations against the Turks. H.M. has had letters from Leccia saying that Otranto can still hold out for more than a month, and that the Turks are no longer scouring the country, but have encamped, and are waiting to take it, as I expect you know. H.M. also asks in these letters that the Duke of Urbino may be sent to Naples. Here to-day there is news that the Lord of Forlì, who was besieged in the citadel, is dead, however there seems some doubt about it. No more. I am always at your service and I commend myself.

From Rome, August 12, 1480, at the 24th hour.

Your Servant PAPINUS DE ARTIMINIO CANCELLARIUS.

To the Magnificent and Worthy Lady Lucretia de Medicis, my most singular benefactress, Florence."

[80] *Ibid.*, lxxx. 96.

" My last letter of the 2nd of the month was in reply to one from you of the 26th of last month, and in that I told you all the news to date.

To-day I must tell you that I went this morning to visit the ambassador of the King [of Naples] to hear if he had any news, and he said that he had heard from the Venetian ambassador that the Turks encamped at Rhodes had gone away, and the army had returned to Constantinople, and that the Venetian ambassador had letters to this effect. If it is true it seems good news.

On Monday morning a children's school was destroyed here, and at first it was thought that twenty children had been killed, but only the master that kept the school perished, which has been regarded as a great miracle. The cries of the fathers and mothers cannot be described. God helped the innocent in that hour. He continues to work wonders. Let us pray that He will not see our great sins.

Messer Antonio Ridolfi, the ambassador of this Republic, acts in a way to make this people greatly obliged to him, for he does not cease to work day and night. I hope that by the grace of God and His glorious mother the Virgin Mary it will bring him great honour, and that there will be an end to much tribulation. May it please God.

In my letter of the 23rd of last month I said that, if you and Lorenzo agreed, it would be a good thing if he would write a letter to the Cardinal of Milan and one to the Cardinal of Portugal, fortifying them and begging them to hasten the holy work, for although they are acting with good will in the matter none the less I know this will be welcome. I am continually with their Lordships, who are well disposed. Farewell.

From Rome, October 4, 1480.

Your faithful servant, PAPINUS DE ARTIMINIO CANCELLARIUS.

To the Magnificent and Worthy Lady Lucretia de Medicis, Florence."

[81] Levantini-Pieroni, *op. cit.*

" In spite of my tears and grief I cannot but inform Your Excellency of the sad fact of the death of Madonna Lucretia, my beloved mother, who to-day passed from this life. Wherefore I am as unhappy as I can say, for besides losing my mother, the thought of which alone breaks my heart, I have also lost a helper who relieved me of many troubles. However it has pleased God that it should be so, and we cannot and should not go against His will, and I am sorry not to be of that strong and steadfast mind that is seemly. I pray that the Lord will give patience to me, and to her rest for her soul, which I hope, considering her blameless life. I have informed you in order that you may know the condition of your servant, and I commend myself as much as I can.''

[82] Levantini-Pieroni, *op. cit.*

'' It is but my duty to tell you of the great and terrible blow which has struck me to-day in the death of my beloved mother, Madonna Lucrezia. You can imagine how disconsolate I am, for I have lost, not only my mother, but my only refuge from my troubles and my relief in many labours. It is true that we must be patient under the will of God, but my mind is not sufficiently constant to be consoled by this. But I pray Him to give me a little patience and comfort, and that He may give her peace and rest. You, to whom I have confided my great loss and tribulation will understand the condition of your servant, who commends himself with all his heart.''

[83] *Ibid.*

'' What part of the state did the wisdom of Lucrezia not see, take care of, or confirm ! She concerned herself with the greater as well as the lesser and the least of all the citizens, and in this way, upon occasion, her actions, from the political point of view, were more prudent than yours, for you attended only to great things and forgot the less, which nevertheless required attention. She both sought and gave advice to the most important persons and the magistrates, and she also admitted the humblest to her presence, and all she sent away happy and contented. But you know all this better than I do, for you never did anything without consulting her, as she did nothing without knowing your views. . . .
The woman is regarded as brave who does not lack prudence in great things, and at the same time does not forget small ones. And such was, O Lorenzo, your mother, who knew how to manage the most important affairs with wise counsel, and how to succour the citizens in time of calamity.''

[84] Pieraccini, *op. cit.*

[85] *Archivio Mediceo avanti Principato*, xcix. This document is too long to reproduce here.

[86] Young, in *The Medici*, says the gold florin weighed 72 grains of gold and represented 12 francs, and was worth about £5 in pre-war money.

[87] *Archivio Mediceo avanti Principato*, lxxx. 17

[88] *Ibid.*, lxxxv. 180.

CHAPTER VI

[1] *Tre Lettere di Lucrezia Tornabuoni a Piero de Medici ed altre lettere di vari concernenti al matrimonio di Lorenzo il Magnifico con Clarice Orsini.* Ricordo di Nozze nel gennaio 1859. Florence.

[2] *Ibid.*

NOTES

[3] *Ibid.*

" I have had your letter by Donnino, and I see what you have decided, and I am glad. For I think that when I am back and have told you everything, you will be satisfied, especially as she pleases Lorenzo. We have not seen her again, and I do not know if we shall do so, for there is no reason. You say I speak coldly. I do so on purpose, but I do not think there is a more beautiful girl of marriageable age here at present. On my return I will tell you my opinion, and, as I said above, we will come to an agreement, so now I will say no more on this matter.

I arrived here rather worn out, for we had a bad journey with little else but rain, but now I am rested and feel well. We should have left on Monday, but it does nothing but rain here, so they have persuaded me to wait a little. But we are quite ready, and as soon as the weather is better we will start, for it seems a thousand years till we return. I commend myself to you.

April 5, 1467.   Your LUCREZIA."

[4] Ross, *op. cit.*, p. 120.

[5] *Ibid.*, p. 120.

" By Giovanni Tornabuoni I received your letter, and he has given me the message from Your Magnificence. It pleases me mightily ; I do not think that in these times Your Magnificence could have done better. I could not be better pleased or more gratified, considering that it is for the benefit and common good of all ; therefore I congratulate Your Magnificence. And that Your Magnificence may be amply informed about everything, although I know that you will hear all from Giovanni, nevertheless it is my duty to tell you that this very day, in the name of God, everything has been concluded. The reason why the contract is not ' per verba dei presenti ' is that Monsignore [Cardinal Orsini] does not wish it to be divulged, therefore we send a sketch of the contract according to his desire ; the one sent to us was simple enough. Everything has been agreed in the following fashion *videlicet* :—That they give a dower of 6000 Roman florins, in money, jewels and dresses ; which they stipulate should return to their heirs should she not have children or dispose of it by will. They agree that you should not give her the fourth part of the dower as is customary here ; and in this and in all other matters the Florentine custom and usage is to be followed, save in the restitution of the dower if she dies *sine filiis et intestato*. Thus neither the custom here nor the custom there will be absolutely adhered to, so that both parties will be content. I have been present at all the arrangements, and they seem to be honest and reasonable ; for you do not need her fortune, and your own remains to you. It is but reasonable that they should have their way in something.

Magnificent Piero, I value the connection much, but they are even more desirous and glad to be related to you. Of a truth, their pleasure is not to be described. This must be a satisfaction to you, and every day, if it pleases God, you will be better satisfied and we also ; for truly if I had a hundred tongues I could not tell Your Magnificence how pleased I am. Send the contract soon, for it will be impossible to keep this affair secret, as Pietro d'Arcangelo, chancellor of the Duke of Urbino, has spoken of it, and these Pazzi have begun to spread the news.

You have not sent the letter I asked Your Magnificence for ; probably because you had letters from the King to send here concerning the affair about which I wrote. If you have them it would be well to send them, as I can assure Your Magnificence that if the friend takes up the business I have good hopes of success. Whatever Your Magnificence does in this and other matters about which I shall write will be well done, as I am certain that Your Magnificence values my well-being and my honour as much as I do myself. I commend myself to Your Magnificence *et quam Deus felicem conservet.*

Rome, November 27, 1468.

Magnificentie Vestres Filius PHY. ARCHIEPISCOPUS PISANUS, *manu propria.*

I said above that I had good hopes if the letters are sent, not because I rely on the benevolence of him who is to do the affair, but because he, if he wishes to gain a place, must give his companions a share, who will either do nothing or be obliged to act according to the will of the other. But he has a great desire to succeed, and will not give heed to what people say, and therefore will not care much for those who may claim their share at any cost. The aforementioned affair [the marriage] has not been announced yet to our Lord the Pope, because it did not seem good to Monsignore to do so before the contract is here.

To Piero de Medici.''

⁶ B. Felice, *op. cit.*

⁷ I. del Lungo, *La Fidanazta di Lorenzo de Medici ; per norre Bondi-Levi,* 1897.

⁸ Ross, *op. cit.*, p. 123.

⁹ *La Fidanzata di Lorenzo de Medici, op. cit.*

¹⁰ Armstrong, *Lorenzo de Medici, op. cit.*, p. 74.

¹¹ Pieraccini, *op. cit.*, p. 128.

¹² Ross, *op. cit.*, p. 126.

'' A few days ago I heard, but not by any letter of yours, of the tournament and the honour done to you. God be praised for all, and especially that you emerged safe and unhurt ; in which I think you were aided by the prayers of your Clarice. Now I have been informed of the wishes of the Magnificent Piero and your own as to Clarice's journey to Florence. Although I should certainly have desired, albeit I have not been consulted, that your wishes should be followed in this matter, always subordinate to those of Madonna, our mother, who is very sorrowful at her departure, yet it would only have been seemly if I, as well as other people, had been written to about this business, for you have no nearer relation here, nor one who is more desirous to please you in this as in other matters. So when you want an explanation, or anything done, write openly to me, and I shall do my best to satisfy you. Say also to the Magnificent Piero that in future he is not to apply to middlemen, for he must dispose of me as he would of a son. *Bene valete.*

Rome, February 26, 1469.

RAINALDUS DE URSINIS, Apostolice Sedis subdiaconus."

[13] *Ibid.*, p. 127.

" I have had a letter from you which is most welcome, in which you say that your coming depends upon the will of the Magnificent Piero, and the opinion of His Lordship the Cardinal. I am quite content with whatever pleases them. How glad I should be to see you before sending my daughter I cannot express, but I am sure the Magnificent Piero knows best, and that we shall never err by carrying out his commands. At all events I hope you have the wish to know me and all your relations here. No more. God preserve you all in good health and happiness. Clarice is well and commends herself to all.

Rome, March 4, 1469.   MAGHDALENA DE URSINIS."

[14] Fabroni, *Laurentii Medicis Vita.* Pisa, 1784.

" I do not know how to begin to tell you with what pleasure and consolation I have to-day on your behalf espoused the magnificent and generous Madonna Clarice degli Orsini. She is a maiden who, in my opinion, by her looks, her presence and her manner, does not merit any other husband than the one whom I think Heaven has bestowed upon her. Therefore you should thank God who, no less in this than in other things, has made you happy by His protection. Since I rejoice in all your well-being and honour, and have for a long time desired this day, I congratulate you from the bottom of my heart, and wish you luck, and pray to our Lord Jesus Christ that He may give you a long and happy life together, and may grant you to see your children's children unto the fourth generation. I will not say more, since Giovanni will have informed you of everything. If I can do anything for you, let me know, for I will do it gladly, as I think you know. May God preserve you in happiness."

[15] Ross, *op. cit.*, p. 129.

" An account of the Wedding of Lorenzo di Piero di Cosimo, according to what was told me by Cosimo Bartoli, one of the principal Directors of the Festival, particularly as regards Sweet-meats and Sugar-plums, and also what I saw myself.

On Friday, which was the 2nd of June, the presents offered by the countryside began to arrive from the principal towns, Pisa, Arezzo, and other communes, villas and castles. All presented eatables, such as calves, fowls, geese, wine, sweetmeats, wax and fish. I send you the exact list as far as I could get it. The presentations of these went on all day on Saturday with great noise and rejoicings : and on that day pieces of veal from 10 to 20 lbs. in weight were given to 800 citizens. You and I were among the number.

Calves, 150.
More than 2000 couples of capons, geese and fowls.
Sea fish and trout in large quantities. I do not yet know how many.

Sweet things in abundance ; sugar-plums as big as arbutus berries,
almonds, pine-seeds, sweetmeats, also the imitations thereof
from there [Naples ?]. The number I do not yet know.
Wax I know not how much.
Many hundreds of flasks of wine and several casks of foreign
wines, such as malvasy and the like, and of native red wine.
Of corn, oats and the like, I do not think there was much.

On Sunday morning the bride left the house of Benedetto
degli Alessandri on the big horse given to Lorenzo by the King [of
Naples], preceded by many trumpeters and fifers, and surrounded
by the youths usually in attendance on marriage festivities, well
clothed. Behind her came two cavaliers, Messer Carlo and Messer
Tommaso, on horseback with their retainers, who, according to the
usage of the city accompanied her to her husband's house which
was most sumptuously adorned, and where a stage had been erected
in the street for dancing. As she dismounted the bride's retinue
arrived from the house of the Alessandri : thirty young matrons
and maidens most richly dressed, and among them was your Fiammetta, one of the two handsomest there. They were accompanied
by another set of youths dressed for dancing and preceded by
trumpeters. Thirty other maidens were in Lorenzo's house to
receive the bride and her retinue. After the olive-tree, to the sound
of much music, had been hauled up to the windows, all went to
dinner. The tree was arranged in a vase like those used on the
triumphal cars for the feast of S. Giovanni and was almost like a
trionfo.
The order of the banquets, of which there were five, was alike on
the mornings of Sunday, Monday and Tuesday.
The bride, with about fifty maidens who were the dancers, ate
in the garden under the loggia which you know, and the tables were
set at the sides as far as the doors, one of which leads into the house,
the other outside. In the loggia which surrounds the courtyard of
the house sat the citizens who had been invited. The tables were
placed on three sides, beginning from the garden, and following the
wall were six tables : here sat from seventy to eighty citizens. In
the ground-floor hall the youths who danced, about thirty-two or
thirty-six, were seated. Forty or more men of mature age were
occupied in marshalling the banquet, and at every table were two
who acted as seneschals. On a balcony in the great room upstairs
dined the women of a certain age, among them was your mother-in-
law, Monna Antonia, and like her were about forty others in the
company of Monna Lucrezia. In short, at the principal tables dined
about two hundred people.
The order observed in serving was marvellous. For all the dishes
were brought in at the door opening into the street, preceded, as is
the custom, by trumpets. The bearers turned to the right in the
loggia and returned to the foot of the staircase up which some went,
while others passed into the hall to the youths, and others to the
maidens in the garden, and others again remained under the loggie
where were those who had been invited, so that all were served at
the same time. The like order was observed in taking away the
dishes, and each man knew his service and his place and did nought
else. The dishes were according to the tables, and among those who

brought them in were the stewards, each of whom directed his own men to the proper table. There were fifty large dishes, the contents of which were sufficient to fill two trenchers, and one trencher was placed between every two guests, a carver being in attendance.

The banquets were prepared for a marriage rather than for a magnificent feast, and I think this was done *de industria* as an example to others not to exceed the modesty and simplicity suitable to marriages, so there was never more than one roast. In the morning a small dish, then some boiled meat, then a roast, after that wafers, marzipan and sugared almonds and pine-seeds, then jars of preserved pine-seeds and sweetmeats. In the evening jelly, a roast, fritters, wafers, almonds and jars of sweetmeats. On Tuesday morning, instead of the roast were sweet pies of succulent vegetables on trenchers; the wines were excellent malvasy, trebbiano and red wine. Of silver plate there was but little.

No side-boards had been placed for the silver. Only tall tables in the middle of the courtyard, round that handsome column on which stands the David (*) covered with tablecloths, and at the four corners were four great copper basins for the glasses, and behind the tables stood men to hand wine or water to those who served the guests. The same arrangement was made in the garden round the fountain you know. On the tables were silver vessels in which the glasses were put to keep cool. The salt-cellars, forks, knife-handles, bowls for the fritters, almonds, sugarplums, and the jars for preserved pine-seeds were of silver; there was none other for the guests save the basins and jugs for washing of hands. The table-cloths were of the finest white damask linen (†) laid according to our fashion.

About four hundred citizens were invited to these five banquets, and among them the first of your house was your Lorenzo, and then Agnolo and Ludovico; I was also there.

On Monday morning to all who had received veal, jelly was given, and then about 1500 trenchers full were presented to others. Many religious (monks and nuns) also received gifts of fowls, fish, sweetmeats, wine, and similar things.

After the guests at the first tables had finished many hundreds ate. They say that between the house here and that of Messer Carlo (‡) more than a thousand people ate, and at Messer Carlo's every day one hundred barrels of wine were drunk.

In the house here, where the marriage feast was, every respectable person who came in was at once taken to the ground floor hall, out of the large loggia, to refresh himself with fruit, sweetmeats, and white and red wine. The common folk were not invited.

The feasting began in the morning, a little before dinner-time, then everyone went away to repose. At about the twentieth hour [4 o'clock] they returned and danced until supper-time on the stage outside, which was decorated with tapestries, benches and forms, and covered in with large curtains of purple, green and white cloth, embroidered with the arms of the Medici and the Orsini. Every time a company came on the stage to dance they took refreshments

* By Donatello, now in the Bargello.
† *Tel di Rensa*, so called because it came from Rheims.
‡ Cosimo's illegitimate son.

once or twice, according to the time. First came the trumpeters, then a great silver basin, then many smaller ones full of glasses, then small silver jars full of water, then many flasks of trebbiano and then twenty-three silver bowls full of preserved pine-seeds and sweet conserves. To all was given in abundance and all the dishes were emptied ; and the same with the flasks of wine. The account has not been made, but from five to . . . thousand pounds of sweet-meats and sugar-plums were consumed.

The bride has received about fifty rings, costing they say from ten to fifty or sixty ducats each ; one piece of brocade ; a sweet-meat dish of silver, and many other such things ; and a small book of the Offices of Our Lady, most beautiful, the gift of Messer Gentile, written in letters of gold on blue vellum and covered with crystal and worked silver, which cost about two hundred florins. On Tuesday the bride left (a tournament was held first), and returned to the house of the Alessandri in the same dress in which she came to be married. This was a robe of white and gold brocade and a magnificent hood on her head, as is used here. She rode the same horse and was accompanied by the same youths, whose rich dresses of silver brocade embroidered with large pearls and jewels baffle description. From what they tell of courts of great Princes nothing was ever seen like it save certain jewels of great value worn by some great Lords. Of the women I say nothing ! Such jackets and robes of silk, all of them embroidered with pearls. I rather blame than praise this height of civilisation. And thus ended this marriage.

One day it rained ; on the Monday, just when the feast was at its highest. It seemed as though done on purpose. It enveloped everything and wet the beautiful dresses, for the rain was so sudden and so heavy that many could not get under shelter soon enough. But the youths and the women had not put on the finest clothes which they had reserved for that day, the most important of the feast, so that to many it seemed their money had been spent in vain, not being able to wear them. However, on Tuesday morning, when the bride went to hear Mass in S. Lorenzo, accompanied by all the youths and maidens who had attended her at the wedding, every-one was in their finest clothes. I warrant you that there were about fifty maidens and young girls and as many or more youths, so richly dressed that I do not think that anywhere among so many people could such a splendid and fine spectacle be seen.

I know that though I have written you many things and in much detail there is still much to be said ; and although it is not worth your reading or my writing, yet I have done so for your information, as I know you to be curious, and that you like to know exactly how things went. So I have written thus thinking it would please you better than a more serious style.''

[16] *Lettere di una Gentildonna fiorentina, op. cit.,* p. 600.

[17] *Ibid.,* p. 592.

[18] B. Felice, *op. cit.*

'' From Messer Francesco we have heard the good news about your whole family; which makes us so happy and contented, that there is no better news to give you. We therefore all beg and desire you to be willing and to act so with everyone that you will become ever more dear to Piero, Lorenzo, Giuliano, Madonna Contessina and

Madonna Lucrezia, and to your sisters-in-law, and to everyone else with whom you come in contact. If it is possible for us here to do anything for Lorenzo or for any of the family, please assure them that we shall neglect nothing in order to please them. In the same way, if there is anything to be done for you, let me know, and I will show that I do not love you any the less than Organtino, who, being a man and therefore necessary to our house, is as dear to me as my own life. Commend me to the Magnificence of Piero and the ladies and salute Lorenzo and Giuliano on my behalf. It so happens that Messer Baptista da Augubio is coming to Florence ; you know how devoted he is to us ; if it should be necessary, speak to Piero and Lorenzo so that, for love of us, they may favour him in every way.

Rome, June 15, 1469.   RAINALDUS DE ORSINI."

[19] Fabroni, *Laurentii Medicis Vita.*

" On our departure Your Magnificence commanded me to give you news of the Magnificent Lorenzo every eight days. Now therefore I will obey for the first week. You will have heard from Francesco Nori and Gugliemo de' Pazzi that the morning we left you we arrived at Prato while it was yet cool. We lunched there with the Proto-notary de' Medici, together with the Podestà of the place and his companions, who had accompanied him and Giuliano. When we left there was a little wind, but we arrived at the twentieth hour on that same Friday at Pistoia, whence several citizens came out to meet us. He descended at the Bishop's Palace, for he had been told by the messengers that Monsignore expected him. After greeting the Bishop, whilst the things were being unpacked, he visited the two Rectors, the Captain and the Podestà of the place, who were also bidden by Monsignore to bear him company at supper. He was visited by four citizens on behalf of the Priors of the City, who asked pardon in the name of the people that, owing to his unexpected arrival, they had not etc., and begging that on his return etc., all in most affectionate words. On the Saturday morning following he was on horseback at the ninth hour. He lunched with the Vicar of Pescia, Baptista Nasi, for there was no better inn. He was visited there by some of the Commune, who presented wine, marzipan and corn, and the same was done by some others personally. He rested in the house of the Grand Master of Altopascio, who had accom-panied him to lunch, and left at the twentieth hour, and met some citizens who wished to honour him in their own houses. He passed through Lucca and at the twenty-third hour he dismounted at the Corona Inn, on the other side, by the Pisan gate. He intended to leave on the following Sunday morning. But after supper six Lucchese citizens came with torches and accompanied by the servants of the Signoria. They found Lorenzo taking the air on the Piazza and receiving visits from individuals. Paolo Trenta and Piero Guidiccioni addressed him, regretting that in this place, where he was so popular and could do so much, he had not felt safe, but had lodged outside the town. They begged him in a long oration to remain until the Signoria had been able etc. Lorenzo replied that, on seeing them, whom he reverenced like fathers, he felt he could better bear such a visit, and felt obliged to reply in person, so that he would postpone his departure until at least after lunch, and in the morning he would go with them to show his love for the Signoria.

On Sunday morning Niccolo da Noceto, Paolo di Poggio and many citizens came for him, and placing him first among them, then Bernardo Rucellai, and then the Chancellor, they conducted him first to Mass in the chapel of the Holy Cross, and then to the Signoria, where he spoke so well in a large assembly that he won the hearts of all these people. As soon as he had returned to his lodgings presents began to arrive ; torches, both large and small, pine-seeds, boxes of other sweets and wine. He thanked, gave presents in return and kept some to lunch with him ; and took out his silver. But seeing that some were ready to move and that the wind was rising, he anticipated the hour of departure. All the same he was followed by many citizens, who wanted to accompany him, and speak with him at length. He rested on the way at Chiesa and Mazarosa and Capezano, all very pretty places, and arrived at Pietra Santa at the twenty-third hour. He lodged at the Campana, outside the gates, for this is a doubtful place, and S. George does not greatly trust S. Zita. Then the Vicar, who is a gentleman of Fiesco, sent to offer him a visit and anything that lay in his power. He saw him and thanked him, and then, accompanied by all these men, who could not see enough of him, he supped, together with some of them, under an arbour which is in a beautiful place opposite the sea, with a fruitful plain behind. This morning he was on horseback at the eighth hour, and came these sixteen miles very happily. At the foot of Monte Tignoso he met the Chancellor of the Magnificent Marquis of Fosdinovo, who came to invite him on behalf of his master. Then at Venza, or a little further, at Luni, he met the Signor Marchese Gabrielle himself, who conducted him to Serezana, to his own house, where, on dismounting, he visited first the Rector who governs this place on behalf of the Florentines. Then he lunched, and after he had rested a little, he went to see Serzanella, which, as seen from the citadel, seemed to him a good purchase. After supper he visited Messer Francesco, the Ducal chamberlain, who was lodged outside the city, and badly provided with supper, so he provisioned him handsomely. To-morrow morning he will go and lunch at Villa Franca, and in the evening he will be at Pontremoli. The whole journey has been done according to plan, and on Saturday he will reach Milan, and as soon as he has done his Magnificent Father's commission, he will return with all speed to you, which is the only reason why he regrets his absence. He is very well and happy, and so is Bernardo. You can tell Nannina this. The whole party is the same as when we left, all in agreement, and most obedient, without any discomforts, and we have not lacked even a nail. There have been no delays or complications. Everything has gone well and happily. May it please God that we find you the same, to Whom we commend ourselves.

July 18, 1469.''

[20] Armstrong, *op. cit.*, p. 81.

[21] *Archivio Med\iceo avanti Principato*, lxxx. 14.

[22] B. Felice, *op. cit.*

. . . . '' Considering your great love for me, you might have left everything else in order to answer me, for you know that I have no greater joy in this world than to have good news of you, of Lorenzo and of the whole family. Please comfort me for your absence with

228

some letters, which, when I receive them I will keep in such a place that it will seem as if I had you always in my arms. I commend myself to you and beg you to command me to do something here for you."

[23] *Archivio Mediceo avanti Principato*, xxxiv. 64.

" You will see from this that by the grace of God we are all well, and we always hope to hear the same of you. Beloved as a sister, the reason why I write is that I hear that your husband, Lorenzo, has the right to appoint, or cause to be appointed, whomsoever he will as preacher at Santa Reparata, and that the position will be given to his candidate. I should be very glad if you would obtain the appointment for my venerable spiritual father, a monk of the Order of S. Augustine, named Maestro Bartholomeo da Padoa, who was to have preached in the afternoons this Lent in Florence in Santa Reparata. He came to Rome this winter on business, and preached at Christmas in S. Agostino, and the Cardinal of Rouen, the protector of his Order, together with some other courtiers, kept him here. He was very well received and preached nobly, so, as I bear him, who is my spiritual father, love and spiritual affection, I am moved to write to you to beg Lorenzo most earnestly to appoint him to preach in Santa Reparata in the morning. I am certain you will have great honour and pleasure therefrom, as all his other hearers have had, and I can tell you that nothing similar has been known in Rome for years and years. You need have no doubt of his acceptance, for I have already spoken to His Reverence, and he says he is willing. But you must send him his appointment or some reply as soon as possible, for I know for certain that very soon he will be summoned to another place. No more, except that may God preserve you.

Given in Rome 1472, March 19.

Your loving as a sister, AGNOLELLA URSINA.

To the Noble and Generous Lady Madonna Clarice degli Ursini, in the house of Lorenzo di Pietro di Cosimo, may this faithfully be given."

[24] *Ibid.*, xxxiv. 76.

" By this you will know that, by the grace of God, I am well and hope to hear the same of you. I wrote to you during Holy Week, but so far have had no reply from you, and since I fear the letter may have gone astray, I will now repeat what was contained in the other letter. I begged you most earnestly to ask Lorenzo to appoint my spiritual father, Maestro Bartholomeo da Padoa, of the Order of S. Augustine, as the morning preacher in Santa Reparata. He was to have preached there last Lent, but was unable to do so because he was kept here by Monsignor de Rouen. He preached very successfully, for he is an excellent preacher, and every day I and many other people received much consolation from his sermons. Now, to honour your country and give joy to me, and also to you, I begged you in my other letter, and I do so again now, to persuade Lorenzo to give him this post. If Lorenzo has made other arrangements since I wrote on Monday in Holy Week, I beg you if possible, to rearrange matters, for I was the first to ask, and am very surprised at receiving no reply from you, for I hoped that the affair was arranged. I beg you to do what you have to do quickly. No more except that may God keep you all in prosperity.

Given in Rome 1472 on April 10.

Your loving as a sister, AGNOLELLA DEGLI URSINI.

To the Noble and Generous Lady, Madonna Clarice di Lorenzo di Pietro di Cosimo, may this faithfully be given."

[25] B. Felice, *op. cit.*

" By this you will know what has happened since we left. We arrived the first night at Figline, and stayed at San Cerbone with Giovanni d'Antonio, who received us very honourably, and entertained us with all his women and other relatives. On his advice, and that of Filippo, we turned aside to Levare, and came on the second evening to Arezzo with Morello, that is Antonio da Pantaneto, who is held in such honour there that we were filled with the greatest admiration. We were visited by the Captain and the Podestà, and also by the Commune, bearing such things as they thought would do us honour. At our entry and our departure we were accompanied by many men of importance with music, and before we left we were prayed and exhorted by the Podestà of Castiglione, through one of his messengers, to lunch with him next day, which we did gladly, knowing him to be devoted to you. There we were also visited by the Commune, and this evening we are at Cortona with the Captain who, having been told of our coming, sent to meet us as far as Castiglione, and here we have been received gladly and with great honour, both by the Captain and the Commune. We shall go on our way rejoicing, as we have done so far, if we know by your letters that we have been remembered to Mona Contessina, and Mona Lucretia, and that my Lucrezia and Piero are well. Commend me to Bianca and Nannina, and if you have any news which you do not think it necessary to keep secret please let us have a line, we shall be most grateful. No more by this.

April 24, 1472."

[26] L. Pulci, *Lettere, op. cit.*

" I wrote to you from Savina, and Ardito will have brought the letter. Afterwards we stayed at Monte Rotondo for some days, and were much honoured, in truth. Yesterday we entered Rome very honourably, with about eighty horsemen, and everywhere Madonna Clarice does you honour and receives it. I shall return in a couple of days to the Marches, and then to you. In my opinion the stay here will be brief, for there is no wedding at present, as you will have heard. That being so we should only lose time and reputation. And besides little Lucrezia and Piero draw us to them like magnets, and you had better beg her to return. . . . Send for us, for we shall take the road by Siena, and shall stop on the way, and then we shall arrive in triumph.

In Rome, May 6, 1472."

[27] *Archivio Mediceo avanti Principato*, xxviii. 89.

[28] L. Pulci, *Lettere, op. cit.*

" I had not time to write everything from Rome. Now, so that there may be no exception to the rule of always telling you some scandal, I must tell you that our Madonna went the other day to visit the Pardon of S. Angelo. Afterwards she visited the daughter of the despot of the Maremma, I mean the Morea. . . . I will therefore give you a short description of this cupola of Norcia, this mountain of fat that we visited. I did not think there was so much in Magna, or even in Sardinia. We entered the room in which this babbler was seated, and she had wherewithal to sit, I can assure you. I will begin in the middle, where virtue resides. Consider that Madonna Mea and Madonna Cosa are consumptive ants in size, and Gratiano a fine fellow. Two large Turkish tambourines on her breast, a huge chin, an enormous face, a pair of pimply cheeks, and a neck between the tambourines. Her two eyes looked like four, and were surrounded with so much flesh and fat and grease, that they were greater than the banks of the Po. And you need not think that her legs were thin, like Giulio's. If they had had a pair of bellows attached they would have been large enough to sow three bushels of seed . . . a noise in the middle and fat everywhere. I do not know whether I ever saw a joint or anything so oily and fat and soft and sticky, and funny as this strange witch. All day they talked through an interpreter, and one of her brothers, with legs no thinner than Jacopo's, acted as dragoman. Your lady, dazzled by this mountain, and thinking it amusing to speak through an interpreter, said how beautiful she was. Benedetto did nothing all day but say what a lovely, clever little mouth she had, and how beautifully she spat. It is true her mouth is small, but nature usually does everything justly. They talked of many things in Greek until the evening. But there was no mention of eating or drinking, neither in Greek, nor Latin, nor the vulgar tongue. She went so far as to tell our Madonna that the dress she wore was mean and tight, for her own was plump and swollen, and must have contained six pieces of crimson satin, enough, I think, to decorate the cupola of S. Maria Rotonda.

In everything else our lady is wise and discreet. She has borne herself like a sybil, and has received great honours. I am returning to Rome to-day to perform my duty and accompany her home, as I was instructed when I left. I only came here to attend to some business which I had left unfinished.

From Foligno, May 20, 1472.''

[29] *Archivio Mediceo avanti Principato*, xxi. 300.

[30] *Ibid.*, xxiv. 282.

'' I am always anxious to have news of you and beg you to let me know how you all are whenever you can. We are writing a letter to Lorenzo on behalf and in favour of Girolamo di Zarzano, about a benefice which was conferred upon him by Monsignor the Papal Chamberlain. It seems that it has also been given to another than Girolamo, and there is great controversy. Wherefore I beg you earnestly to remind Lorenzo on our behalf several times that we recommend the said Girolamo to him, and we shall be very grateful. No more. A thousand blessings from me on you and your children. We are all well.

Rome, November 25, 1472. MAGDALENA DE URSINIS, mater.

Item. My daughter, you will be blessed if you will take good care of Girolamo in this matter.

To the Magnificent Lady Clarice de Ursinis, my blessed daughter, Florence.''

[31] Poliziano, *Prose Volgari, op. cit.*

[32] *Ibid.*

[33] *Ibid.*

" This morning I wrote and told you that Lorenzo was well. I expect you will receive this letter and that one at the same time. Now I have nothing else to say except the same thing, but in order to act as usual I thought I would write these few lines. As I wrote to you, we have lost Galasso. I do not think he wanted to have anything to do with me, especially in Latin, but I do not want to find myself in the deserts of Barbary. I do not think the other children are as worried as you are about our staying here. I go round looking for these things in order to have something to fill my letter. Lorenzo laughs at the spots on my clothes, and recommends your specific, which seems to me the best there can possibly be. I thank you that, even though I am not present, you have thought a little about my affairs. May God grant that I may repay you in some measure. There is nothing else. Please make my excuses to Ser Niccolo that owing to lack of time I do not write to him. Possibly he has received two of my letters to-day. I have written this with great difficulty, for I have a very bad headache, and my stomach is out of order. God grant that it is nothing more. I have gone without my supper this evening and hope this will do me good, for I suspect a little fever. But this is beside the point. Lorenzo is well and happy and so are the rest of the family. I commend myself to you and pray that God may keep you happy.

Pisa, April 19, 1476.   Your servant ANGELO."

[34] Pieraccini, *op. cit.*, p. 129.

[35] *Archivio Mediceo avanti Principato*, xxiv. 7.

" This is to tell you that your brother Organtino has arrived and is staying at Monte Rotondo, and is in good health, by the grace of God. But he cannot come and visit you at present because he only has leave for a short time, and could not get permission for the necessary time to come to you. So please forgive him. But he intends, if God gives him grace, to come soon to visit you, if nothing more happens in Puglia, where he is engaged. I should be glad to hear of your journey. No more. May God keep you in health. Take care to keep happy. We are all well here.

Rome, May 7, 1477.   MAGHDALENA DE URSINIS, *tua genetrix*.

To the Magnificent Lady Clarice de Ursinis, my blessed daughter, Florence."

[36] Poliziano, *Prose Volgari, op. cit.*

[37] *Archivio Mediceo avanti Principato*, xxxi. 191.

[38] *Ibid.*, xxxi. 207.

I am sending you a hundred little birds that have been given me, and a pheasant. I have kept some for ourselves. We are all happy, by the grace of God, and we pray Him that you may be the same. We are very well received by this whole city, and the children all seem in splendid health. It is true that no guard is kept here, and everyone is allowed to enter, which makes me rather suspicious. I beg you to see about it. I am well and pray you to beware of the plague. I commend myself to you.

Pistoia, August 23, 1478.   Your CLARICIA.

To the Magnificent Laurentio de Medicis. Florence."

[39] Poliziano, *Prose Volgari, op. cit.*

[40] *Ibid.*

"Madonna Clarice is well, and so are all the family. Here we had not heard anything of the rumour of which Franco tells me by the hand of this same bearer. This, however, has relieved us of all anxiety, for we have faith in his letter. Madonna Clarice feared it might be something more serious, and that you were purposely making light of it. Now she is content and agrees. We lack nothing, and are only worried by your troubles, which are so great. May God help you. *Spes enim in vivis est, desperati mortui.*

Madonna Clarice would be glad if, when you do not need him too much there, you would send Giovanni Tornabuoni back here, for she is lonely without him, and for every reason she thinks that his presence here would be desirable.

I look after Piero, and exhort him to write, and in a few days I think you will be very surprised, for we have here a master who teaches writing in fifteen days, and he does marvels at his work. The children play about more than usual, and are quite restored in health. May God help them and you. Piero never leaves me, nor I him. I would have liked to serve you in some greater thing, but since this has fallen to my lot, I will do it gladly. . . .

Pistoia, 26 August, 1478.   Your servant ANG. POL."

[41] *Ibid.*

[42] *Nonna, Mamma e Nipotina, op. cit.*

[43] Poliziano, *Prose Volgari, op. cit.*

[44] *Ibid.*

"All this family, by the grace of God, are well. We are awaiting your coming with the greatest anxiety. Here we are preparing to honour this Marquis or Captain, whoever he may be. I have no more to say, except to commend myself continually to you and pray that God will keep you in happiness.

Pistoia, September 2, 1478.   Your servant ANG. POLITIANUS."

[45] *Archivio Mediceo avanti Principato,* xxxi. 278.

[46] Poliziano, *Prose Volgari, op. cit.*

"Since last night Madonna Clarice has not been feeling very well. She is writing herself to Madonna Lucrezia and says that she fears she may have a miscarriage, or else may suffer in the same way as Giovanni Tornabuoni's wife. After supper she lay down on the couch, and this morning she rose late, lunched well, and after lunch she lay down again. The women of the Panciatichi family are with her, including the mother of Andrea, who is a very wise woman. Andrea tells me that she says that Madonna Clarice is not without danger of miscarrying. I thought I had better tell you everything. But all these women say they do not think things will go badly, and to see her, she does not look ill, *nisi quod cubat, et quod paullo commotior et quam consuevit.*

Piero was the first this morning to greet His Lordship. He said a few words of the speech you wrote for him, and said them very well. His Lordship lifted him up in front of him, and entered Pistoia in this manner. Madonna Clarice sent him a fine bunch of partridges, and this evening we are going to visit him at the twenty-second hour, it being now the nineteenth. Piero was accompanied by Giovanni Tornabuoni, who completed his speech. According to his people, His Lordship has come with the greatest desire to do you honour and to satisfy the Signoria and especially yourself.

Clarice sends you I do not know how many partridges, which were given to her to present to His Lordship. I will note carefully what happens and will do my duty to the best of my ability, and will tell you all. May God preserve you. I commend myself.

Pistoia, September 7, 1478."

[47] Pieraccini, *op. cit.*, p. 134.

" M. Stefano has just arrived here, and by the grace of God, has found me a good deal better, as I think, and has comforted me greatly. He is writing to you himself at greater length. The rest are very well and commend themselves to you.

Pistoia, September 7, 1478."

[48] Poliziano, *Prose Volgari, op. cit.*

" Maestro Stefano is writing at length about Madonna Clarice. She has been without further trouble so far. Last night the Maestro thought she had a little fever, and every evening she seems rather exhausted. She supped very well at the fourth hour, and afterwards she was in the best of spirits. It has probably been rather an attack of catarrh than anything else, for she says her hands have been tormented by itching, which the Maestro says is a sign of catarrh. At night she sleeps very well, and is the same in the day, except at about the twenty-third hour. She was greatly cheered by the arrival of the Maestro, and thinks she is well again. The Maestro makes her rest in bed, as a precaution. She has continually with her the mother of Andrea Panciatichi, whom she greatly esteems, and who is a great comfort to her. Either Andrea or his brother is always in the house, and one of them is never absent. We shall take every care, not only of her, but of the rest of the little family, who are well, and in good spirits. Madonna Clarice is cheered by the letters and news from Florence. I wish I could do more, but I will do my best.

Pistoia, September 8, 1478.   Servitor ANG. POL."

[49] Pieraccini, *op. cit.*, p. 134.

" I find that your Madonna Clarice has more the symptoms of serious trouble, than the trouble itself. I was in doubt, but I am not sorry she was worried, as things have not gone too far to be remedied. I hope that with the grace of God we shall be able to take such measures that the birth will take place safely, and that we may be able to stop the flux which has begun. So take comfort, for everything will go well. No more, except that I commend myself to Your Magnificence.

M.V. SER STEFANO DE LA TURRI."

234

[50] *Ibid.*

"I have just had a letter from you telling me not to be frightened. This is to tell you that I am much encouraged, as the trouble has not progressed any further. It is true that I feared at first, and told you what I feared, but M. Stefano has told me, as have the other doctors, that I am in no danger, and I feel almost well. May God keep you happy.

Pistoia, September 8, 1478."

[51] Poliziano, *Prose Volgari, op. cit.*

"I think my letters must be acceptable to you, for I only write to give you news of your family. All, by the grace of God, are well, and Piero is still learning to write, and is becoming quite a good scribe, so that I hope he will soon relieve me of this burden of writing *sine argumento*, as I do, for I am ashamed of it. But may God grant that I have always to say the same thing to you, which is that we are well. Madonna Clarice is cheerful, and quite well again. We keep good guard, but are anxious both about the news from there and about you. May God preserve you, for it seems to me that all depends on that. Do not worry about us, for we are most careful about everything. As far as I am concerned I will not lack diligence, nor goodwill, nor loyalty, for I know how much I owe you, and I love Piero and your other children almost as much as you do as their father. If sometimes something hard and strange happens, I will force myself to bear it for love of you, to whom I owe everything. I commend myself to you.

Pistoia, September 29, 1478.   ANGELO POLIZIANO."

[52] *Ibid.*

"Herewith is a letter from Piero written and composed by him. He and all this family are well, and anxious to see you. I commend myself to you.

Pistoia, September 21, 1478.   Servitor ANGELUS POLITIANUS."

[53] *Letterine d'un Bambino Fiorentino, op. cit.*

[54] Poliziano, *Prose Volgari, op. cit.*

"Piero is well, and so is the Count's son. We take care to keep as good a watch as possible, and also to make them take exercise, nor do we neglect our usual studies.

Antonio Manetti and one of the monks of the Badia write to tell me that I must return certain books they lent me a long time ago, and they have been asking for them since before I went to Pistoia. When I returned I could not send them back, for there are several books, and I could not send a porter back with them when I was with the children, for such were Madonna Clarice's orders. They are in the box, and it is necessary, in order to return them, that I should come to Florence for half an hour. I beg you to allow me to do so, for without your permission I will never leave Piero to go into the desert. The children could stay with Monsignore for that short time, for I do not think they could be safer. There is nothing else, except that I commend myself as usual.

Fiesole, October 18, 1478.   Servitor ANG."

[55] See Chapter 6, Note 64.

[56] *Archivio Mediceo avanti Principato*, xxxvi. 1361.

"Your messenger Andrea has been here, and has begged me to intercede with you for him, for he is very sorry for his fault. Please either keep him with you, or find him a place, for since he has shown himself faithful to you, it would be contrary to your nature not to pardon him for an error, and to cause him to go astray and end badly. For thereby you might discourage others who are faithful to you. His mother was so glad that he should be in your service, and now she is so unhappy for she fears that her son, if he is not with you, will get into bad ways and bring sorrow upon her. He has been punished for his fault by his sorrow and shame, for they say that when he was sent away he was beside himself, and could not regain his spirits, and I really think he feels the slight on his honour, which is a good sign. So I beg you that, either because of his proved fidelity, or for the sake of his mother, or because of his own character, or because of my pleadings, you will favour him, and either take him back or find him other work. I commend myself to you.

From Cafaggiuolo December 13, 1478.   Your wife CLARICIA.
To the Magnificent Laurentio de Medicis. Florence."

[57] B. Felice, *op. cit.*

"Thanks be to God that He has made an end of Lorenzo's many troubles and worries and those of this city. We have just made peace and concluded an alliance in the manner you will have heard, for we sent the terms some days since, and you will have heard everything from Lorenzo. Let us trust in God to bring everything to a good conclusion. Let us thank God a thousand times for giving us this grace. . . ."

[58] Fabroni, *Laurentii Medicis Vita, op. cit.*

[59] *Letterine d'un Bambino Fiorentino, op. cit.*

[60] *Archivio Mediceo avanti Principato*, xxxvii. 261.

"This is only that you may know that, by the grace of God, we are all well. Except for his trouble, Giuliano is very well and is a good boy. Maestro Stefano has seen him, and thinks he is much the same, and no different than before. I will take care of him as a mother should. I beg you to take care of yourself for the sake of your children and for my sake. All commend themselves to you.

From Cafaggiuolo, April 25, 1479.
To Lorenzo de Medici, Florence."

[61] *Ibid.*, xxxvii. 262.

"We are all well. Giuliano is the same, and I do not think that Maestro Stefano finds him any weaker than before. I will take every possible care of him. No more. I commend myself to you.

April 25, 1479.   Your daughter, CLARICE.
To Monna Lucretia de Medici in Florence."

[62] Poliziano, *Prose Volgari, op. cit.*

[63] Fabroni, *Laurentii Medicis Vita, op. cit.*

"I hear that the plague is even worse than usual. All the prayers of your wife and children beg you to take care of yourself, and if you could with safety come here for this festival it would cheer us greatly. I leave it all to your prudence. I should be glad not to be turned into ridicule by Franco in the same way as was Luigi Pulci, nor to hear that Messer Angelo can say that he will stay in your house against my will, and that you have given him your own room at Fiesole. You know that I said that if you wished him to remain I would be content, and though he has called me a thousand bad names if it is with your approval, I will endure it, but I cannot believe that it is true. I can well believe that Ser Niccolo, who wishes to make peace with him, has implored me so much. The children are all well, and long to see you, as do I most especially, for it is my greatest torment that you should be in Florence at such a time. I commend myself to you always.

In Cafaggiuolo, May 28, 1479.''

[64] See Chapter 6, Note 67.

[65] B. Felice, *op. cit.*

[66] *Archivio Mediceo avanti Principato*, lxxx. 67.

'' We are now all well in Gagliano, where you know there is nothing but the walls. And since the annual sickness is not yet over I am suspicious of Cafaggiuolo. I would like you to send me various things from Florence, for I have nothing for the use of the family. Please send two pairs of forks, four pairs of sheets for ourselves and four pairs for the servants, and two tablecloths.

I am asking you for these things although I do not doubt that Lorenzo will come, though I am not sure. Please send me twenty braccia of linen cloth, so that I can make some shirts for these children. No more. I commend myself to you.

June 2, 1479.

Please show this letter to Lorenzo as I am not writing to him.
Your CLARICE in Gagliano.

To the Magnificent Lady Lucretia de Medici, greatly honoured as a mother. In Florence.''

[67] *Ibid.*, xxxvii. 430.

'' Our exiles at Fagna are all very well and happy, and I think we are all out of danger, though Maestro Stefano is still in doubt, but there would have been some signs by now if there was anything. If you think we ought to return we will do so, and if it can be done without danger I would like to get the clothes and things belonging to these children, which are there, for they need them. Please tell me what to do, for without these things it is very inconvenient. No more, except that we are all very well, thanks be to God, and we beg you to take as much care as possible of yourself, for your health is our happiness. I commend myself to you.

In Gagliano, June 9, 1479.   Your CLARICE.

To the Magnificent Lorenzo de Medici, my lord, in Florence.''

[68] *Ibid.*, lxxxv. 228.

'' I have a letter from you which rejoiced me greatly, since you are well, and it also gives me pleasant news. You want to know where we are in Gagliano, and how. We are in the old house, on the right as you enter, and we have arranged things so that, if you care to come here at any time, there will always be a room ready for you. As I told you, Anna and the other one are free of infection, for there would have been certain signs by now. But Maestro Stefano is still in doubt. For myself I would send her back, but I await your views. We are very well here, thanks be to God. I commend myself to you, and please tell Lorenzo to come and see us sometimes.

In Gagliano, June 15, 1479.   Your CLARICE.

To the Magnificent Lady Lucretia Medicis, who is like my mother. Careggi."

[69] G. Volpi, *Affetti di Famiglia nel Quattrocento*, 1890.

[70] B. Felice, *op. cit.*

"Magnificent Madonna. It is now four days since we had a messenger from Rome. This morning Niccolo da Ugolino Martelli showed me a letter he had received with news from there. It says that the people of Cavi are holding out well, and that they have received and are receiving help and favour in money and men from the Prince of Bisignano, their relative, and it is thought that this will be a longer and more desperate undertaking than anybody believed. They say also that the wife of Count Girolamo when she went to the camp to see the Count was almost captured by the men of the valley, the partisans of the Colonna, but she received much help. To-day we hear that M. Alberto de Arengheris, a noble Sienese citizen, with all his goods and possessions has taken the road for Venice, in order to go to Rhodes, since he is discontented and suspicious of the present state of Siena, and it is thought that many other gentlemen, his friends, will do the same. I will give you news of what passes in Rome, and I commend myself to you.

July 19, 1480.   FILIPPO REDDITI."

[71] *Archivio Mediceo avanti Principato*, lxxx. 90.

[72] *Un Viaggio di Clarice Orsini de'Medici nel* 1485, *descritto da Ser Matteo Franco (edito da Isidoro del Lungo)* in *Scelta di Curiosità letterarie inedite o rare, dal sec. xiii al sec. xvii. Disp. xcviii. Bologna,* 1863.

" 'Ser Piero, good-bye, good-bye Franco, good-bye Lorenzo, good-bye Butto, good-bye Francesco, good-bye, good-bye, etc. etc.' The place is between Bagno and Capitulo at the time of our departure. Florence having parted from Pisa we came, singing joyfully, to the other side of Monte Castelli by the mill, where we found, on looking down from above, about twenty-five soldiers with shields and pikes. We began to say among ourselves ' Who are these people ? ' but when we cried ' Palle, Palle ' they replied ' Palle, Palle ' and ' Orso, Orso ' and as we drew near they cried the more, and we found that they were men sent from Monte Castelli to accompany us. They wanted to take us into the town, but as we were unwilling, they came down with us into the plain, where there was a swarm of women with faces like chestnuts, but all happy and cheerful, with tables spread with wine and puff pastry. We drank on horseback, and having sent away all the soldiers except one whom we kept as a guide, we left, still singing and rejoicing. We passed by deserted Monte Guidi, and half-way down we met a priest with his frock tucked up all round, and as much out of breath as if he had come from Assisi. He said he was a friend of Donnino's and pressed us to dismount and enter the town where he has his church and his house. He tired himself so, and ran to and fro so often that, if he did not get himself bled, I fear he must have been dead by eight o'clock. God help him. We left without stopping at all, and passed Casoli without entering. About four miles beyond Casoli, Martino Ghezo and Martino Moro rejoined us, for they had not been able to keep up with us as we had been riding very quickly, and so they had remained behind. They said that in Casoli they had met the much-desired Nannina in a litter. She made them stop and asked about Lorenzo and Madonna Clarice, and hearing that Madonna Clarice had gone on ahead, and Lorenzo had gone to Pisa, she said she was in despair, and was very sorry not to be able to see Lorenzo, or at least to speak to Madonna Clarice. When Madonna heard this she said several times on the road that she regretted her bad luck in not having at least met her.

Thus until about two miles from Colle we continued to sing and joke and talk. Then we stopped, for all the words fled into a brother of Antonio da Pela who came to meet us, and conducted us as far as the broken-down and ruined township of Colle. When we reached the house the said Antonio da Pela came out with such a flood of talk that we, and his brother, and everybody else were drowned in it whence it is obvious that he is the elder brother. When we came into the room we found about thirty-five of his relations, children, women and babies, and we had barely entered when the bore began to say, ' Madonna Clarice, this is my daughter—curtsey and touch her hand—and this and this. And this is my granddaughter—curtsey and touch her gown. And this and this. And these children are all my grandchildren—stand up, be courteous. This one is to be a priest, this one a nun, this one is Madonna Lucrezia's god-child, this one is just married, this one makes Venetian lace, and this one ribbon.' May he get dysentery. If I had not got him away he would have bewitched us all. By saying how tired Madonna Clarice was, and the rest of us, I stopped him for a little while. We arrived at the hour of twenty-two and a half or twenty-three, and when we had rested a little Ser Giovanni Antonio and I went to see paper made ; and when we returned we took Madonna Clarice, who thought it a fine thing, and was pleased, not only with the work, but with the water and the fresh air. On our return we supped at about the first hour ; some crisp cakes, puff pastry, and trebbiano wine, salad and pickles, boiled chicken, and kid, and then roast pigeons and I do not know how much chicken, almond paste, and how many boxes of sweets.

Before supper the community of Colle presented Madonna with corn, wax, marzipan, wine, and sweetmeats, brought by many fine ambassadors, three of whom spoke for the rest. The substance of it was that they had expected Lorenzo, but as he had not come, they made their presents to her, who was another Lorenzo. They begged pardon for the smallness of their gifts owing to their poverty, and begged that she would commend them to Lorenzo, both themselves and their territory. Madonna replied shortly and well, saying that they should have had faith in her and in Lorenzo without making presents, for such things are done rather by strangers and foreigners than by good friends. ' On the one hand you complain, and ask me to tell Lorenzo of your poverty and your needs, and then you spend money on these things. I accept them all and return them to you, for if I kept them I should have them distributed in the country-side for the love of God, so I give them to you, who need them more than I.' There was a great fuss, for they would not take them back on any account, alleging that there were plots, etc. Ser Giovanni Antonio and I sent the things back to them by the servants, but kept four flasks of wine and a piece of marzipan, so as not to seem angry. And that was the end of that.

We slept excellently. In fact, if Pela had not worried us with so much silly chatter, we should have been full of joy and love for him, for in truth one must regard the spirit more than anything else.

In the evening, after supper, there came a Sienese ambassador, a certain Messer Ricco, who remained in the room with Madonna Clarice and Ser Giovanni Antonio for half an hour, speaking of the Sienese troubles. He said he had come expecting to find Lorenzo, for he had written a letter saying he was leaving with his wife, but not saying where he was going. As I know that in other matters the ambassador pleased Ser Giovanni Antonio, I will say no more.

In the morning we left, but first Ser Giovanni Antonio and I went to visit the Podestà. We came as far as Tavarnelle with a guide, and then to Passignano, whither Donnino had preceded us, and we arrived about the fifteenth or sixteenth hour. After a little rest we lunched; boiled liver and kid, and broad beans, curds and good wine. Afterwards we saw the whole house and the church, and the relics. I cannot tell you how pleased Madonna was with the house and her room, and we stayed there all day, examining and looking at everything. In the evening we supped on salad, an excellent herb pie, fried curds, beans and cheese, etc.

In the morning, that is yesterday morning, we left as soon as we had heard Mass. We took the road of San Casciano, and below Fabrica we found a horseman, who galloped up and said : ' Your Piero has sent me to find out which road you have taken, for last night he came several miles this way to meet you, and now he has gone towards S. Maria Impruneta with Messer Giovanni and everybody.' We replied that we were going by San Casciano. He at once departed at top speed to tell them. Finally, on the other side of San Casciano, at the crossing of the river, we met Jacopo Salviati and his friend, Tommaso Corbinelli, who had come to meet us : and, having embraced with great joy, they came with us. Then near the Certosa we met Paradise full of the angels of feasting and joy, that is to say, Messeri Giovanni, Piero, Giuliano, and Giulio riding pillion, with their attendants. As soon as they saw their mother they threw themselves to the ground, some by themselves, some with the help of others, and all ran and put their arms round the neck of Madonna Clarice, with more joy and kisses and content than I could tell you in a hundred letters.

I too was so overcome that I dismounted and before they remounted I embraced them all, and gave them two kisses at once, one for me and one for Lorenzo. Sweet little Giuliano said, with a long Oh, ' Oh, oh, where is Lorenzo ? ' We said, ' He has gone to Poggio to find you.' He said, ' Oh no ' and nearly cried. You never saw anything sweeter. Piero has become the finest boy and the most graceful thing you ever saw. He has grown a little, and has features which make him look like an angel ; his hair is long and more spread out than before, which suits him. Giuliano is pink and fresh, like a rose ; sweet and shining and clean like a mirror, happy and with those contemplative eyes. Messer Giovanni too, looks well, he has not much colour, but looks healthy and natural, and Giulio has a brown and healthy skin. All, to conclude, are a natural joy. Thus, with great rejoicing, the whole party went by Via Maggio, Ponte S. Trinità, San Michele Berteldi, Santa Maria Maggiore, Canto della Paglia, Via de Martigli, and arrived home. . . .''

[73] *Archivio Mediceo avanti Principato*, xl. 268.

" By yours of the 5th I see what you say about Alfonsina, and the demand they make. Personally I am of your opinion, that you are doing enough if, according to their custom, you secure to her that which they give her, and I have not seen it done as they ask, except by some of the Sanseverini. I spoke of it with the Countess and with Signor Virginio when I was at Bracciano, and when the Countess asked me what had been done in your case, I replied that we had done this freely, and I thus persuaded her to leave it to you. When the Signor wanted to know my views I told him that it ought to be according to the custom here, but that he should not make too much fuss about it, but I said I had no instructions from you to conclude the matter more in one way than another. From Baccio I heard, before my journey, that they would in no wise be content with this, but I did not find them so definite about it, but I have no doubt that if you stand firm they will not balk at this, for they are anxious that you should force their hands and take Alfonsina away. They are as anxious to meet your wishes as you are to meet theirs. So, if shortly you decide to send for her, I think they will yield of their own accord, and I will be patient and stay here until the matter is settled. If I spoke of wishing to return it was because of my desire to see you and the family again, not because I lack anything, nor that I cannot endure that desire for your convenience and benefit. As for the expense, I think I have arranged so that it will be all right, but if it is necessary that I should economise more, I will do so gladly as soon as I see that I must stay longer. But I do not think they will break it off for this reason, and I cannot believe it after what passed between us at Bracciano, for, as I told you, they do not make much of it, especially Signor Virginio. I have not spoken to Baccio since my return, for he has not been in Rome, and I have not had a chance of discussing it with him, but I will do so as soon as I see him, and I will report to you.

As to the Archbishop, I can assure you that he never spoke the words you write to His Holiness. He did say them to the Cardinal, for the reason I wrote you the other day, owing to the difference between Signor Virginio and the Cardinal, for in this way he has some part with them, otherwise he is excluded. But he would not speak thus to His Holiness for anything in the world. Someone has reported this to you in order to do him an injury, for he is entirely devoted to your interests, and he can show this better by deeds than words.

I am, as usual, always between the two, sometimes well and

sometimes the contrary. But on Monday and Tuesday and to-day, up till now, I have felt fairly well, without that blessed stomach trouble which will not let me rest. I commend myself to you.

April 9, 1488.   CLARICE in Rome.

To the Magnificent Laurentio de Medicis, my beloved husband. Florence."

⁷⁴ Fabroni, *Laurentii Medicis Vita, op. cit.*

" I am writing to you on behalf of Lorenzo, and there is nothing else to say except that since Saturday I have written several letters to you, so that I will now send you details of the present sent by the Sultan to Lorenzo. I sent these details also to Piero, but his letter will come more slowly. There is a fine bay horse, strange animals, sheep and goats of various colours, with long ears down to their knees, and tails trailing on the ground nearly as big as their bodies ; a large beaker of balsam, eleven sable skins, more aloe wood than one man can carry, great vases of porcelain such as have never been seen, and most cunningly worked, cloth of various colours in one piece, fine dimity, which they call turban cloth, cloth treated with gum, which they call sexe, great vases of sweetmeats, dried plums and ginger."

⁷⁵ Quoted by Reumont, *Lorenzo de Medici*, Leipzig, 1874, vol. iii. 355.

⁷⁶ *Lorenzo de Medici. Lettere a Innocenzo VIII.* Florence, 1830.

" I am too often constrained to trouble Your Holiness with the griefs fortune prepares for me ; and since they are the gifts of Heaven and cannot be resisted, it is better for everyone to support them as far as possible, since they come from the Divine Goodness. But the death of my wife Clarice, which has just occurred, has over-whelmed me with such grief, sorrow and pain, for an infinity of reasons, that it has overcome my patience, and obedience to the trials and persecutions of fortune, for I did not think that anything could happen to me that would hurt me so much. But being thus deprived of her sweet accustomed company has grieved me so much that I can find no remedy. However, I do not cease to pray God to give me peace, and I have a firm hope in His Divine goodness, and that He will make an end of my great pain, and will not thrust upon me more such trials as I have suffered for some time past. And I most humbly beg Your Holiness from the depths of my heart, to deign to pray for me, for I know how anxious you are to help me. I commend myself to you and to your Holy Feet.

From Filetta, July 31, 1488."

⁷⁷ Ross, *op. cit.*, p. 397.

". . . I wrote that Madonna Clarice was ill. She died three days ago, but I did not send the news at once as it did not seem to me of much importance. Now that I am despatching the courier with letters from Naples I inform Your Excellency. She died last Wednes-day at 24 of the clock and was buried without pomp that evening. The Magnificent Lorenzo is at Filetta taking the waters and the baths, and the doctors advise him strongly not to come to Florence, also his friends have written to persuade him to finish his cure, and thus he will do. To-day, according to the custom here, the funeral service will take place at 21 of the clock. The whole city and the ambassadors of H.M., of Milan and myself, have been invited. But before I received the invitation, I went with the Milanese ambassador to the house of the Magnificent Lorenzo, and we condoled with Piero, the Magnificent's eldest son, in the names of our Lords, in such words as seemed fitted to the occasion.

Florence, August 1, 1488."

CHAPTER VII

[1] See Chapter V.

[2] *Letterine d'un Bambino Fiorentino, op. cit.*

" That pony does not come, and I am afraid that if he waits so long Andrea will turn him from a beast into a man, instead of curing his foot.

We are well and are studying. Giovanni can already pick out words. You can see how far I have got with writing, but in Greek I am rather keeping in practice with Martino's help than making any progress at present. Giuliano thinks of laughing and nothing else ; Lucrezia sews, sings and reads ; Maddalena knocks her head on the wall without hurting herself ; Luisa can already say a few words ; Contessina makes a great noise all over the house. All the others attend to their business, so that nothing is lacking except your presence.

We hear that things in general are going better than last year, and we hope that, if you are well, everything will come to a good conclusion. For good and valiant men are of little use in treachery, but of great value in open war. We have confidence in you, for we know that besides your goodness and valour, you remember the state which our ancestors left us, and the havoc and the injuries we have suffered. May God keep you.

Your son PIERO."

[3] B. Felice, *op. cit.*

[4] Pieraccini, *op. cit.*, p. 245.

[5] *Archivio Mediceo avanti Principato*, xxiv. 502.

[6] Pieraccini, *op. cit.*, p. 232.

[7] Fabroni, *Laurentii Medicis Vita, op. cit.*

[8] This letter is printed in the Italian edition of Roscoe's *Leo X·* Milan, 1816.

[9] Pieraccini, *op. cit.*, p. 233.

[10] *Lettere di Lorenzo de' Medici, op. cit.*

" It is almost with shame that I write to you about the affairs of Sig. Francesco, for it seems absurd to have to remind Your Holiness of a thing which must be dear to you above everything else, nor should my letters carry more weight with you than Sig. Francesco's natural condition. However, as I see the matter is being drawn out at length, I have not been able to abstain from this appeal, nor from anything else I can do for Sig. Francesco. He writes that he is very pleased with Maddalena, and this should constrain you to provide for him in such a manner that I may remain content and satisfied, as I shall be when Sig. Francesco's affairs are in a state which conforms to the dignity of Your Holiness and the repose of my mind. I have never desired that Your Holiness should despoil anyone in this world for the aggrandizement of Sig. Francesco, but insomuch as this would be a shameful thing, and alien to your nature, it seems to me unlike your innate goodness and kindness not to provide him with means to keep up his position, without doing injury to others. I beg you in all humility, to relieve yourself and me of this trouble, and to provide for him in such a way that I shall no longer need to approach you in this matter. By doing this you will perform a deed worthy of your clemency and goodness, not only a pious and a reasonable act, but one that is necessary, and most pleasing to me, and which will give a good example to all who have hopes of you. I commend myself to you.

Florence, February 26, 1487.

E.S.V. SERVITOR. LAURENTIUS DE MEDICIS."

[11] Fabroni, *Laurentii Medicis Vita, op. cit.*

" You have expressed my wishes about Maddalena's dowry. You know that when Maddalena went there, I did not think the marriage would take place so soon, for her age was not suitable. Since it was hurried on, there has been a slight delay about the dowry, but I thought it had been settled through the Archbishop that it was to be four thousand ducats. I do not know what kind of ducats nor on what conditions. I have given my other daughters two thousand ducats all told, including the two hundred ducats in the Monte, which are paid at the times and on the conditions you know. I should be glad to have it settled in one of the following ways, either that the whole dowry, with the exception of the few things Maddalena takes with her, should be secured on our account for the alum, and I would pay the same rate of interest as the Monte ; or else that il Signore should receive the interest from the Monte and the things brought by Maddalena, and the rest should come from the alum account. In fact, there is no difference, except that either the whole sum is taken from that account, or part is taken from the Monte, whichever Sig. Francesco prefers. It would be best to get it all from there, and then there should be no difficulty in raising this sum. I have no other means at present, and you know how many holes I have to fill. See what you can do about it and let me know.

August 8, 1488."

[12] Reumont, *op. cit.*, vol. ii. p. 345.
[13] Staffetti, *Innocenzo Cibo, op. cit.*
[14] I. del Lungo, *Florentia, op. cit.*

" I see what you say about Clarice, which grieves me, though her illness is no news to me. I have written to tell her the reason why Piero may be delayed for a little while, but she need not consider this if she thinks it better to return, though I should have liked her to wait for Alfonsina. I would like Maddalena to accompany her, for she is but a child, and her husband's house is in disorder, and it would be a comfort to Clarice. But I would like to achieve this with the goodwill of the Pope and of Signor Francesco, and not otherwise. I should regard it as a favour, but I will be content with whatever you arrange. And if Signor Francesco would like to come and visit this place at the feast of San Giovanni or any other time that would please him, I should be glad, as I have told Messer Giorgio Italiano, his man, who is here at present. He seems a good fellow, and very fond of Signor Francesco, and we have had much speech together about his master, and he shows how much he is doing to settle that matter of Santa Severa for him, for I understand that it is important and useful. It seems to me that in this matter and the others that concern his son, His Holiness is acting very coldly, and so far he has had great difficulty in getting the little he has. I am sorry, not only for the sake of Sig. Francesco, but because my daughter has to be stinted, and I am in despair about this and other things, considering the delays, the changeability and the little care that is taken of these matters there."

[15] Ross, *op. cit.*, p. 289.

" . . . I came, and on the road, and whilst in Rome, with all the love and economy I was able to employ, was so useful to my masters that they showed their appreciation by words and deeds many times; particularly when I stood aloof and they tried others. Of the money received by me for the expenses, my enemies twice carefully dissected, like anatomists, my accounts, shop by shop, day by day, entry by entry; and everything was in such order that calumny had a fall, and they were laughed at and put to shame. Thus my affection, fidelity and diligence were established and talked of publicly by them (as I heard privately) so that I pardon all. When I made up the final balance only twenty-eight lire were missing, which must have been forgotten by the man who buys retail. This would be of small account if I had not lost so much in brains, soul and body, instead of only twenty-eight lire, in all these devilries and persecutions, etc., so that I once even cursed both thee and Lorenzo who sent me into this hell. But God has helped us, for of a certain Lorenzo, thy, and my own good intentions, could not have a bad ending.

All this, my Ser Piero, must be a comfort to thee as it is to me. Also I cannot describe the kindness and love shown to me by Madonna Clarice, twice or thrice she even said that the Count showed small discretion in taking me from her, exclaiming: ' See how I am left, I will not allow any man to have the spending of my money but Franco; and I will eat nothing but what has passed through his hands; we never intended to give Franco to him in order that he might be buried alive in a wood, he would be far more useful to Madonna Maddalena and to his house if he were here at hand etc.' She talked of this a hundred times, and has already sent for me twice since I have been at these baths, and kept me two or three days until his Lordship drove me back to the baths."

It was rumoured that Maddalena was to go to Florence with Alfonsina, and a list was drawn up of the things she was going to ask of the Count for her journey; among other things she desired :—

" As chaplain I wish for Franco.

And someone to write my letters, for this Franco will be good.

And I should like Your Excellency's necklace for the time I am in Florence, and such a dress and such footmen, etc., if it please you etc. The list was given to my lord in the evening and after reading it he replied : ' All thou askest I give thee willingly, save only Franco and my necklace.' The girl replied : ' Madonna Clarice desires that he should come.' ' And I desire that he should stay. They have nought more to do with Franco once Lorenzo has given him to thee, and I desire that thou leavest him to look after thy interests for the income of the baths I intend for thee. Thou seest how I am robbed by all. He has done more in the fifteen days he has been there than all my other people since I had Cervetri.'

These words were repeated to me by my angel mistress and lady, who has doubtless wept more than once with Madonna Baccia over my coming to stay here, for Madonna Baccia writes that she talks of me and calls for me every hour. Were it not for this, and for the thought of him there, who is my soul and my heart, of whom I think in all my tribulations so that by the true God, Ser Piero, melancholy then flies from me and my heart is so consoled that my soul is kept in my body. Otherwise I should have died a hundred times. Enough. I might go on and tell that every day I hear how my lord praises me, and I hope from these baths to get great honour etc. and a hundred other expectations from friends and models made in Rome. But as I do not want to break thy head I skip : enough that I have let off a little bile ; I wanted to tell thee something about my life. I have been here at the baths of Stigliano since March 12th, saving the few days Madonna Clarice sent for me as I said ; and have already arranged the baths Tuscan fashion. The rooms are disgusting, Bagno a Morba is a Careggi in comparison ; the air is accursed, the men are like Turks ; everything as bad as can be. Day and night I have to struggle with *bravi*, with soldiers, with swindlers, with venomous dogs, with lepers, with Jews, with madmen, with thieves, and with Romans. Now I run to the cook, now to the baker, then to the tavern, then to clients in the inns ; then I argue with the discontented, with the sick in the hospital, then with the pedlar, then with the grocer, then with the chemist ; then I go to the washerwoman, then to the grooms, then to the courier, then to the doctor, then to the priest. For I have transported all these people here ; there were but bare walls and only half of them standing. In short I have had to bring from the smallest to the largest thing which may be needful for perhaps ten thousand people into this forest, so that every man may have, by paying, every convenience he wants. And I am alone to manage all. During this month of May never a day has passed but there have been a hundred or a hundred and fifty persons ; rooms, beds, even the courtyard, all are full, and some days there have been more than three hundred. Most of them stay three days and then go ; and I have to receive them all, to see to their food, to provide what they want and have not brought with them, grass, oats, hay, in short, everything. For all this they have to pay me, so I hope to glean more than four hundred ducats for Madonna Maddalena if God gives me health. With cooks, innkeepers, bakers and so on I have about twenty-five men in my pay ; and if you could see your Franco in this tempest and purgatory and whirl, host of this great inn of the Devil, by God you would pity him. They comfort me by saying that Christ must wish me well if I escape without a beating, a knife in my ribs, a quarrel, or an illness, for no one has ever returned whole from here. God be praised for His mercies. Yet I am of good cheer, and have such faith in my fair dealing that I hope to do myself honour, if it pleases God. Till now I have pocketed about a hundred ducats, and all sorts and conditions of men have come. If I have not gained with the bad ones I have not lost ; most went away contented. From those of the better sort, couriers, gentlemen, and the like, I think I have gained affection and esteem, for since they returned to Rome they have written to me and sent me presents. Some day I hope to find a great joy, I even hope in the —— of Lucifer the Great, serving for the love of God, of Lorenzo and of what is his.

Vale. May 6, 1488.

Your FRANCO, fighting at the Baths of Stigliano.''

[16] Biagi, *La Vita Privata dei Fiorentini*, in *Vita Italiana del Rinascimento*. Milan, 1893.

'' In all the shops a display was made of fine and rich things, hangings and brocades, and pearls and jewels and silver plate, which was a thing of marvellous and stupendous beauty. For San Giovanni a show with clouds and demons and triumphal cars was prepared and other erections and popular fancies for passing the time, as well as all the usual festivities customary at this season.''

[17] Serdonati, *Vita di Innocenzo VIII*. Milan, 1829.

'' When Francesco went to Florence to celebrate his marriage he took with him many knights and noblemen, the flower of the Roman nobility. He was received with great magnificence in Florence, and richly lodged, together with his suite. But Lorenzo, who liked to have his son-in-law with him in his house, and perhaps hoping thereby to gain the greater goodwill of the Pope, made him dine with him continually at home, without any pomp, and as one might say *en famille*. Therefore, since the Florentines are generally considered mean in their expenditure, he began to think that the gentlemen who had accompanied him to his wedding might be being treated in the same manner. This grieved him, for he feared that afterwards in Rome, he and his relatives might be held up to ridicule. He did not dare to ask them how they fared, in case he should hear that which would displease him. But one day one of these Roman gentlemen, who was very intimate with him, seeing him so thoughtful, asked him the reason. He replied that although he knew that his father-in-law, Lorenzo, was a very great man, he was grieved that, owing to the custom of the country, or for some other reason, these gentlemen should be treated too intimately, and that it worried him for their sake, but that as soon as they returned to Rome he would recompense them for any discomfort or displeasure they might have had. The Cavaliere was surprised, and having heard the reason for this, he said that he was certain that if the Pope himself were lodged as they were, he could not be treated with greater splendour or pomp, better served, cared for and honoured than they were, and that no one could desire more than they had received. Francesco was very pleased to hear this and could not resist telling his father-in-law, who replied to him very kindly, that children, among whom he now reckoned him, were treated differently to strangers and noble personages, such as those who had accompanied him. They were treated splendidly, partly for their own merits, and partly out of respect for him, but he made no difference between Francesco and his own children. These things gave great pleasure to Francesco, and when the Pope heard of it he was greatly pleased, and all admired the judgment and prudence of Lorenzo in public matters as well as private.''

[18] *Giornale Storico della Letteratura Italiana*, vol. xvii. These letters are given in this volume, but are much too long to quote here.

[19] Staffetti, *Il Cardinal Innocenzo Cybo*. Florence, 1894.

[20] Pieraccini, *op. cit.*, p. 127.

[21] B. Buser, *Lorenzo de Medici, op. cit.*

'' As you commanded me, I will tell you all I have heard about the daughter of that Capuan gentleman from your friend and my relative. After I had seen him I consorted so much with these youths that you would think I had gone back several years. By this means I managed to see her one day. She does not seem to be particularly good or bad, but I rather dislike her throat which is somewhat thick at the back. If it were in proportion it would not matter. But when I spoke of it to that merchant you know of, through whom I saw her, he said that she did not have it as a child, and he would enquire if it was by chance, for he thought, as I did, that her throat seemed swollen at the back. Otherwise she does not displease me, for if she is only thirteen years of age, as our friend tells me, she is not small, but one can easily be mistaken, as you know. But her arms, which are usually a guide to the legs, are good, and also her hands. She seems to be straight, but about this and her height I will tell you another time. Her skin is good and she has a good natural colour. Her eyes are light, but not unpleasantly so, she has a good nose, and her mouth, though a little heavy, does not destroy her charm. But I may be mistaken, for I have only seen her once, and then with respect, and anyhow I may be mistaken in some of the details I have given you, for you know how easy it is for a man to be deceived, for a mother would rather show her daughter to ten men than to one woman.''

Letter from Bernardo Rucellai to Lorenzo de' Medici.''

[22] B. Felice, *op. cit.*

[23] Zobi, *Delle Nozze del Magnifico Giuliano de' Medici con Filiberta di Savoia*. Florence, 1868.

Nearly all Alfonsina's letters, both those printed in this work and those in manuscript in the Archivio Mediceo in Florence, are very long and full of politics, so that they cannot be quoted here in extenso.

[24] W. Roscoe, *The Life and Pontificate of Leo X*. London, 1893, vol. i. p. 378.

'' Your Mother has been told that you practice yourself in tilting, wearing heavy armour, and managing the great horse, which may in all probability be injurious to your health. I can scarcely express to you how much she is dissatisfied with these proceedings. In the greatest distress she has enjoined me to write to you on her behalf, and to observe to you that although your ancestors have displayed their courage on similar occasions, yet you should consider who and what they were. When Piero di Cosimo appeared in a tournament, his father, who governed the city, was then living, as was also his brother. At the time Lorenzo appeared his father was also in being, and he had a brother, Giuliano, the father of our most reverend Cardinal ; and when the same Giuliano tilted, Lorenzo himself governed. When your father appeared in the lists he had two sons and two brothers ; notwithstanding which he did not escape blame. You are yet young, and the magnificent Giuliano and yourself (both of you yet unmarried and he infirm in his constitution) are the only support of the family. You cannot therefore commit a greater error than by persevering in such conduct, and she recommends that you should rather engage others in the contest and stand by and enjoy the entertainment ; thereby consulting your own safety and preserving the hopes of your family.

APPENDIX

LETTERS OF CONTESSINA DE' BARDI

LETTERS OF LUCREZIA TORNABUONI

Piero from Florence to Lucrezia at Bagno a Morba	October 1, 1467.
Lorenzo from Florence to Lucrezia at Bagno a Morba	October 4, 1467.
Piero from Florence to Lucrezia at Bagno a Morba	October 5, 1467.
Contessina to Lucrezia	October 25, 1467.
Lucrezia from Bagno a Morba to Lorenzo in Florence	October 27, 1467.
Piero from Florence to Lucrezia at Bagno a Morba	November 13, 1467.
Suor Bartolommea to Lucrezia . .	1467.
Lucrezia from Bagno a Morba to Lorenzo in Florence	May 31, 1468.
Lucrezia from Bagno a Morba to Piero in Florence	July 1, 1468.
Francesco de Justinis from Foligno to Lucrezia	September 7, 1468.
Piero from Careggi to Lucrezia in Florence .	July 13, 1469.
Bishop of Cortona to Lucrezia . . .	April 27, 1470.
Antonio di Pacis from Pisa to Lucrezia in Florence	December 13, 1470.
Tanai de' Medici to Lucrezia . . .	January 14, 1471.
Filippo de' Medici to Lucrezia . . .	March 10, 1471.
Francesco di Ser Antonio from Certaldo to Lucrezia in Florence . . .	July 31, 1471.
Mariotto, General of Camaldoli, to Lucrezia	December 18, 1471.
Piero Bruni, from Cassero di Arezzo to Lucrezia	January 12, 1472.
Giovanni Aldobrandini from Pisa to Lucrezia	January 12, 1472.
The Queen of Bosnia from Rome to Lucrezia in Florence	January 18, 1472.
Francesco di Antonio to Lucrezia . .	June 5, 1472.
Clarice from Siena to Lucrezia in Florence .	June 20, 1472.
Francesco di Antonio from Bibbiena to Lucrezia in Florence . . .	August 28, 1472.
Lucrezia to Clarice	August 30, 1472.
Jacopo, priest of Fucecchio to Lucrezia .	September 20, 1472.
Pagolo di Macchiavelli to Lucrezia . .	January 4, 1473.
Pagolo di Macchiavelli from Vico Pisano to Lucrezia	February 28, 1473.
Papinio de Artimino from Certaldo to Lucrezia in Florence . . .	March 12, 1473.
Lucrezia to Lorenzo	August 7, 1473.
The Ancients of Galatea to Lucrezia . .	August 23, 1473.

LETTERS

Poliziano from Florence to Lucrezia at Bagno a Morba	May 31, 1477.
Bernardo Rucellai from Florence to Lucrezia at Bagno a Morba	June 7, 1477.
Lucrezia from Bagno a Morba to Lorenzo	June 8, 1477.
Niccolo Michelozzi from Florence to Lucrezia	June 14, 1477.
Katerina, the wife of Nicholaio the tailor, from Volterra, to Lucrezia	June 16, 1477.
Lucrezia from Bagno a Morba to Lorenzo	June 18, 1477.
Piero Malegonelle from Bagno a Morba to Lucrezia in Florence	September 16, 1477.
Lotto Mancini from Mugello to Lucrezia	October 15, 1477.
Andrea di Mazzanti from Spoleto to Lucrezia	November 15, 1477.
Antonio da Pela from Colle to Lucrezia	November 16, 1477.
Some criminals of Barbaricine near Pisa to Lucrezia	February 8, 1478.
Filippo Popoleschi to Lucrezia	March, 1478.
Giovacchino Bardi from Volterra to Lucrezia	April 3, 1478.
Giovanni from the Stinche to Lucrezia	April 4, 1478.
Piero Malegonelle from Pomerance to Lucrezia in Florence	April 5, 1478.
Abbess of S. Margherita at Prato to Lucrezia	May 11, 1478.
Francesco d' Antonio from San Martino to Lucrezia	May 27, 1478.
Prioress of San Domenico at Pisa to Lucrezia	June 1, 1478.
Rinaldo da Panzano to Lucrezia	June 12, 1478.
Leonardo Tornabuoni from Pistoia to Lucrezia	September 8, 1478.
Niccolo Martelli from Pisa to Lucrezia	December 11, 1478.
Clarice from Cafaggiuolo to Lucrezia in Florence	December 16, 1478.
Poliziano from Cafaggiuolo to Lucrezia	December 18, 1478.
Andrea, Prior of San Piero Maggiore, to Lucrezia	1478.
Lodovica Torella from Milan to Lucrezia	1478.
Atalante, priest of Bientina, to Lucrezia	February 4, 1479.
Paolo Riccialbani from S. Gemignano to Lucrezia	May 22, 1479.
Poliziano from Fiesole to Lucrezia	May 25, 1479.
Lorenzo from Trebbio to Lucrezia in Florence	May 31, 1479.
Clarice from Gagliano to Lucrezia in Florence	June 2, 1479.
Gerardus de Bobbio from Florence to Lucrezia	June 17, 1479.
Carolus dei Medici from Varano to Lucrezia	June 18, 1479.

255

LETTERS OF CLARICE ORSINI

S

257

BIBLIOGRAPHY

Archivio di Stato, Florence. *Archivio Mediceo ante Principato.*

Alberti, L. B., *Della Famiglia*, ed. by C. Capasso, Milan.

Allegrini, *Chronologica Series Simulacrorum Regiæ Familiæ Mediciæ Centum.* Florence, 1761.

Armstrong, E., *Lorenzo de' Medici.* London, 1896.

Baccini, G., *Le Ville Medicee di Cafaggiuolo e Trebbio.* Florence, 1897.

Bode, W., *Florentine Sculptors of the Renaissance* (Eng. trans.). London, 1908.

Booth, C., *Cosimo I, Duke of Florence.* Cambridge University Press, 1921.

Boulting, W., *Woman in Italy.* London, 1910.

Burckhardt, J., *The Renaissance in Italy* (Eng. trans.). London, 1909.

Buser, B., *Lorenzo de' Medici als italienischer Staatsmann.* Leipzig, 1879.

    Beziehungen der Mediceer zu Frankreich. Leipzig, 1879.

Cambridge Modern History. Vol. I. Cambridge University Press, 1904.

Cappelli, A., *Cronologia.* Milan, 1906.

Cartwright, J., *Painters of Florence.* London, 1901.

Casini & Morpurgo, *VII Lettere di Contessina dei Bardi dei Medici ... per nozze Zanichelli-Manotti.* Florence, 1886.

Cionacci, C., *Rime Sacre di Lorenzo de' Medici e Madonna Lucrezia, sua Madre.* Florence, 1680.

Dante, *The Divine Comedy* (trans. Cary).

La Donna Italiana descritta da Scrittrice Italiane. Florence, 1890.

Ewart, K. D., *Cosimo de' Medici.* London, 1899.

Fabroni, A., *Laurentii Medicis Magnifice Vita.* Pisa, 1784.
Vie de Laurent de Medicis (trans. Serionne). Berlin, 1791.

Magni Cosmi Medicis Vita. Pisa, 1789.

Felice, B., *Donne Medicee avanti il Principato.* Florence, 1905–1906.

Gardner, E., *Florence* (Mediæval Towns Series). London, 1910.

Giornale Storico della Letteratura Italiana. Vol. XVII and others.

Guasti, Cesare, *Tre Lettere di Lucrezia Tornabuoni a Piero de' Medici.*

Ricordo di nozze del gennaio, MDCCCLIX. Florence.

Lettere di una Gentildonna Fiorentina ai figliuoli esuli. Florence, 1877.

Scritti Storici. Prato, 1894.

Guasti, Gaetano, *Cafaggiuolo e le altre fabbriche di ceramiche in Toscana.* Florence, 1902.

Hare, C., *Ladies of the Italian Renaissance.* London, 1904.

Heyck, E., *Florenz und die Mediceer.* Leipzig, 1902.

Horsburgh, E. L. S., *Lorenzo the Magnificent.* London, 1908.

Hyett, F., *Florence.* London, 1903.

Landucci, L., *Diario Fiorentino*, 1450–1516. Ed. I. del Badia. Florence, 1883.

Levantini-Pieroni, G., *Lucrezia Tornabuoni.* Florence, 1888.

Litta, P., *Famiglie Celebre Italiane.*

Lucas, E. V., *A Wanderer in Florence.* London, 1912.

Lungo, I. del., *Women of Florence* (Eng. trans.). London, 1907.

La Donna Fiorentina del buon tempo antico. Florence, 1906.

La Fidanzata di Lorenzo de' Medici. Per nozze Bondi-Levi. Florence, 1897.

Lungo, I. del., *Un Viaggio di Clarice Orsini descritto da Ser Matteo Franco. Scelta di Curiosità letterarie inedite o rare xcviii.* Bologna, 1868.

Nonna, mamma e Nipotina, Lettere femminile di Casa Medici. Florence, 1892.

Florentia.

Macchiavelli, N., *The Florentine Historie* (trans. by Thos. Bedingfield, 1595). Tudor translations, London, 1905.

Maulde la Claviere, R. de., *The Women of the Renaissance* (Eng. trans.). London, 1900.

Medici, Lorenzo de', *Lettere a Innocenzo VIII.* Florence, 1830.

Meyer, *Donatello* (trans. Konody). Leipzig, 1904.

Poliziano (Angelo Ambrogini), *Prose Volgari inedite.* Florence, 1867.

Pulci, L., *Lettere*, ed. S. Bongi. Lucca, 1886.

Pieraccini, G., *La Stirpe de' Medici di Cafaggiuolo.* Florence, 1925.

Reumont, *Lorenzo de' Medici.* Leipzig, 1874.

Roscoe, W., *Leo X.* London, 1893.

Vita e Pontificato di Leone X. Milan, 1816.

Lorenzo de' Medici. London, 1846.

Ross & Erichsen, *Pisa* (Mediæval Towns Series). London, 1909.

Ross, J., *Lives of the Early Medici as told in their Letters.* London, 1910.

Florentine Palaces and their Stories. London, 1905.

Florentine Villas. London, 1901.

Serdonati, F., *Vita di Innocenzo VIII.* Milan, 1829.

Smeaton, O., *The Medici and the Italian Renaissance.* Edinburgh, 1901.

Staffetti, L., *Cardinal Innocenzo Cybo.* Florence, 1894.

Symonds, J. A., *The Renaissance in Italy.* London, 1910.

Tenhove, *Memoirs of the House of Medici* (Eng. trans.). London, 1797.

BIBLIOGRAPHY

Trapeznikoff, T., *Die Porträtdarstellungen der Mediceer des XV Jahrhunderts*. Strassburg, 1909.

Trollope, T. A., *The Girlhood of Catherine de' Medici*. London, 1851.

Verdi, A., *Gli Ultimi Anni di Lorenzo, Duca d' Urbino*. Este, 1905.

Villari, P., *Life and Times of Macchiavelli* (Eng. trans.). London.

La Vita Italiana nel Rinascimento. Milan, 1892.

Volpi, G., *Un Cortigiano di Lorenzo de' Medici*. (Giornale Storico della Letteratura Italiana XIII.)

Young, Col. G. F., *The Medici*. London, 1894.

Zobi, *Delle Nozze del Magnifico Giuliano de' Medici con Filiberta di Savoia*. Florence, 1868.

INDEX

For Product Safety Concerns and Information please contact our EU
representative GPSR@taylorandfrancis.com
Taylor & Francis Verlag GmbH, Kaufingerstraße 24, 80331 München, Germany

www.ingramcontent.com/pod-product-compliance
Ingram Content Group UK Ltd.
Pitfield, Milton Keynes, MK11 3LW, UK
UKHW021013180425
457613UK00020B/925